Huna: A Beginner's Guide

HUNA

A Beginner's Guide
by
Enid Hoffman

Para Research
Rockport, Massachusetts

HUNA: A Beginner's Guide
by Enid Hoffman

Library of Congress Catalog Card Number: 75-41901
International Standard Book Number: 0-914918-03-6

Typeset in 10 pt. Paladium
Typesetting by Elizabeth Bauman

Printed by Alpine Press, Inc.
on 55-pound Surtone II Antique

Published by Para Research, Inc.
Whistlestop Mall
Rockport, Massachusetts 01966

Manufactured in the United States of America

First Printing, April 1976
Revised Edition, November 1981
Fifth Printing, November 1982, 4,000 copies
Total copies in print, 20,000

Contents

Dedication

I dedicate this book to all who have suffered with me through thick and thin and stuck it out, to those wonderful people who have shared my good times and bad times, and especially to my children: Marlee, David, Mary-Joy, and Robert. Without them, this book never could have been written.

My part is done; the rest is up to others. I will never cease to watch over this book, to love it, to encourage its activity. But at this moment I accept it unconditionally as I let it go, with perfect trust in my High Self and all the other High Selves, The Great Poe Aumakua.

I ask The Great Poe Aumakua to care for this child. I ask them now to use their power to ensure that no sin of hurt is contained in any action of this book.

And I give it to society, as I have given four other children. To you, the reader of this book, I present my brainchild. I will clothe it with a handsome cover and send it out to meet you, hoping you will give it a warm reception. For with warmth, it will expand and embrace others.

Preface

Over the years since I wrote the first edition of *Huna: A Beginners Guide*, I have continued my research on Huna through literature and experimentation. These activities helped me refine and expand my original understanding of Huna and led me into new ways to apply it.

Working with my three selves has occupied a major portion of my time. Communicating with my low self and praying to my High Self have helped smooth the path I follow.

These processes have proven productive for me. Through personal experimentation, I've been able to develop new techniques based on Huna. As I make contact with my three selves, they become a working team, contributing more and more to each other. This process allows for expression of ideas and theories that benefit others.

Using Huna I perceive the world through a basic concept which underlies all theories of human nature. This kind of perception reveals a deeper and broader view of the individual experience of others. What is revealed becomes material I can use in developing further theories. As the years go by, Huna becomes even more important and valuable as a guide to understanding others.

Using Huna enables me to reach the basic experience of others, drawing us closer together and alleviating some of the separateness we all experience in our relationships.

It has been gratifying to know that others have shared my experiences. Your mail has proven that to me.

It has also been exciting to find new developments in psychological research validating the Huna concept and offering new avenues of exploration to all students of Huna. This new edition of my book includes some of the interesting results of recent research.

Many new ideas have risen into my mind which I have developed and offered for the reader's consideration. One such idea concerns the power of Hawaiian language sounds to affect consciousness.

Max Freedom Long created the context within which I, and many others, was able to utilize Huna. He was inspired to look within the Hawaiian language for a code that would reveal the psycho-religious system used by the Kahuna of Hawaii. The meanings of the words and combinations of words gave forth definitions of what it meant to be a human being and the tenfold concept of an individual person. He used the Lorrin-Andrews dictionary written by a missionary who recorded, as faithfully as he could, the spoken language which had never had a written version.

The original language used by the Hawaiians was a spoken language and as Huna students we have missed out on the sounds of their spoken words. Our oral cavity is a resonating chamber in which words, silent or sounded, reverberate in specific vibrational patterns. Situated below the brain is a palate, a sounding board in the roof of our mouth. The vibrations passing through this palate resound in the brain in specific patterns of vibration. In this edition you will learn a new way to use Huna. Hawaiian sounds each have a unique vibration pattern that can change the quality of your speech, your throat, your sinus passages and your brain. Working with tiny speech muscles, some new vibratory patterns can be utilized to create changes in your experiences of life. I suggest that as you come across the various Hawaiian words you try chanting them in order to gain deeper insight into the meaning behind each individual word.

There are five vowel sounds, seven consonant sounds and one consonant glottal (silent) sound. Thirteen in all.

The Hawaiian language is a member of the great Malayo-Polynesian family of languages which is the most widespread traditional language family in the world, rivaled now by English. It spread to every part of the world during the eighteenth and nineteenth century. Within Polynesia, Hawaiian belongs to the East Polynesian group of languages and is closely related to Maori, Marquesan, Tahitian and Cook Island languages.

The internal structure of the Polynesian language indicates its high antiquity. The laws of euphony which regulate the changes of consonants are fixed and uniform in the New Zealand, Samoan and Hawaiian languages (New Zealand being considered the most primitive in its form).

In Hawaiian an unbroken rule says that no two consonants are heard without a vowel between, and all words end in a vowel. Most Hawaiians who speak the native language have a sharp ear for the slightest variation of vowel sound, but do not clearly distinguish differences in consonants. There is no distinction between B and P, T and D, G and K, L and R and V and W. Actually the consonant sound lies between these pairs when spoken.

There are three classes of Hawaiian words—words depicting sensation, images and abstract ideas. There are also three styles; every day language, oratorical and religious or poetic.

Just for fun, here is an example of how the Hawaiian word *Kahuna* is translated into other dialects near its own: *Tufunga* (Fakaafo, Samoan and Tongan); and *Tuhuna* (Nukuhivan).

In Hawaiian when k is found at the beginning of a word it is not sounded, but is dropped. When found in the middle it becomes a gutteral catch or break and is often found in the written word as an apostrophe rather than a k.

Included in this revised version is a list of Hawaiian words and some instructions on how to pronounce them. Directions for your development into fluidic and harmonious expression of them to create vibratory patterns to improve your health are found in the breathing exercises and will furnish you with a lot of fun as you experiment and experience these wonderful sounds, in addition to your practices based on the Huna Concept.

I will be happy to hear of your experiments and experiences as you develop these ideas further, and will answer letters addressed to me in care of the publisher.

Introduction

Speaking of two lectures he had given, Carl Rogers once said, "The response to each of these talks has made me realize how hungry people are to know something of the person who is speaking to them or teaching them." Since I intend to talk *to* you rather than write *at* you and hope to become your teacher during the span of time it takes to read this book, I shall now set down what I hope will satisfy your hunger. Of necessity, I will confine myself to aspects of my life that pertain to the material in this book, but interestingly, those aspects are the most important features of my life.

Where do I start? Where is the beginning of a book like this? How far back in my life do I look for the germinating seed of this book? I think the real beginning was when I first began to get some answers. We'll start there, then go through the first stumbling efforts, and on to the techniques that brought favorable results, arriving finally at the stage where I developed the urge to share my success with others, to teach them the concepts that had brought me answers.

So I shall start with the first idea that enabled me to begin the process of learning who I am, why I am here, and where I am going. That first idea was, "I am not my self." This led to my becoming very curious about the self that I was not.

Picture a little girl with brown curls and blue eyes in a freckled face, rather tiny for her six years. I lived in a small New England town with my parents, a sister three years older, a sister three years younger, and a brother who was a year and a half younger than I. My father taught physical education to men in state normal schools—teacher's colleges. My mother, active in community affairs, had a professional background in the theater. The only characteristic that set me apart from any other normal little WASP female of that time was that I started school with two "bad" habits: sucking my thumb and sitting with one leg tucked up under me or both heels tucked under my buttocks. I'm sure you'll be relieved to hear that I had kicked both these habits by the fourth grade.

Like all children, I was learning to know myself by the way others reacted toward me. Gradually I built an image that I adjusted to as well as any other person does, I guess. That image was based mostly on what was Nice and what was Not Nice. So most of my efforts were directed toward being a Nice girl, at least on the outside, and avoiding behavior that would bring disapproval and punishment. I was well aware, even when I was very young, that I really wasn't Nice at all, but I found it the better part of discretion to behave as if I were.

So my life proceeded through the usual experiences of a middle-class child, until I reached high school. By that time the strain of living up to expectations was beginning to tell.

I had learned I could not take credit for all the "blessings" of being white and Protestant and belonging to a respectable family. In fact, I sometimes wondered if there had been a mistake. I had learned that much was expected of a young woman with all these advantages, and the expectations seemed impossibly high to me. "*Naturally* we are all smart!" That was the clincher, and inwardly I gave up trying to fulfill expectations. My decision wasn't obvious as I recall. But very gradually the family seemed to accept the idea that I wasn't as smart as my sister, that I did not care much about my appearance, and that probably I would never amount to much.

So through high school I went, gathering mostly C's in my studies, learning little, and managing to escape my parents' attention most of the time by behaving like a Nice girl as much as I could. Marriage beckoned as a way to move on to a better role than that of Disappointing Daughter, so I was married right after high school graduation.

That was during the Depression. My parents thoughtfully rearranged their home to give us a two-room apartment. I became pregnant immediately and was then caught between two authorities, my mother and my doctor, each of whom had different ideas of prenatal care. And I had other ideas. Pleasing neither my mother nor doctor, I gave birth after seven months to a three-pound boy, who died at the age of one month.

As I wrote those words, up came all the grief I could not release at that time. All those unshed tears flooded out as I left my typewriter, and with them the feelings I had suppressed when I was eighteen years old. All the guilt, all the pain of loss which I could not face then.

And then I was pregnant again, which wasn't quite Nice then, but not much was said. On October 27, 1936, my daughter Marlee was born. How can I express the delight she gave me then and has continued to give me all these years? There I go again! Tears flooding out, but this time, as they blind my eyes to the typewriter keys, they are expressing the delight and joy that I could never fully reveal before.

I doubt that I was a very good mother, being young and inexperienced. Because of financial difficulties, my husband and I lived apart and gradually became near-strangers. When my daughter was only a few months old I became solely responsible for our support. The Depression was on in earnest and times were hard for everyone. My father lost his position and went to work for the WPA, and I soon followed him there. Many people will remember the WPA, President Roosevelt's answer to unemployment.

Some of my experiences then were really funny. I was given the job of teaching both photography and bowling, knowing nothing of either. Using books and catalogs, I survived by staying one jump ahead of the students. After that I had various jobs in different programs and developed some skills that proved very useful later.

Keeping my head above water was an awful strain. Life often seemed a nightmare of earning money to pay bills so that I could continue earning money to pay bills. Just to keep going was an effort. So when a man came along who was willing and eager to have me as a wife, to support and care for me, I went into marriage headlong, with love and willingness to give my all to it.

Those first years in Connecticut were some of the happiest and most fulfilling years of my life. Although I saw little of my husband, I had a lovely home, a daughter, and soon a son. His birth was a new high point in fulfillment for me. This son came into my life approved by all, welcomed with enthusiasm. An adorable baby, David grew into a fine son and is now a man any mother would be proud of. Life was great. Living in a typical little colonial house in a typical suburb with a typical station wagon, I began to spread my wings.

I became a Girl Scout worker, secretary of the PTA, and a community service volunteer. In January of 1950 my second daughter was born. I named her Mary-Joy after my older sister whom I have always loved and admired very much. She was a loving and exuberant child who enjoyed tagging around after her brother. Marlee became a second mother to these two and was often given responsibility beyond her years for their welfare.

So my family grew, and through them I grew and expanded my knowledge and expertise as housewife and mother and a member of my neighborhood and my community. Finally my family became complete with the addition of another son, Robert. How can I possibly describe him? Robert is unique. He was so easy to love and spoil, but he has never been spoiled in any sense of the word. His charm persists to this day, spreading warmth to everyone he encounters.

My children and I shared a typical suburban life with all its ups and downs, all its fun, and all its disappointments. Holidays developed family traditions, and the family developed its own personality. Those were the days!

Then a major shift—a divorce and moving to another town. New schools and new friends forced the children to make difficult adjustments. I had to work outside the home and provide most of the support for my household. My oldest daughter married and left the family nest. Adolescence hit David with no father to help him through the transformation.

But there were compensations, including a delightfully big old house in which we could spread out, develop hobbies, and create a new family atmosphere. We had difficulties, but there were fun times, too. I became interested in little theater, developed my skills in crafts, made new friends, and held various interesting jobs. It was at this time that my interest began to focus on the psychic sciences. I've always loved to read, and slowly I began to build a library around the subjects of the occult and parapsychology.

My first psychic experience happened in that lovely old house, my third marriage lasted its brief six months there, and I was living there when I met my fourth husband.

Although my image of myself had undergone many changes, it still held a picture of one who was not very Nice, not *really* very strong, and, above all, not worthy of being loved. So when this big, strong man came into my life and wanted to marry me, I took it as an opportunity to change my image and become a valuable person. Again the problems in my life were becoming more difficult to solve. Being a mother, homeowner, and wage earner, as well as trying to satisfy some of my own desires, was getting to be quite a strain. I was acutely conscious of my children's fatherless state and wanted to share the responsibility of being a parent.

Actually, that marriage taught me the most important lesson I have ever learned. It was extremely painful. I believed I could become the ideal wife, according to my husband's description of the role. And I tried. Oh, how I tried! I became so absorbed in this endeavor that I truly believed I had achieved it. For six years I lived under that illusion.

Because of this illusion, our life changed radically. We moved to Vermont and became a small-farm family. We had many wonderful experiences on the farm. I could write a book about all the funny things that happened, the fascinating world of animals and beautiful country landscape, the swimming pool in the river, and the interesting Vermonters we met. I became a farmer's wife, rising at dawn to milk the goats, making all our bread, and creating an old-fashioned homey environment for my husband and three growing children.

But behind all this there lurked disaster. I was leading a completely false existence. Whenever anyone does this, there is pain in store for all involved.

We spent our first year in Bethel, learning to become farmers and adjusting to village existence. Our herd of goats increased, and I developed skill as a milker of dairy animals and explored ways of using goat's milk. We kept chickens, and raised two little pigs to maturity. The whole family learned to include farming chores into lives already filled with school and personal activities. We did not succeed in our attempt to be self-sufficient farmers, probably for lack of experience. But our experiment forced us to reconsider our life style and try to make changes that would remedy our situation. By now, I was becoming aware of some inner personal conflicts that I couldn't resolve.

I felt responsible for my own happiness and also for the happiness of everyone else I contacted. I felt my unhappiness would make others unhappy if they became aware of it. Therefore, I must never reveal feelings of sadness, anger, or displeasure. This became a great burden. I had placed myself in a family situation where I felt I had to decide which person's happiness had priority. More and more often I had to choose between my husband and one of my children. The agony of deciding whose happiness was more important became very great. I realized that I had to resolve this inner conflict.

Help came in a strange way. After a year in Bethel, we moved to Kirby, Vermont, purchasing a much larger farm. This move necessitated closing our Vermont house for one winter and living in a rented apartment in Derby, Connecticut. Having heard much about the Spiritual Church's psychic development classes, my husband became very interested in joining one. So we visited the nearest Spiritualist Church, which was the Albertson Memorial in Stamford. Our psychic training began when we were admitted to the Friday evening class there. Attending church every Sunday, we became familiar with the eleven affirmations they made every week.

The fourth affirmation attracted my attention, and I puzzled over it for months. "I am morally responsible for my own happiness or unhappiness." On pondering this, I realized that it is either true for everyone or true for no one. So each person is responsible for his own happiness or unhappiness! What a revelation this was to me! I became acutely aware of other people's attitudes about this. I listened to people's conversation from a different point of view and found much food for thought. It took me nearly a year to digest this principle and then begin to use it in my life. At that point I found that by taking responsibility for my happiness, I was able to choose how I would react to other people. As I began to choose more often not to accept unhappiness, other people lost the power they had formerly had over my life. And I tried more and more to make others take responsiblity for their own reactions and stop blaming me for their unhappiness or holding me reponsible for making them happy. This caused a good many arguments!

After our year in Derby, we returned to the farm in Vermont and resumed the life of farmers, but now my husband had taken a job outside the farm to ensure our survival in a difficult life style. But our life was not the same as before, for I was beginning to change, working very hard to resolve some of the inner problems that had brought me and my children into a difficult relationship with the man I married. Communication between myself and Bernie, my husband, worsened, and a gulf in understanding yawned wide and deep. As we were unable to bridge the gap, separation was the only solution.

When I had accepted the image of wife, as designed by Bernie, I had accepted it totally, including the principle that the husband always comes first. This conflicted with my deeply held feeling of responsibility for my children, who I thought came first. Feeling responsible for their happiness, I found it excruciating to choose between husband and child. But Bernie resolved that problem for me by attacking the children whenever I took their part. I dealt with this by falsifying my real feelings, disguising my love for them so as not to arouse his antagonism. This proved quite unsuccessful, and he grew more and more resentful of my attention to them. This problem brought an end to our Vermont venture. On a snowy, cold December morning, Robert and I left carrying our personal possessions on a toboggan, coasting down to a neighbor's house to hitch a ride into St. Johnsbury, where we took a bus to Connecticut.

An amazing transformation took place in me on that bus ride. All the created personality of six years fell away and I was my old self again. By the time we reached Marlee's house, the transformation was complete. I realized what had taken place when David greeted me with, "Welcome back, Mother."

I now hope that my children will be able to look back on that period as a time of growth and learning. I do. I hope that seeing me try to live someone else's image of me has taught them the futility of it and has given them the strength to assert their own individuality.

And so, starting out again, I continued my search for my identity and the meaning of my life. I settled down in Connecticut and went back to working outside the home and creating a home for my now smaller family. Outside of work, I pursued my interest in resolving my problems by turning to psychic development. I joined groups with like interests and attended many lectures pertaining to spiritual and psychic themes. I became an avid reader of occult and esoteric books and eventually discovered the work of Max Freedom Long on the *Kahuna* of Hawaii. Here I found what I had been looking for all my life: a model of a human being that would give me a solid foundation upon which to rebuild my life and personality.

The origins of the psycho-religious system called Huna ("secret" in Hawaiian) are lost in pre-literate antiquity, but certain legends have come down to us through oral tradition. Long, long ago, when the Sahara desert was green and fertile, twelve tribes lived in the area. In each tribe there were people who practiced what we would call magic, based on their knowledge of man and nature. When the Sahara gradually dried up and turned to sand, the tribes moved on. They spent some time in the valley of the Nile and helped to build the Great Pyramid. They also must have been involved in the mystery schools of that period, for their secret is well-illustrated in the Tarot cards that we know today.

The Kahuna had control of psychic abilities, and those who practiced precognition foresaw a time of darkness to come. They decided that the tribes must move to an area where their beliefs and practices would be safe. Using clairvoyance, they saw uninhabited islands in the Pacific, which they chose as their future home. One tribe, for unknown reasons, went instead to the Atlas Mountains of North Africa where some Huna words and practices reportedly survived among the Berber tribesmen as late as 1917.

The folklore of Hawaii is full of the miracles of the Kahuna: They were also excellent psychotherapists, treating what we would call complexes, fixations, and psychoses. Hewahewa, a great and wise Kahuna, saw in a vision the coming of Christian missionaries. When their ships arrived at the islands in 1820, Hewahewa and his people were on the beach to greet them. But soon the missionaries outlawed all the practices of the Kahuna, and even today they are looked upon with contempt by pious Christians in Hawaii.

So far as I know, the first non-Hawaiian to investigate Huna was Dr. William Tufts Brigham, who became curator of the Bishop Museum in Honolulu in 1881. Max Freedom Long came to Hawaii in 1917 and worked with Brigham until Brigham's death in 1921.

Long stayed on in the islands for ten more years, studying Brigham's notes and working with the few remaining Hawaiians who had any knowledge of the ancient lore. (The last of the expert Kahuna whom Brigham had known had died before Long arrived.) Brigham had amassed a great deal of data on what the Kahuna could do. He had watched them walk on hot coals and had even done it himself under their protection. He had recorded many cases of healing, controlling the weather, calling sharks to the beach, and other exploits. But they had never told him *how* they did these things.

In 1931 Long left the islands in despair of ever discovering the Kahuna secret. It was not until 1934 that he succeeded.

"Starting with the idea that the kahunas must have had words in the native language with which to tell budding kahunas how to perform miracles," he wrote, "I began to study any and all words in the Hawaiian dictionary which might have named something that had to do with man's mental and spiritual nature." Embedded in the root vocabulary of the Hawaiian lanuguage and its symbolism, Long found what he and Brigham had looked for in vain, the secret of the Kahuna!

Long's first book, *Recovering the Ancient Magic*, published in 1936, has been out of print for many years. However, all of the material in it is included in Long's second book, *The Secret Science Behind Miracles*. After the latter work was published, Long founded Huna Research Associates, a society devoted to the study and development of Huna techniques. Long's later books, *The Secret Science at Work*, *Psychometric Analysis*, *Self-Suggestion and the New Huna Theory of Mesmerism and Hypnosis*, *Growing Into Light*, and *The Huna Code in Religion*, report their work as well as his own.

I first became acquainted with Huna in 1966 when I read *The Secret Science Behind Miracles*. Since then, I have devoted considerable time to studying, testing, developing, and teaching the Huna system and relating it to modern discoveries in the fields of psychology and parapsychology. The present book is a revised and expanded edition of a pamphlet titled *You Two Can Be A Kahuna*, first privately published in 1973 for use in my classes.

Because this book is for beginners, I have not always identified the source of the various ideas and techniques. While the basic Huna concept comes from the Hawaiian tradition, the use of the pendulum is Long's contribution. My students and I have developed further techniques for using the pendulum to communicate with one's own low self. I also wish to acknowledge my debt to Dr. Otha Wingo, the director of Huna Research Associates, and to Dolly Ware, curator of the Max Freedom Long Museum. For those interested in a more detailed history of Huna studies, I recommend Long's books.

Huna is no longer secret. Since the publication of Long's first book, Huna has belonged to everyone who cares to use it. It is not so much a rigid discipline as a model or pattern of the universe that can explain events that may have been mysterious. When you finish this book, Huna will be as much yours as you wish to make it—quite possibly as much yours as it is mine or Max Long's. Perhaps you will become, like me, another link in the chain of Huna tradition that has its beginnings in the remote past and extends into the future as far as the mind's eye can see. Perhaps you will become a Kahuna.

The basic philosophy of Huna enabled me to understand how my personality had been constructed and how I could reconstruct it. I determined to master the secret myself in order to use it to gain power over my own life and become successful in my goals. Huna enabled me to make my life self-satisfying and productive.

Arriving at the University of Connecticut in 1968 as a Resident Counselor, I soon began teaching non-credit courses and workshops at the Experimental College and Yggdrasil Drop-In Center. Through these, I taught some of the knowledge I had gained and shared my experiences. Continued study, research and sharing has developed my ability to understand and use Huna. Re-interpreting it as new research reveals new aspects of its universal validity, and developing it into a system easy to use and simple to apply to everyday affairs.

This book is the culmination of my efforts to find a system that offers a means to self-knowledge. It will enable you to find for yourself what I have found. And if it saves you any of the pain and bewilderment of not knowing who you are or what you are doing here, it will have served its purpose. If my hard-won knowledge of what a person is can make the path easier for others, my goal will have been reached.

And so my book is born. How do I feel at this moment? Very, very tired, but so very pleased with myself. And very grateful to my High Self.

"Coming to know Huna is like coming to know the alphabet of psychology. We do anything better when we have learned WHY each step is to be taken." (Max Freedom Long—*Self Suggestion*)

1

The Huna Concept

Within Huna we find a very simple logical concept. Each persn has three selves. Using Max Long's names for them they are: The High, middle and low selves. In Hawaiian they are called *Aumakua, uhane* and *unihipili.* In modern psychology these are called the superconscious, conscious and subconscious. Each self has an invisible body of subtle substance called kino-aka in Hawaiian. These subtle bodies are composed of etheric substance, much finer than physical matter and invisible to our physical eyes. The three kino-aka bodies interpenetrate each other and the one physical body they use.

Each of the three selves uses energy or life vitality during its sojourn in a physical body. Unihipili uses *mana,* the basic life vitality. This energy or force is used to keep the physical body functioning and for all physical action. Uhane has *mana-mana,* a higher voltage of life vitality to use to think and feel with. This mana-mana is produced from mana and must come from the low self, unihipili. The life vitality used by the High Self, Aumakua, is called *Mana Loa* and it is the highest voltage energy. Mana Loa can effect an instant healing as well as perform other types of miracles.

These three selves, in their kino-aka bodies, use their unique vital force to activate them. They live together in one physical body during the person's lifetime. Three selves, three kino-aka bodies and three levels of force are contained in one physical body.

There is only one sin in the Huna concept. That is the sin of hurting another self. The Huna way of life is a harmless, hurtless way. Working with one sin, awareness is focussed on the acts and omission of acts that result in hurt to another being. There are Huna techniques to make amends or gain forgiveness for each and every sin committed, so humans can live free from guilt.

Considering the multitude of sins and taboos existing in our social structure, it can come as a relief to know that in Huna, we only have to work with one sin. Keeping within the rule of a harmless, hurtless life, forgetting all other sins, can enable us to live without regret, shame or guilt.

The Huna concept is very simple, easy to use, and yet very broad. It gives us a pattern of being we can work with to aid us in our search for answers to the basic philosophical questions: "Who am I, why am I here and what should I be doing with my life?"

When I first looked at my own life in this framework, I began to feel with rising excitement that I was on to something very valuable and real. I learned that this concept was at the bottom of all the practices of the Kahuna. Their miracles and magic were the result of their profound knowledge of forces and substances, visible and invisible, and how to work with them. Their powers were released by a deep understanding of the natural sense of guilt which we feel when we have hurt another. Their understanding of interpersonal relationships and the relationships between the three selves in one being, plus their knowledge of the physical world, gave them incredible power.

These are exciting realizations, holding the potential for everyone to grow in knowledge and power. If the Kahuna did it, we can do it by studying the Huna concept and the Hawaiian language. By practicing their techniques until we are as skilled as they, we can produce miracles too.

What is a miracle? To me it is a miracle when I can project a thought and have it become a reality. It is a miracle when I can set a goal and see it achieved in mysterious ways. It is a miracle that by using the sounds of Hawaiian words changes can take place in my consciousness. We do not understand the many miracles happening all around us. Let us start our search, not only to understand miracles, but to find ways to cause them to happen. To begin let us use the Hawaiian language as spoken by the Kahuna, examine the simple Huna concept, and then correlate both with philosophy, psychology, religion and physics.

We will use some Huna techniques, change them to suit our personal preferences, practice them until we are skilled, develop new ones based on what we have learned, to become more productive and happier than before. This book will tell you about some of the understandings my students and I have achieved, some of the techniques we have used and the results we have had. I hope it will give you ideas that stimulate your thinking and give rise to more questions that need answers. A question is a challenge, the pursuit of answers is an adventure and discovering answers an exaltation and a spur to continuing.

Share with me the excitement of discovering the selves, share the fun I've had in getting them to work together. Come with me, get to know my low self as you learn about yours, become friends with my middle self and meet my High Self, who as a member of The Great Poe Aumakua (the family of High Selves) already knows your High Self. Through the study of Huna, meet all the wonderful people who have discovered the delights inherent in the process of becoming a Kahuna.

Each self comes from one of the main streams of life forms moving along the evolutionary path. From the realm of nature comes the elemental self to join with a human self, and from the angelic realm comes the High Self to make a threefold team of selves that make up one being, growing together through cooperation.

Max Long used the words "middle" and "low" for uhane and unihipili because of the locations of their centers of consciousness in relation to the physical body. Low does not mean inferior in Huna, just uniquely different. Uhane, the middle conscious self has its center of consciousness in the head area and unihipili centers in the area of the solar plexus, the center of the central nervous system in the physical body. That center is in the pit of your stomach below your breast bone.

The High Self, Aumakua, has its center of consciousness in a subtle body that is so large its center is above our physical head. The least condensed of all the subtle bodies, it permeates all the lower, more dense bodies, but expands outward much further than the other two. Next in size and density is uhane's subtle body. Most dense and most compact is the subtle body of unihipili. All are called kino-aka bodies in the Hawaiian language.

These three kino-aka bodies interpenetrate each other and the physical body. Imagine them as three ovals of three different sizes. They resemble that ancient Chinese egg trick, where by opening the outer, largest egg you find one within which is just a little smaller, open that and you find another, still smaller. Nesting within one another they are a beautiful illustration of how our kino-aka bodies are within each other, except the living kino-aka bodies interpenetrate one another.

My research shows unihipili's kino-aka body is a shade of blue. The shade is much like the blue shown in photographs of Earth taken from space. Those photographs showed the Earth bathed in its blue atmosphere, what I would call its unihipili-kino-aka-body.

The kino-aka body of the low self is the densest of the three and has been labelled the "etheric body" in other cultures. Aka has been called etheric substance. In India we find the word "akasic" or "akashic" for the universal substance within which all memory is held. Huna teaches us that the low self preserves all our personal memories in its kino-aka body.

Aka, or etheric substance, is also called ectoplasm and is a very fluid, sticky and versatile substance. It can be extended outward in a thread or rod. It clings to all it touches, drawing out a fine thread between itself and that object. We might be compared to spiders in the web of universal life, connected to all we have ever touched or focussed our eyes on. We have woven webs of relationships with objects and people ever since we were born. Thoughts and energies can flow along these threads of kino-aka substance, allowing us to silently communicate with others.

The ability of the low self to manipulate its kino-aka body and extrude substance from it may explain some of the mysterious events that take place in a seance room. Examples would be the tipping of a table, the ringing of bells and the movement of a trumpet. Other manifestations of what is called psychic energy can also occur. Under a red light in a completely darkened seance room, kino-aka or ectoplasm appears as a white cloudy matter that issues in streamers from a trained medium. But under red light the blue substance appears white. Kirlian photography, which uses an electrical device to record phenomena that are invisible to our physical eyes, has produced pictures of this blue substance around the fingertips of human beings. A narrow band of blue is seen around each finger. Radiating from that are other colors which have been related to the emotional states of the subject being photographed.

In Carlos Castaneda's book, *A Separate Reality*, there is a wonderful description of a low-self ability to extend portions of itself outward and fasten onto objects outside the physical body. This description is found in a scene where a master crosses a waterfall. He extends a rod of aka substance from himself to a rock, then moves on that rod to the rock. In this way, extending a portion of subtle substance ahead of him to each rock, he crosses the waterfall.

All three subtle bodies are connected to each other and to the physical body by cords of aka substance. The cord that connects unihipili to the physical body, and the one connecting it to uhane, is a silvery-blue-white. As long as there is life in the physical body, these cords hold the two selves connected to the body. The cord connecting the High Self to the physical body and its other two selves is a golden color and is rooted in the physical heart.

Uhane's kino-aka body, less dense and larger than unihipili's, is often called "the astral body." From the outside it resembles a soap bubble, reflecting many colors off its surface, but in contrast to a soap bubble, the inside is filled with shifting clouds of color. Those clouds are many hues and shades of color that reflect uhane's thoughts and feelings. Uhane has a latent ability to temporarily rise out and have experiences outside the physical body. These experiences are called "astral travel" and "out-of-body-experiences" (OBE). This separation of uhane from its physical home is often spontaneous, and happens under great stress or serious illness. However, after training in specific techniques, it can occur at the specific intention of uhane. There have been occasions where individuals have looked back at their reposing physical form and seen, stretching out between them, the silvery cord of aka substance connecting them to their physical-etheric body. The elasticity of this aka substance is limitless. It can be drawn out to such a tiny thread that it becomes absolutely invisible.

Each self uses a form of life vitality. Unihipili has mana, uhane has mana-mana, and the Aumakua has Mana Loa. Each of these differing life forces has unique powers and qualities. Mana is the power to build forms and maintain them in their growth and decline. It is the power that builds and maintains the physical body keeping it as close to the precise blueprint in the kino-aka body as possible. From this mana also comes the physical energy we use in our everyday life to keep the physical body functioning.

Mana-mana, the life force of uhane, is divided between thought and feeling. Both are creative will power. Every thought and every emotion are taken by unihipili as the "will" of uhane to be manifested in form. Uhane has the capacity, using this mana-mana, to think, imagine and create thought patterns willed with feeling. Unihipili takes these designs and patterns and manifests them in our life.

Mana Loa, the life force used by the High Self or Aumakua, contains the power of compassion, or the highest form of unconditional love. This force has a cohesive quality that keeps forms pulsing in a contraction-expansion motion that animates them. The golden cord from the Aumakua is rooted within the heart of the physical body and keeps it beating rhythmically. When Mana Loa is used to heal, its power is so great that the healing occurs instantaneously.

These three life streams of intelligent force; angelic, human and elemental; unite together so that each may evolve in cooperation with the other two.

Unihipili is in charge of creating, re-creating and maintaining our physical bodies. It looks to uhane for commands, decisions, wishes and desires to bring into reality, and its devotion to uhane is uncritical, unchanging and ever obedient to uhane's will. It hungers for goals to achieve, plans to fulfill.

Uhane lives as a guest of unihipili in the physical body. Hungering for love and wisdom, uhane exercises its power of will to bring into being the contexts within which these two needs can be filled.

Aumakua sends its love, along the golden cord into our hearts, encouraging us to share this love with others and pour it out even as it is poured into us.

Each self exists in a specific realm of intelligence and consciousness. These three realms are known as the elemental realm of consciousness, the human realm of consciousness and the angelic realm of consciousness. All beings in these three streams of evolution progress according to their cooperation with each other. Each of the three selves is dependent on the other two for its own growth and progress, and therefore cooperation is needed between them.

The Great Poe Aumakua are known as our loving parental spirits, loving us without judgement or conditions. They work to guard and guide, as wise parents would, and their goal is our growth and gain of wisdom through experience. They cannot hurt us by denying that expansion of our intelligence and will. The High Selves are all in close communion with each other, and each works closely with the low selves of their own being. Huna teaches us that the path to the High Self is through the low self. Through the nature spirit, we reach the divine spirit.

Uhane has human consciousness; intellect and intuition, the abilities to reason and intuit. Uhane thinks and feels and all its processes are suggestions or commands to its unihipili to be manifested in personal reality.

Unihipili has elemental consciousness. El-e-mental means "Mind of God" and is an unchanging wisdom of divine imagination manifest. The elemental life stream is a realm of beings called elementals, and they function in all forms within our world. They build forms from the tiniest atoms to the huge mountains and lakes we enjoy so much. Our own elemental being, our own low self is a nature spirit. it has been trained throughout many eons in form building, from the very simple to the now complex job of building a physical body from its etheric pattern for a human spirit to come into as a guest.

We could use other words for these main lifestreams. We could call them natural, human and divine. A nature spirit, a human spirit and a divine spirit are other names for the low, middle and High Selves: unihipili, uhane and Aumakua.

On examining the three selves, we find that each has its own particular kind of consciousness, talents and functions. Each has its place in the tri-self complex. They are equal, but different from one another. Each contributes its own particular nature or essence to the total being. Let us examine them to find their unique differences.

The three realms of consciousness that exist parallel to each other, in harmony with each other, are co-workers in intelligence and evolution. First the realm of nature, biological intelligence, is called "elemental intelligence" and it is in all animated, physical bodies.

The second, called human consciousness, belongs to the social being that we are, in a society of other human beings. One of the species called human among the mammalian species within our biological world.

The third level of consciousness is called divine, for it has the aspects of the divine nature. Natural, human and divine; we live in all three worlds simultaneously.

In the Hawaiian language all three selves are called spirits. A nature spirit controls the human physical body, a human spirit lives in it as a guest, and hovering over these, as a guardian angel or great parent, is the High Self, Aumakua.

Uhane is aware when awake, but loses that waking awareness when sleep overcomes it. During its waking hours uhane works with unihipili and during sleep it is presented with dreams from the higher self to help guide it in its daily actions so that the higher aspects of being can be actualized in daily life.

Uhane both thinks and feels. Uhane uses the neo-cortex part of the brain which has two hemispheres. On one side feeling and intuition are active and on the other side rational thinking and logical processes occur. While awake, you can narrow awareness down to a concentrated point or expand it to include the whole world. You can shift your attention to the past, remembering, or you can daydream about the future. You can also live in the "now," aware of what you are feeling in the moment and responding to ongoing events. You have free will by which you make your choices. You can give love, approving warmly, or display dislike by withholding your approval. You can hate, displaying the fire of anger, or cut another with the sword or criticism. You can act from what you are feeling now, or react from past emotional experiences. You have choices. Because you are external to the low self, you can do all these things to your own low self as well as to others.

Your low self has elemental consciousness. Literal consciousness, meaning that it does not reason or use logic. It does not make choices. It experiences everything literally—exactly as it occurs, including all your thoughts and feelings. We are very fortunate that this is so, for it makes that self an extremeley dependable one which we need in order to survive physically. This elemental consciousness never sleeps. Its constant awareness, even during the condition of an anesthetized physical body, enables it to keep the physical machine running and functioning at top quality. It always lives in the "now." Under hypnosis, many people have reported events that happened during sleep or surgery, proving that awareness is always present. Unihipili thinks deductively but is unable to reason inductively as uhane does. This is a very important factor in communicating with the low self, for the communication must be very literal for it to be understood correctly.

There are universal laws governing each mode of intelligence and consciousness. Understanding these laws is the path to achieving unity between the three independent selves. When united in intention and purpose, all is well. Uhane must always remember that unihipili is in charge of the physical existence and there has the power to control events. With its strength in the physical world, it can pit itself against uhane's desires and wishes and come out the winner. If unihipili rebels against following uhane's plans to take a trip, it has the power to break a leg and prevent the trip from being accomplished! All of uhane's big plans can go for naught when it is in conflict with its unihipili! Unihipili demonstrates its power by creating events beyond our conscious control that demonstrate its opposition if we would but notice them as such. Unihipili is in charge of body weight, body temperature and all other homeostatic functions of the physical body. Unihipili always tries to maintain the balance between the two polarities of hot and cold, overweight and underweight. When there is a disagreement between uhane and unihipili over the most desirable weight, we find the war is usually won by unihipili who has the last say in every case. Do you know someone who went on a diet to lose weight, only to have that weight return when they relaxed their efforts?

Unihipili works with images, pictures, sounds and other input through the physical senses and from the mind of uhane. Unihipili is normally silent, but can sneeze, cough, moan and even cry. On the other hand, uhane has the power of speech, while Aumakua communicates telepathically and through symbols in dreams.

All three selves are perceptive. Aumakua has a more highly evolved view of reality, broader in scope and with greater perceptive powers. Each self has a world view, but they are uniquely different. Uhane sees much of reality through social conditioning and is often programmed to be obedient to the wills of other human beings, Uhane often becomes nearly a total social being, accepting others' ideas, concepts and beliefs and imposing these on their own unihipili rather than exercising their own creative will and powers of discriminating the valuable from the valueless, the meaningful from the meaningless.

Unihipili builds a self-image, a self-concept for uhane to live by from the material accepted by uhane. The low self is in charge of the memory bank, and one of its services to uhane is to furnish any item of memory when asked. Unihipili must also keep contained all unexpressed thoughts and feelings that uhane has repressed or suppressed into the memory bank. These fill the mind of unihipili and keep clamoring for the fulfillment which has been denied them. Sometimes it seems as if we had a tape recorder running steadily, rephrasing over and over every thought we ever created!

Uhane reasons, develops an intellect and develops powers of intuition or knowing through its power of willingness to know. Uhane has free will or the power to make choices of what it "wills" unihipili to do for it through its direction, imagination, suggestion or comand. Uhane's consciousness often wanders, moving into many states or levels. Uhane daydreams, remembers the past, imagines what the future may be or what it wishes it would be. Uhane often functions in a self-induced trance, spacing out from the here and now. Uhane can also be sharply aware of the present, and can focus attention concentratedly. Uhane is constantly making choices; to love or not to love, to despise or approve, to think or remember.

Uhane has the choice of responding to what is actually happening "out there" or reacting to what is occuring within. The reader of this book is uhane, a human spirit, a human being. Unaware that your low self takes your every thought and wish quite literally, you have been creating the context within which you are experiencing this lifetime as your low self manifests the forms within those contexts. You are the source, for your unihipili, for the design for living that you enjoy or dislike. Your low self looks up to you as its lord and master, its parent and its teacher. In particular, your low self sees you as the architect of your life cycle. You plan, and unihipili will faithfully carry out exactly what it receives by way of instruction, suggestion or command. It needs your "will-in-action," for it has nowhere to go, nothing to do without it. It also hungers for love, as uhane does, and uhane has the choice of either loving its own inner self in emulation of the high self, unconditionally, or it may choose to despise and look down on the self within as inferior.

We are very fortunate that our elemental self is so dependable. We can rely on it completely to faithfully carry out our every wish, our every desire, for these are "will" for unihipili, to be obeyed. Unihipili never sleeps as uhane does. Its constant awareness and hovering consciousness that permeates the physical body, even when it is anesthetized, assures us of continued physical existence.

Of course all elemental low selves are in evolution, growing more adult all the time, so now and then we get a "beginner" who forgets to breathe (as trained to) and a crib-death results. Can you imagine that poor little elemental reporting back to its superiors? When they ask "How did you do this time?" it must hang its head in embarrassment and humiliation as it replies "I forgot to breathe!"

Unihipili thinks deductively, but is unable to reason inductively as uhane does. This is important to remember when communicating with the low self, for all communications must be very literal in order that they can be correctly understood by your own self.

The High Self, Aumakua, is two in one, the great parent, both male and female. It is everything that unihipili and uhane are, and much more. It is a self that is above our level of understanding, so we have to take a lot of information about it on faith until we begin to experience communication with it.

We already know much about the two selves, uhane and unihipili, for we have had direct experience of them ever since we were born. They are known as the conscious self and the subconscious self and our life experience is full of their interaction. They make up the team of two selves that produce what we experience. They have many features of polarity, and are either complementary or in opposition, depending on the circumstances.

The following chart is a list of the features of unihipili and uhane that have been covered in the text up to this point. Use it to review what you have learned about uhane and unihipili.

MIDDLE SELF	LOW SELF
Uhane	Unihipili
Conscious self.	Sub-conscious self.
Human spirit.	Nature spirit.
Centers in the head.	Centers in the solar plexus.
Has a subtle body called kino-aka. An astral body.	Has a subtle body called kino-aka. An etheric body.
Uses energy called mana-mana.	Uses energy called mana.
Has the power of will.	Has the power of wisdom.
Has thoughts and feelings.	Retains thought forms and emotional patterns.
Has short term memory.	Retains all memories.
Ratironal and intuitional mind.	Literal mind.
Inductive and decuctive reason	deductive thinking only.
Has free choice.	Ruled by uhane's choices.
Plays social roles.	Serves the social self.
Vocal.	Mute.
The initiator.	The completer.
Decision Maker.	Carries out commands.
Goal setter.	Goal achiever.

SOME OF THE ROLE PLAYING

Teacher	Student
Master	Servant
Parent	Child
Programmer	The programmed

Within the Huna concept, a sense of sin is considered a natural response to knowing we caused another pain. Many of us are not aware of how much and how often we hurt our selves. Because of that we do not feel guilt for having done so. By using Huna techniques and understanding the Huna concept, our awareness of causing pain can eliminate any further hurting acts. We can also begin a life style in which we do not allow others to hurt our low selves anymore.

Working with Huna we begin to realize how much in our lives is holding us back from the life we want to live. Much of this is due to pain inflicted in the past on our own low self. We tend to begin at home, with our low self. We resolve to stop any kind of speech or behavior that is hurting our own inner self. Denigrating remarks, insults, self-deprecation are all integrated into the low-self image. A context is created within which the low self feels unloved, unappreciated and inferior.

Moving into a harmless, hurtless life style we become aware of what we say about our own selves, think about our own selves and feel toward them. We are also alerted to other people's speech concerning their own selves. Gradually and painlessly our world view changes. We see these all in a different light, and begin to change our attitudes.

We begin to stand up for our own self. We stop others from hurting it in any way. We let them know our low self feels hurt and become the protector and defender of our own low self. We stop attacking our own self and begin to appreciate its contribution to the whole person. We begin to recognize its function within us and appreciate the enormous contributions it makes. No longer do we put ourselves down as unworthy, unlovable or inferior in any way. That change is reflected outwardly in our world.

Working with Huna, we see the value in living a life in which we never hurt another intentionally and begin to stop the unintentional behaviors that result in another's hurt. We begin to make amends for any hurt inflicted as soon as possible. Gaining forgiveness for any offense we have inflicted is a major goal. Keeping ourselves free of any guilt feelings or patterns frees us to live more fully and accomplish better goals.

You must accept that your own low self comes first. Your own low self is the one you have the first obligation to. Be certain you and others do not hurt it further. Work to eliminate harmful actions that hurt others as your secondary task. Drop any behavior that you find results either in hurt to a self or causes you feelings of guilt.

We cannot go through life without hurting our self or another now and then. Huna provides a solution to these events. Gaining forgiveness dissolves guilt as does making amends. To be forgiven is a state within yourself. It is something you feel or experience. Words are unimportant if one does not *feel* forgiven. Many times another says "I forgive you" and yet you retain a sense of guilt. It is our own inner experience we must deal with and that is the most important. It is that state of guilt within that must be dissolved.

Making amends is one way to absolve yourself from guilt. Uhane's function is to plan a program of making amends. Uhane's consultation with the low self will determine if the plan will be sufficient to dissolve all feelings of guilt. As we work with Huna we sometimes discover we have guilt feelings about past deeds. Often, the people we hurt are no longer around and therefore we cannot make amends. In those cases, a program of giving to others as substitutes often works. Make amends by giving to another what you could have given to the one you hurt long ago.

Begin now to help your own low self by controlling impulses to action that would hurt another and developing patterns of remedying any hurt as quickly as possible. Apologize to your own self for any past hurts; ask it for forgiveness. Repeat this daily until you actually feel that forgiveness flowing upward from the solar plexus. Explain that you hurt the low self, through ignorance, and now in your new-found wisdom, your intention is to avoid continuing any harmful speech or action. Each time you find you have hurt yourself or someone else, apologize and ask your self to forgive you.

Be sensitive to the inner experience of others. As you become aware of their hurt feelings, respond in ways to alleviate that hurt. Respond to their inner pain appropriately as it happens, and without any reference to past feelings or actions. Today is now. Being hurt is now. Past hurts are only triggers for what we may experience in this moment.

Planning programs to obtain forgiveness or make amends can be tricky. You may have to work at them. Re-work your plans and put a lot of energy and thought into them. Keep checking with your low self until a plan you both like is created and then proceed. We must differentiate natural guilt from social guilt. In our society there are many sins. Social sins masquerade under other labels. When we are wrong we feel guilty. When we behave badly by social standards we feel guilty. So these are truly social sins. Most of us carry a load of guilt from being programmed by our society to feel guilty when we flout society's rules. From early childhood on we are programmed to accept a set of values already established by others—what is right and what is wrong, what is good or bad. Our social survival and fulfillment of social needs depends on whether we accept these values and integrate them into a personal system. For most of us they become our own. We forget their origin, and we become convinced they are our own values. When young we need a set of guidelines in order to survive, but we soon forget that they are truly guidelines for survival and not our own.

As we mature, and our ability to reason develops, some of us change the value system we hold. This often causes rifts between the low self, who clings to the social set, and the middle self, who has developed personal values that are meaningful to it. The two selves lose touch with each other and become alienated from one another. Many of us walk around with a tremendous load of guilt, yet we don't know why. We would love to shed it, and be free of guilt, but we don't know how. We've even lost track of how we got it in the first place! Huna helps us to understand how guilt has collected and gives us techniques to rid ourselves of guilt.

How can I convince you of the importance of working with the Huna concept of guilt and hurt? Perhaps you are tired of being hurt, tired of feeling guilty and want to change your life style so you can function without them. If so, great. For you who are still content with things the way they are, let's explore a little more the effects of being hurt and not expressing that hurt.

Unexpressed hurt becomes anger, and suppressed anger becomes hostility which can be destructive. If we hurt others and their hurt is held in, it can boomerang later and hit us with destructive force. We have all had experiences of being the target of someone's anger over something we have done without them letting us know it hurt them. When they blow up, we usually say "Why didn't you tell me?" Or, perhaps they say that to us when we explode after a similar situation. Start to express your hurt when it is in a small and current state. Let people know when they have hurt you. Expect them to remember that and not repeat it. If they do, hold them responsible for it. If you feel angry that they have done what you told them would hurt you, express that mild anger before it becomes hostility. You will be doing them a favor! Not allowing others to hurt you is one way you can show them you love them, and care about them. Just as much as you desire to lead a harmless, hurtless life, you should encourage others to do it as well.

Begin to eliminate conditions that allow you to become a target for another's anger, resentment, hurt feelings or put-downs. Stop them right at the start! Become more aware of making others targets for your own feelings of hurt, anger, guilt and self-blame. Begin to change your world view to encompass awareness of all harmful acts and you will have a beneficial effect on others' lives as well as your own. Awareness begins the change that gradually leads you into a harmless, hurtless life style.

When we look around us and see the increasing violence in our society, we become fearful and distrusting. And, we wonder, where is it coming from? Mindless acts of violence are seeming to become commonplace. Deep down we fear our own repressed anger and hostility. Others expressing their anger threaten our tightly reined-in violence.

In our early religious instruction many of us have heard an unforgettable story of our begining as human beings. The story relates that man and woman were created as perfect beings, without fear, anger or guilt. "Original sin" is the part of this story that illustrates disobedience to authority. By disobeying the one in authority, this original man and woman first experienced guilt and shame. We have carried this potential for feeling shame and guilt within our very bones from the time we first heard that story.

Our fear of those in authority and their powers to punish and hurt us colors our whole childhood experience. It lies in our subconscious like a slow-moving poison, inhibiting us and creating a context wherein it is better to hide what we feel, hold back our natural impulses and suppress expression. Doing what we want becomes a sinful act if it is in contradiction to what others wish.

Our parents, religious leaders, government officials and others become the authorities who can cause us pain. We fear being hurt or restricted by their power. We mature ignorant of the high price we pay for suppressing our expression of our true feelings. In a sense, this common process leads to the outbursts of violence and hostility we are experiencing throughout our society today. We are vulnerable to infection as long as we continue to allow the same repressions to simmer within us.

As stated previously, there is only one sin in Huna. It is not disobedience to authority. It is to hurt another. And the more intentional the hurt, the greater the sin. When we are fully aware that hurt will result from our acts, our guilt is greater. Just like the crimes that fill our news, the targets for our rage are not the original causes of our anger. Misplaced because of taboos ingrained in our psyche, our acts sometimes seem inexplicable. It is natural to feel hurt, natural to feel guilty, when hurting another. Our natural response to alleviate pain in others has been buried beneath a social structure that trains us to mind our own business and to ignore others' pain.

You may experience a paradox working with this one sin of Huna. There are those individuals who *choose* to be hurt. You may be one of those, or some of your friends may be. An example of this would be when something is said with no intention of hurting another, and yet the recipient chooses to take it as a hurtful remark. Dealing with this paradox can be difficult, but being aware of it means there are methods we can use to overcome it. Begin to take responsibility for your own choices, and start to hold others responsible for theirs.

I had a friend who "chose" to feel hurt whenever she realized how seldom I called her on the phone. She let me know about this when she called me. My response to this was "Who needs friends like this!" I told her that if she chose to feel hurt and neglected by my lack of attention to her, that I would sever our relationship in order to "cure the situation." I let her know I had no intention of hurting her, no feeling of neglect was manifested in my not calling but that she had a knack for making me feel guilty about what I did not do. I told her I carried enough guilt without her adding to my burden! Being quite intelligent, she perceived the logic, and we agreed that I was free not to call her without her interpreting that as neglect or hurt.

Do you hold people up to shame or blame when they forget your birthday? When they neglect to do something you want them to? Would you like to feel you have some power over their actions and that you can wield this power by making them feel guilty? If so, become aware of it, and reconsider your attitude. Become aware of those who wield power over you by creating feelings of guilt within you. Realize you have a choice in the matter. If you continue to feel guilty, it's your responsibility, not theirs. It's a game people play within the power struggles of relationships. You can choose to refuse blame or shame just because someone else places it on you. Anyone who hurts us deliberately, in any way, does not have our best interests at heart. You hurt someone when you make them feel any kind of emotional pain. We must learn to be responsible for our own choices, our own unhappiness or happiness, and move out from under the control of others. We must drop our efforts to control others through their avoidance of pain and through their fears of incurring our displeasure.

Begin to be authentic, to express what you feel and think as honestly as you can. If these sincere and truthful expressions of your experience are not related as caused by another but as a state of being within you, they will be effective in better relationships with others. There is a big difference between similar statements. "I feel unhappy" is a far cry from "You make me unhappy." Begin to be responsible for your own inner experience. Begin to tune in to the inner experience of others. Respond to that with genuine caring so their pain can be alleviated. But always be aware that another may choose the painful experience. You must respect that choice.

Are your relationships nurtured by caring and concern for others? Or, are they games you are playing with others to vent your anger and spite? Do you seek out those who will deliberately hurt you to validate some concept of yours that this is the way the world is? Do you seek to be a victim of others' unkindness? Or, do you know someone else who always finds that they are the victim of others?

Here is an exercise. You use your own imagination to bring into experience the differing world views of unihipili, uhane's social self, and Aumakua. Keep in mind that unihipili represents the inner mind that has been shaped and organized according to the choices you have made, and that the social self is that which has been shaped by society's will. Your Aumakua's love for you will be expressed through its concern for your welfare and growth.

The following technique will help you get in touch with your three selves. You can either memorize the procedure, or dictate it onto a cassette tape so that you can play it back as you go through the technique. A tape recorder is a good investment for a student of Huna, for there are many ways it can be used to help you. It shortens the time spent and is much more effective than using your recall.

Begin every Huna technique by relaxing. There are two popular methods you can use. Sequential relaxation or tension relaxation. For sequential relaxation you focus on each part of your body in turn, mentally instructing it to relax, go limp, become peaceful. Starting with your toes, tell them to relax, become limp. Move to your ankles, instructing them to relax and become limp. Move on up your legs, focussing on your calves, knees, thighs and hips, instructing each one to become relaxed and peaceful. Continue on through your buttocks and torso and on up to your chest, shoulders, neck and head. When you reach your head tell your scalp to relax, then your forehead, nose, cheeks, lips and chin. When you have completed the succession of body parts from toes to head you will be completely relaxed.

While both techniques work, I prefer tension relaxation. Choose a time and place where you will have at least half an hour undisturbed. Wear loose fitting clothes and pick a comfortable chair. Stretch out one leg in front of you until it is level with your hips then stretch it outward as you tense the leg as hard as you can. Hold it a moment and then let your leg drop as you stop tensing. Do the same with your other leg. Now stretch out one arm to the side as far as it will stretch, hold for a moment and then let go. It will drop to your side. Do the same with your other arm. Next sit up very straight, stretching upward as high as you can. Hold for a moment, and then stop tensing, allowing your body to resume its natural posture. In order not to slump, imagine an invisible hook coming down from above and attaching to your head. Allow it to draw you upright without using any of your own energy to do so. Now you are ready to begin your adventure in imagination. The following directions can be either taped or memorized.

As I move in to greater awareness, I relax more and more. Counting from ten to one will narrow and concentrate my awareness and relax my body further. As the count proceeds my awareness becomes more focussed.

Counting from ten to one, I move clockwise around an ascending staircase, spiral in form, within my mind. Ten, my experience begins, nine, I move around the spiral staircase as my body relaxes and my awareness sharpens and focusses. To eight, alertly aware, I move to seven. From seven I continue to move, my awareness more focussed, my body more relaxed. Six, five, awareness keen, comfort and ease of body greater. Four, three, deeply relaxed and fully aware. Two to one brings me to a focussed awareness and a relaxed state. Here I poise myself.

Clarity is reached and my target is the program I am about to complete. First I will imagine my social self in front of me to my right. I allow that social self to form in figure, posture and pose. I observe carefully what I perceive. I *will* that this experience and all my observations remain as vivid memories, to be recalled at my desire at any time in the future. Now I observe the clothing, facial expression and any other details within this image. I allow this image to move and change, the pantomime a teaching experience for me. I stay with this moving image for a short period of time, absorbing all it has to teach me.

As I move to the next experience, I reiterate that all I have experienced will be recalled easily in the future.

Smoothly I repeat in reverse succession the numbers ten to one to move spirally, (clockwise) to my next phase. Ten, nine, eight, seven, six, five, four, three, two, one. At this level uhane's feeling nature can be externalized.

To my left let an image of the feeling part of uhane appear. It will be in motion, either sitting, standing or moving about freely. Let this image appear as a person of a specific age to symbolize my emotional maturity. I keep my attention focussed on this projected image and observe carefully the picture, the pantomime, and the body language of this expressive part of me. I stay with it to learn of my current state. I notice all relevant details, and I will remember all of this to be recalled at a future time. I stay with it in silence and repose as an observer. As I feel this image completed, I release it and move on.

Now moving to encounter my unihipili, who will appear in front of me as a small creature, I count ten, nine, eight, seven, six, five, four, three, two and one. As I pause the objective image of unihipili is projected in front of me as if I were looking through a telescope which brings this tiny creature into view. Remaining silent to enter this realm where unihipili lives, I keep my awareness focussed on what is presented to me. I observe each detail of form and movement. Each color, each object. I will remember all of this later, and now I willingly learn from what is presented to me at this moment. Before I leave this image I project toward it my love and care and my full acceptance. I express my gratitude and appreciation for all services performed on my behalf. I close this part by blessing my own unihipili and releasing it from my experience.

Moving up the spiral staircase again, clockwise, I count from ten to one for my encounter with a projected image of my Aumakua. Ten, nine, eight, seven, six, five, four, three, two, one. Love is here. I feel it. Unconditional love and acceptance flow to me from this projected image. I am receptive to the love and radiance that I can imagine, and my focussed awareness reveals to me the specific telepathic communication I need now. I relax even more in recognition of the great protection this love gives me, and experience that which I realize I will give to others in the future. As I experience its power I know it is to be shared by flowing through my own expression and action. I release this projection in my imagination, and sit quietly for a few moments.

Now I resume my daily affairs by returning to waking consciousness and full awareness of the material and physical world around me. I stretch my arms and legs as a cat does, arousing from a nap. I stretch all over as I open my eyes and orient myself to my surroundings. Relaxed and refreshed I am ready to proceed with mundane affairs.

During one of my experiences I reached my low self first and got the impression of its holding a lot of guilt. When I touched on the feeling side of my nature I saw a young girl, crying because of making so many mistakes. She felt upset about them but was helpless to do anything. Moving next to my social self I saw a grown woman trying to make up to all those she had hurt. She felt guilty and responsible for their difficulties because of her mistakes, I saw her wishing she could be forgiven, but feeling that she could not.

Moving to the high-self level of consciousness, I did not see any images, but I heard a telepathic conversation. It seemed that two people were conversing about forgiveness. One said to the other "What is this about getting our forgiveness? We don't have any of that commodity here. For here there is nothing to forgive. We accept all with perfect love and never perceive anything as needing our forgiveness. We have none to give." The other commented, "I guess she will just have to deal with this forgiveness need all by herself. If she wants to keep her guilt and regrets we can't prevent her, but we recommend she let them go and dissolve the barriers between herself and others. It is only on the human level that there is such a thing as sin and forgiveness. Guilt is a purely human trait, not a divine one."

I came out of this with a new understanding of what I must do. I had to accept myself as completely as the Higher Selves do.

I have three selves to work with and integrate. The more I use these techniques, the more efficiently I work with the selves and get them into a harmonious team. You have three selves too. The more often you are in touch with all of them, the more you can integrate their world views, desires, experiences and talents. There is a purpose and meaning to your life here and now. Keeping in touch with all three selves is one way to determine what those desires, experiences and talents are. When all three selves are pursuing the same goals, looking for meaning within the same activities and finding the same purpose for being alive, success is assured.

Use this technique as often as you feel it is desirable. You may use it by posing a specific question concerning a decision you want to make or a choice you must make. You are the boss, but the input of your other selves can help you by giving you more information on which to base your decision.

Uhane lives in a world of duality, our cultural society. Love and hate, right and wrong, good and bad, beautiful and ugly. These polar opposites are all part of the framework on which we build our life style. Conditional love is what most of us experience from other individuals and it is what we most often give. True caring is beyond most middle selves capabilities or capacity, however, it is the quality of the compassion of the High Self. Unconditional love is the feeling within each High Self toward all over living beings. The dualistic conceptual pattern that society imposes on all uhanes, which are units within it, is reflected back again from unihipili who so aptly mimics the values of its uhane. These reflections occur as events that naturally flow into being in the dualistic framework. Unihipili builds your personal world—literally—on what you believe, think and feel. Your world view has come into being from the values found in your environment and from those who have had power and authority over you when you were growing up. At this time, your low self has a world view that may be different from your conscious one, for uhane is noted for changing its mind frequently, while lodged firmly in the low self structure are values of good and evil, right and wrong, that were impressed deeply into its consciousness long ago. This gives rise to conflict between uhane and unihipili. The work of Huna is to dissolve these conflicts and restore unity and harmony between all the selves.

Both uhane and unihipili have a self-image. Uhane gets its self-image by reflecting to the world what the world has impressed on uhane of its value system. Unihipili gets its self-image from uhane's opinions of its own self. Its inner self. Many of us hate our self often. We deride ourselves, disparage ourselves. We put our selves down. Unihipili absorbs all these attitudes like a sponge, creating a self-image through repetition or intensity.

All selves need love. They are constructed to give love. The High Selves love unconditionally. There is nothing we can do that will change that unconditional love. To them, we have never been unlovable. The High Selves love us totally. They care about us and about whether we are happy or unhappy. They care when we feel unfulfilled or guilty. They care about our progress through life and try to assist us in fulfilling our reason for being born here in our body.

The middle self seeks love and approval from other humans. Uhane accepts the dual values and standards of its society and follows suit. It gives conditional love or hate. In the United States, it is very common to teach children to despise their inner self, to repress or suppress their natural urges and inclinations. Our culture teaches us to place others' happiness before our own. It impresses on us the need to love others and not ask for love. Many of us grow up with a low opinion of our own inner self, that is reflected in its self-image. We just do not love our own unihipili. Many unihipili are starved for love. You have it in your power to love your own inner self as unconditionally as your High Self loves you both. Being a mirror-like consciousness, reflecting what you think and feel, unihipili will only radiate as much love as it gets from you. An unloved unihipili is incapable of loving anyone else. So begin to love your own self now. When unihipili is filled with love, its consciousness expands. You will feel that rising within you and that love will radiate outward to include all others. Unihipili expands in the warmth of your approval and love. Your admiration for its great contribution to your life will bring you rewards of greater enthusiasm in fulfilling your goals. Any self who feels unloved contracts, hides and pulls away from contact with others. It emanates coolness or coldness and refuses to share what little love it has.

The first selves we are obliged to love are our own. Admire them, approve of them, and accept them unconditionally. You are the most important person to your own unihipili. You are its authority, its ruler, the controlling self.

Do you ever talk to yourself? You know the old saying, "If you talk to yourself, you're either rich or crazy." Well, it's not true. Everyone should talk directly to his own low self, but always in a kind, courteous and considerate manner. Treate your low self as someone you do not want to hurt, for it is sensitive and will flinch at anything unkind. It recoils from insults and contracts from the chill of disapproval.

Do you ever talk about your self? I'll bet you do it more than you realize. I know I do, and for a long time I've been trying to be aware of what I say about myself. Because modesty is so highly valued in our society, we often say demeaning things about ourselves. We're inclined to look down on people who "blow their own horn" and approve of those who depreciate themselves. Thus, you often hear people say, "Oh, I have no talent at all," or "I forget things all the time," or "I'm not very smart," or "I'll never be able to do that," or "That was stupid of me" or "I just can't help myself."

Listen to the people you meet from now on and notice what they say about themselves. Listen to your own words. I think you may be surprised. Remember, everything you say about yourself conditions your low self's image. You either help to encourage the negative image established in the past, or you give your self a new and better image. What kind of self-image do you have? Does your self believe it is careless, stupid, graceless, homely, unlovable or something similar? Are your reinforcing those opinions or counteracting them? Make a resolution to change from a poor image to one that fits what you know about the low self. The low self will live up to the image it believes to be true because the image is built through words and experiences.

The low self is the storehouse of all of uhane's unexpressed feelings. All feeling is happening at the present time in uhane, but if not fully expanded into action or expression, the unfulfilled feeling becomes a stored emotion. All emotions are of the past, stored in the memory held by unihipili and furnishing a basis for reaction in the present.

To clearly understand the differences between feeling and emotion helps clarify one of the basic differences between unihipili and uhane. There are two aspects of consciousness uhane experiences. One is a feeling response to experience, the other a mental response to what is happening. Many of us have lost touch with certain feeling responses, such as anger, guilt or grief from having suppressed them so often, but they are there and impressing our low self with their energy. Unexpressed, they build up in the memory as an emotional framework for future reactions to similar events.

In my own life, I was taught that nice girls do not display anger. I really wanted to be a nice girl. Somehow I came to believe that nice girls don't feel angry. Over a period of time, all my anger was automatically repressed. As a mature woman I could honestly state, "I never feel angry." I was over fifty years old before I discovered that I certainly had experienced anger, but just had not been aware of it. I began to deal with unexpressed, repressed anger that my low self had been storing up. With the help of my High Self, and the willing cooperation of unihipili, I am able to bring into my awareness the feeling of anger when it occurs, as well as some of the fears I had hidden and some of the guilt. You may discover, through Huna, that you can do as I have done and am still doing. You will bring into awareness and be able to express feelings in permissable and acceptable ways. I have learned to laugh more fully and to allow myself to cry. I have learned that the guilt I hold, my regrets, are just so much extra weight. I am slowly unloading them to lighten my life, to free me to fulfill my life purposes. You too can do it with Huna, easily. It is fun and exciting rather than fearsome or dreadful.

Feeling is an experience of uhane in a constant changing response to life itself. Unihipili with its elemental consciousness mirrors back to us everything we feel. In that mirror is all the feeling we held back. Feeling is life itself. The more we experience feeling, the more alive we are. Life flows, and feeling flows from the inside in an ever-outward direction. Turned in on itself its flow is blocked. It becomes a stagnant, non-moving, destructive force.

Tears and laughter are actions that need the full participation of all parts of each human being to work their wonderful capacity for healing mind, emotions and bodies. By the time we move into our twenties, most of us are only crying or laughing with a tiny part of our being. The healing quality is lost. Pain gives rise to the desire to cry. Pleasure gives rise to the desire to laugh. We have all experienced these in their fullness at some time. The pleasure of discovery of something new, or of something understood at last, causes laughter. Mental, emotional or physical pain brings tears to our eyes on many an occasion. Most of us are familiar with the sore throat we get when we hold back unshed tears. Some of us are aware of chest pain when the desire to cry is suppressed or repressed. Many of us have been conditioned to believe that weakness is *bad* and crying is a sign of weakness, and therefore *bad*, too. Many of us have lost the capacity to cry!

When an individual stands dry-eyed at a time of obvious personal grief, nearly everyone joins in the chorus, "Cry, it will do you good!" They realize that tears will soothe the pain of grief and exert a healing effect. Tears are a balm for the whole self, the salve it needs to heal the pain. Who knows what else could be healed if tears were allowed to flow freely? Perhaps we are wrong when we urge others not to cry, to be brave. As parents we stick lollipops in children's mouths when they cry, we soothingly say, "There now, don't you cry."

As you begin to work with Huna perhaps you will be able to release some of your unshed tears. You may be able to learn again the healthy aspect of crying freely when you feel pain. The difficulty you may have is with your own conditioning and in presenting other conditioned social beings with a reaction that may threaten their own unshed tears. They may react with anger or discomfort. Try to work appropriately with Huna techniques, and realize you will be moving away from your usual conditioned responses.

Just as tears have a healing effect on our body, so does laughter. Tears and laughter, the great healers. Norman Cousins tells of his recovery from a very serious illness through the use of humor. In his book *Anatomy of an Illness* he relates finding that a good laugh starts deep within the abdomen, moves upward with tremendous energy and heals the body in the process. His reflections on healing and regeneration are now being taken quite seriously by those in the healing professions. Especially by those who realize that all cures and healings take place within the body and are performed by the intelligence within the body. All others can do is to assist in that process.

Here is a technique you may use to renew yor body's ability to laugh heartily. Many of us do not laugh fully at all. Since laughter "is the best medicine" you should take this technique seriously. However, you may find it more difficult to do than read about. Again, find a place where you can be alone for ten minutes outside the hearing range of any other person. Perhaps you may want to go outside and find a nice spot in a wooded area or an open field. Wherever you go, make sure you feel confident you will not be overheard. Stand up straight, breathe deeply a few times, focus on your outbreath. Breathe in all the way to the bottom of the abdomen. Then press your hand against the bottom of your abdomen as you breathe out. Press inward and upward when you exhale, breathing out until you just can't get any more breath out. Practice this breathing for a few moments, then let your breath be taken over by your low self. Start laughing. Just use a "hee haw" or any other words or sounds that IMITATE laughing. Keep doing it, repeating whatever you have chosen until it transforms itself into real laughter. Keep going until that laughter rises from the very pit of your abdomen. Deep and hearty, let the laughter roll out. You may be able to laugh until you cry! That's great—and is most healing to your system. If you have difficulty with this exercise, go to your public library and get some books that are humorous to read so you arouse your dormant potential for laughter. Then try the exercise again. Once you have been able to get a good belly laugh going you will experience a great sense of relief and relaxation. The healing process is well begun.

The best morning meditation I know of is the laughing meditation. As soon as you wake up, start laughing and keep laughing for five minutes. If you are married get your spouse to join you or you may find yourself in trouble!

Give yourself to these techniques and experience the response that comes. First we have to give of ourselves to receive the benefits that can come from the giving. We must give in order to receive. Giving is primary, gaining is secondary. First we must give something, then its natural response comes to us.

We give attention, and in turn receive attention from others. We give our own low self attention, recognition, respect and caring. Then back come these same qualities to us with even greater power than contained in our gift. All of the aforementioned have penetrating power. When absorbed, that power can transform the well-being of our low self. It in turn transforms our well-being. As we transform our low self, we are transformed.

However it is not just a two-way exchange between the low and middle self. There is a third self involved. As we give to our own low self, we are given to by our High Self. As we love our low self, we are loved by our High Self. The simultaneous action of low self reception and High Self gift to us is a remarkable experience to the Huna student, and well worth working toward.

As the low self has the capacity to grow to human stature, so the middle self can grow from human to divine. Both of these selves are receptive and absorbant to what comes to them from a higher level. Sitting in the seat of power we create the material from which our low self builds and organizes its own structure. As we "do" to our low self, the same is "done" to us by our High Self. The quality of feeling we feed our low self is the quality of feeling we get from our High Self. First we give to the low self and then we get from the High Self. There seems to be no other way! The paradox of first the gift given and then the gift received can be resolved in our own experience.

Most of us came to Huna because of feelings of separation and alienation from our own ground of being, from our own selves, and perhaps from what we call God. We wanted to be whole, united and at peace. We want to "come home," the oft-repeated phrase that is so difficult to understand. What is common for many of us is our experience of feeling we are *away from home*. And yet, we cannot explain why we feel this way.

Coming home is being re-united with our low and High Selves. To be healed of this separation and the alienation between us and our High Self, we must heal the split between ourselves and our low selves. We must give before we can get, and we start by doing what is possible. We give to our low self all that we desire to have from our High Self. As we do, silently and invisibly, the same quality of giving flows to us from our High Self. As we love, so we are loved. As we forgive, so we are forgiven. As we revere so we are revered. As we alleviate pain, our own is eased. As we raise our self, we are also raised up, in consciousness. As we fill our own low self with love, respect and recognition, we receive love, respect and recognition of a different nature from our High Self. The low self cannot know the love we have except by our gifts. And as we give, we receive what we cannot know, except that it be given to us from a self which possesses a nature so different from the middle and low selves it is nearly beyond our comprehension. Let us try to give in line with what we feel we would welcome in greater measure. And as we do, we should recognize that each gift prepares us for the capacity to give more, until we truly become a channel through which high-self qualities flow.

2

Unihipili

Unihipili is your inner self, the child within or the low self. Most any label can be used. Choose the one that will fit your idea of your own unihipili best. You will find your concept of that self will vary according to circumstances, so remain flexible for awhile. Think of each label as a role-playing one that is used under very specific circumstances. The first thing to do is choose a name for your own unihipili. It's not polite to keep saying "Hey, you..." A specific name will clarify to whom you are actually talking. Be sure the name you choose is compatible with dignity, pride and self-worth. These are characteristics we should encourage in our low selves. You might name it after some person whose character you admire or who typifies success in your chosen field of endeavor. The name can be whatever pops into your awareness from your own low self. The name you choose may be a temporary one, usable until a more suitable name can be determined. As you select a name, be alert to reactions to it rising within you. If you get a feeling that it's not right, try another one. Do this until you feel completely comfortable with the name you have chosen. Inform your self that for now you will be addressing it by that name. Later you may want to change it.

Max Long called his low self George. I call mine Junior. One student named hers "subby" after the word subconscious. Another student, Mary, calls hers Mary Jane. Choose whatever seems suitable. All kinds of ideas will occur to you.

In some primitive religions it is believed that each person has a secret "true" or "real" name. It is also believed that a magician cannot effectively practice magic on a person unless he knows the true name. Of course, true names were closely guarded secrets. There is protective value in this practice. If your low self learns to accept values and ideas only when it is addressed by name, you can control what affects it.

Naming your own low self is the first step. Learning about its nature comes next. Then, armed with some knowledge, begin a series of communications with it to find out more and more. Each technique practiced will reveal another facet of your low self and help integrate its personality with your own.

The mind of unihipili has been called a "bio-computer" for it has many of the characteristics of a computer. Its exact, literal deductions about time and space are one of these characteristics. Another is the aspect of being literal and factual in its interpretation of everything fed into it. The low self is different from a computer in that it converts speech into images which it holds in its memory bank. All sounds, sights, smells and tastes are images recorded in its consciousness. It cannot differentiate between the messages it gets from the environment and those from your thoughts, ideas and feelings. It registers them all as facts of life, organizing them into a fantastic web of relationships. It *associates* each input with others already there and classifies the input.

The word "carrot" is associated with its form, color, taste and smell. Different words are associated with other words in some relationship within the mind of unihipili, and the word association test given by psychologists can be used by Huna students at home to find out what some of these relationships are for you personally.

Uhane is a dualistic self, separating what is thought and what is felt—living in a world of dualistic concepts of right and wrong, bad and good. Unihipili puts it all together into patterns. Most of us do more thinking than feeling in our daily life. Some of us are unaware that feeling is a continuous stream of consciousness for uhane. Many of us are unaware of what we are feeling. But the two-way streams of thoughts and feelings are flowing and registering in the mind of unihipili to be translated into action, memory or storage. With the help of our low self, we can recover many past experiences of feelings of which we are not aware. Those memories still have impact on us, though they have been long forgotten by uhane.

Another important fact about unihipili is that it keeps a record of all our conditioning, all the prohibitions we have accepted, all of the outer world's restrictions on our behavior, all the taboos, the no-nos, and other types of input which are what we unconsciously live by after we are grown up.

All the defenses we built into our computers are available to us from unihipili. The record is clear and exact. Our self-image, which developed from others' reaction to our behavior, is there, intact and measurable. It's there whether we feel lovable and worthy, or whether we feel unlovable and unworthy of receiving attention, and whether we feel in control of our own life, or controlled by outside forces.

The difficult task of Huna is not in getting answers, but in learning to ask the questions that have answers. We may have to ask many questions before we hit on one that has an answer. We may have to learn new ways of asking questions in order to receive informative answers. Unihipili has a literal mind; an exact mind. A mind that deals in tangibles, images and real memories whether they come from experience, thought or feelings. Questions must be phrased in literal terms, because the answers will be literal. Ambiguous questions cannot be understood by our low self. Any response to an ambiguous question will be incorrect.

The art of asking questions of unihipili must be developed. Your low self is only too eager to help you become better acquainted. It may even be over-eager to please you. Guard against seeking answers to what you have already decided you want to hear. You have to hold your own desires and opinions in obeyance, not thinking about the answer, just the question, and being open to whatever comes. You will, in the beginning, have to convince unihipili of your sincerity, your earnest desire to hear the truth as unihipili sees it, not as you wish it to be.

When first becoming acquainted with your own low self, you will find it is like getting to know a stranger. Unihipili may hedge a little. It will not be sure of your response to its revelations. Here is where you must play the role of a very wise parent. Being patient, understanding and loving, tell your low self that you realize you have not listened to it in the past, and you are sorry. Admit you have called it names, downgraded it and acted with hatred and disgust toward it. Convince your own self that from now on you will mend your ways, always treat it kindly, always speak of it in positive, loving ways and will care for it, nurture it and protect it as you would your own child. And you must keep your word!

Many of you will find that early life experience taught unihipili not to trust anyone. Those that were supposed to love and care for it may have failed to do so. Expecting love and encouragement, some unihipili found rejection and put-downs. You must convince your own inner self that you will behave differently if this is what happened. It may take a little time for your unihipili to learn to trust you, but if you follow the Huna precepts of loving yourself first, putting it before all others in importance, defending it from others and never rejecting or insulting it, you will find its naturally trusting nature emerging. Communication will become free and honest.

Before you could reason or talk, unihipili was dealing with the outer environment as best it could. It was forced to adopt certain behaviors and attitudes in order to survive. These behaviors and attitudes remain as the background of your life. Most of us cannot remember that period of time before we started to reason and think, before we verbally communicated with our world. But with Huna techniques, and by gaining the confidnece of your unihipili, those experiences can come into your awareness to be dealt with in a reasonable manner.

When your body was in its infant state, before you had any power to care for yourself, it was fully dependent on others for a sense of worth, validation of its lovability and its ability to control others by behavior. It learned through experience to feel differing degrees of lovability, worth and power. Infants who received full caring and loving attention moved outward into the world, confident and self-assured. They trusted the outer world to be as nurturing a place as home was in their early years. The capacity to develop trusting relationships was encouraged in the secure atmosphere of the home.

Early frustration of human needs sets a pattern in unihipili of limited ability to trust other people. You can begin to remove those limits on your low self by being trustworthy. You can love your own self, hold it in high esteem and give it a sense of its own worth and power. Some of us, through forgotten early experiences, turn to the wrong people for satisfactions of our needs. Or, we are unreasonable in our demands on others. We insist they love us and pay attention to us. These unreasonable demands usually lead to our being rejected. That fulfills an inner belief in which we say the world is a rejecting, ungiving place to live in!

In this culture, where we are taught to consider other's welfare before our own, a personality is created that inhibits personal desires in order to please others. To win their acceptance and love is our most important task. We become quite disillusioned to find *it cannot be done.* You just can't please everybody.

When decoding the Hawaiian language for information about unihipili, Max Long found that the low self has a tendency to hide. It is mute, it does not speak. It stays within and in some cases uses its control over the metabolism to add layers of flesh on the physical body to feel more hidden away. It retreats from expression and will escape your probing mind to hide, even from you. It is skilled in hiding. This characteristic sometimes tends to make attempts to know it difficult. Perhaps it has been hiding from you for years. You may have to move slowly and delicately to get it to reveal the opinions, beliefs and emotions it holds. The ease or difficulty of communication may depend on the depth at which your low self has been hiding.

To see low selves before they hide, you must turn to watching infants and children in their uninhibited and unrestrained behavior. You can learn about your own inner self through scientific research into the behavior and tendencies of small children. In one experiment it was determined that each baby has a built-in response to another human being in distress. That response is the desire to alleviate distress. Even small infants demonstrated this by turning toward an adult and appealing to them to act. The low self will do the same.

Unihipili is very sensitive to pain. Unihipili dislikes to see any live creature suffer. The low self dislikes perceiving another's pain almost as much as it hates to experience pain itself. Because it is part of the world of nature, another's pain is felt as its own. This causes unihipili to retreat and hide from a world that inflicts pain.

The elemental consciousness of the low-self mind is like a mirror. It reflects back whatever is put into it. It does not judge, reason or value. It accepts all values, judgements, thoughts and ideas that come to it. It organizes all it encounters and holds in its memory everything that either it or uhane has experienced or perceived. It is a servant to uhane. It is a student of uhane and obeys uhane as the middle self's obedient child.

Conditioning children is like the conditioning of the low self. Giving it a framework in which it feels it can survive is best. Your low self is in charge of physical, mental, emotional, social and personal survival. In the case of extreme physical danger, it can even take action. It has no morals of its own, but adopts the morals of those it associates with. It builds a moralistic framework from the material given to it.

However, you can condition the low self. What is conditioning? Conditioning is the process by which the low self learns to function in this world. Through conditioning, the low self acquires its sense of right and wrong and learns modes of behavior that enable it to maintain the equilibrium that is essential to its nature.

The capacity to accept conditioning is one of the low self's great talents. That is how it learns physical skills such as walking, driving, bicycle riding, and skiing. A skill is a habit, although we often don't think of it as such. Skills and habits are learned by repetition; in order to become competent, we must practice a physical skill over and over. A routine becomes a habit through much repetition. We have habits that we consider good and others we consider bad. Whether they are good or bad to the low self depends on what it has learned by conditioning.

The low self can also be conditioned by authority. Sometimes an authority figure has to speak only once to engrave a commandment indelibly into the low self. Authorities who have the power to give or withhold what the low self wants, needs, or desires are gods to the low self. Insofar as an authority has this kind of power over the low self, the authority is able to condition it.

So, the low self is conditioned by experience and by the voice of authority. Starting at birth, parents are the gods. Later, through repeated experiences with siblings and playmates, fixed attitudes are formed. Then Mary takes her little lamb into the educational system. Although that little lamb would rather frolic and play, it is taken in hand and indoctrinated with society's standards of behavior and of what is true and false.

This is simplified, of course, but my purpose here is to indicate what we are looking for when we communicate with our low selves. Many fixed beliefs that originated in childhood are still retained by our low selves. Some of these beliefs are still useful, some are not. You may think you are well aware of all the beliefs your self holds, but I found neither I nor my students were aware of them all until we began to probe our low selves systematically.

I'd like to tell you about a childhood experience that illustrates what conditioning can do. When I was about nine years old, the family living in the next house was composed of a father, a mother and two daughters, one my age, one younger. These two girls missed school often because of colds. This puzzled me because colds were rare among my family.

What puzzled me most was that the girls' mother took such care to prevent colds, but my mother didn't! I frequently heard the girls' mother say, "Put on your rubbers or you'll get wet feet and then you'll come down with a cold!" "Bundle up well, for if you get chilled you'll be in bed with another cold." "Oh, dear, it looks like you're catching another cold!"

My mother also cautioned us to wear rubbers, but her concern was for our shoes. They cost money. To this day, I am conditioned to care for my shoes. But one hang-up I don't have is about catching colds.

Since I don't believe that getting wet brings on a cold, I can get wet and not get a cold. I do know that extreme exposure could affect my health, but it would have to be pretty extreme before my body would succumb. I also firmly believe that my low self can reject any germ it wants to, therefore, I don't fear contact with sick people.

If I feel the first symptoms of a cold, I start talking to my self and ask, "What's up, Junior?" I usually get a sensible answer as to why Junior (my name for my low self) accepted the prospect of being sick. Then I remove the cause of Junior's desire to be sick and Junior promptly rids our body of the germs.

We do not know our own selves very well. We ought to know them better. In order to know them, we must get them to communicate their thoughts, feelings, attitudes, opinions, and beliefs to us. When we get to know them, we can dissolve unwanted conditioning and start reconditioning. We can begin to assume the role of authority over our own selves and take the responsibility for monitoring all information being fed to our low selves.

Does it seem like a giantic program? To embark on a path of self-discovery and self-removal is a momentous undertaking. But I assure you it is fun all the way—an exciting adventure.

One of the characteristics revealed about unihipili through the study of the Hawaiian language is its "innate tendency to worship the gods." This strong trait has a tremendous influence on the course of our lives. As stated before, in infancy the parents are the gods that are worshipped with adulation and adoration. During adolescence this worship of the gods becomes hero worship and each individual focusses on some social figure for adulation. This shift from parents to others during adolescence occurs more strongly in individuals who lack self-confidence. When we worship a god we achieve identification with one who is stronger, better, freer and more powerful.

An article in the February 1981 issue of *Discovery* titled "The Lennon Syndrome" discussed the shift that normal children make from worshipping their parents to those worshipped by other adolescents. This is called hero worship. The transition in adolescence is from physical gods (parents) to social gods. The new gods have the power to express the things we cannot through inability or taboo. Rudolph Valentino was worshiped by women whose sexual eroticism was repressed, Elvis Presley, as rebellion against sexual morals, mirrored the wishes of many youths and Lennon rebelled against the *status quo* or the mindlessness of everyday life and conformity. Currently our gods are peaceful individuals and contrast the exploitive, materialistic and aggressive gods of the past. Deep inside we believe all gods are immortal. Therefore, the grief is most intense at the death of a social idol. This gives rise to the puzzling phenomena seen at the death of Presley, Valentino and Lennon.

With Huna, we begin to restore a sense of worth and self-esteem to our own inner self. We begin to get that self to look to the High Self for an outlet for its worship. We encourage our low self to be a channel for love and intelligence from the High Self to uhane. We begin to eliminate hero adulation.

In *The Dream And The Underworld*, author James Hillman describes three realms of being. The Upper World, the Underground and the Underworld. They correspond to the conscious, the subconscious and the unconscious. He puts our High Self into the underworld which corresponds to Heaven or the realm where souls live eternally. Into the underground, the realm of nature, he places our subconscious self unihipili. In the upper world, where he finds uhane, he finds the world of our culture and society where our heroes exist. He speaks of Hercules, the classic hero, as being the same as the ego, a part of every uhane. In all the Greek myths it is notable that the hero cannot conquer the underworld. The hero is never able to enter it. This includes Hercules. These classifications enable us to see how misplaced hero worship can be. It becomes a barrier to knowing one's own High Self and always ends in tragedy with grief at the actual death of the hero-god.

Our High Self is immortal—eternally alive in the underworld. That part of us can be communicated with and a close relationship can be formed while we are mortal. To the Hawaiian the highest divinity was each person's

High Self. They claimed anything higher could not be understood and therefore was useless to us. Our own High Self has divine aspects that can be communicated to us, emulated by us and integrated into us through the openness of our own inner self. Flowing through the subconscious, the super-conscious can make itself known.

Uhane has no direct connection with the High Self, just as the ego-hero can never enter into the High Self's underworld. Ego cannot enter the realm of consciousness where our High Self dwells. An illustration of the route the middle self must take to the High Self is found in the Tarot card THE LOVERS. There are three symbols of selves on this card. The male symbolizes uhane and he is looking to the female figure unihipili. She is looking up into the symbol of the High Self, a face with wings extending outward on both sides.

In order for the Huna student to use this precept, it is necessary to become objective to the low self, and in full communication with it. When we fully know our low selves, we can begin the process of using unihipili as a channel to the High Self. So, with first things first, we pursue knowledge of our inner self and get that relationship to uhane integrated and united.

Unihipili performs all autonomic behavior, all learned habits, skills and rituals. We learn through the Hawaiian language that it is called a "ritualistic self." Each habit is a ritual. So is each skill performed, because they are based on the pattern of sequential steps taken to reach a target or goal. Unihipili is *a creature of habit* meaning it likes to perform the same sequences that have been established over and over again. Understanding how rituals, habits and skills are learned and performed by your inner self will be of tremendous help in your retraining and in developing new habits, new rituals and new skills.

A ritual is a series of actions, always performed in the same order, and in the same way, to produce the same desired result. Parents help infants develop rituals by following ritualistic patterns themselves. Parents use rituals to get the infant to sleep, quiet him down or get him to do what they want.

A typical good-night ritual for a small child starts with undressing in a certain way, washing up in a certain sequence, getting the favorite toy or blanket and climbing into bed. Often the ritual does not end there. A drink of water, a bedtime story or some other form of attention from the parent is needed before the ritual is complete and the child can sleep.

The Kahuna made frequent use of ritual, for they well understood its functions and effectiveness. The science of psychology has probed the way people use ritual and has found that we all tend to develop rituals in our everyday life. Apparently, we are ritualistic beings who find comfort in established routines and patterns. Even as infants, we start forming rituals, many of which become ingrained habits that may persist long after we have forgotten the reasons for them.

The low self develops rituals. It groups together similar ideas and sequences of ideas in order to perform its functions. For instance, to drive a car, we must perform a certain ritual, or routine pattern of actions, without omitting any sequence. This is an innate function of the low self that follows a lawful universal pattern. Like all universal laws, this pattern is neutral but functional. It can be used properly, or it can be abused. Let's examine how we use the innate ritualistic character of our low self and see if we can use it in other ways to make life more effective.

We often fulfill our needs for security, power and success by developing rituals that bring us those things. Once these needs are fully satisfied, other needs may develop, but we may be unable to stop following the old ritual which is no longer satisfying. At times we may find that a promise of satisfaction as a result of a certain behavior is never fulfilled, but we go on behaving that way out of habit, remaining hungry and unsatisfied.

How innovative is your behavior? How spontaneous are you? How original is your approach to new events? Perhaps you're so immersed in ritual that you are absolutely predictable! Can you think of a friend who behaves in such set patterns that you can predict his behavior with certainty under most circumstances? Does certainty make you feel secure? What kind of people do you like to associate with? These are the kinds of questions that arise for a Huna student. Let them come into your mind.

We have many social rituals which help society function smoothly. Social rituals allow interpersonal interaction without friction, but it is interesting to look at them from a personal point of view, and consider whether you hide behind social rituals in order to protect your real self. If so, why? What threatens you? These can be very important questions for your personal growth.

Many social rituals inhibit honest expression of feelings, and limit our ability to really know one another. Every society has social taboos which are perpetuated by those who do not want the boat rocked. Let us examine some of society's rituals and taboos about sex, money, security, and spiritual growth—not to mention our churches' rituals, many of which have become empty and meaningless. Even some of the clergy seem to be unaware of their purposes!

According to the ancient Hawaiians, in the mind of the low self, ideas are like bunches of grapes that jostle each other into activity. This is the basis of word-association tests. Once the low self learns a pattern of activity or routine, each step of the sequence triggers the next, and life functions smoothly. Teaching a routine to the low self is a way of setting a pattern we can depend on. We know the low self will not let us down by forgetting one of the steps.

Once the low self has learned a ritual, it is greatly disturbed if the sequence is altered in any way or not completed. One of my children always had to have his blue teddy bear in his arms before he could go to sleep; he never slept without it. When I took him to stay with his grandmother for a few days, we discovered after arriving that we had forgotten to bring the blue teddy bear. I promised to mail it. The next morning I received a call from grandmother telling me that my son had not slept a wink all night, but had been sitting on the living room floor crying for his teddy bear! So, I drove out with it. Within five minutes of my arrival, he was sound asleep. He slept all day. His good-night ritual was finally completed!

Let us examine our rituals to see if they are doing what they are designed to do. If they are not, we can devise a new ritual and teach it to the low self through repetition. Since the low self clings like a vine to everything it has learned, it may not be easy to change. And it will be even more difficult if the ritual is fulfilling some unconscious need.

Creating a ritual and teaching it to your self is a method of teaching your self what goals you want to achieve. To impress some idea on the low self, create a ritual and perform it every day unti the low self has learned it and will do it automatically.

But before designing new rituals, why not redesign some old ones to make them more efficient? Here is a list of situations usually governed by rituals. Add your own suggestions, then perform the exercise so you can review your own rituals, and change those that are impeding your successful pursuit of happiness.

Meeting new people.
Greeting old friends.
Getting a disagreeable job done.
Earning your living.
Getting to sleep.
Getting started in the morning.

Sit quietly and allow your mind to project a movie of one of your rituals. Notice whether it produces satisfaction and exactly what the satisfaction is. Probe your feelings regarding this ritual, then image doing things differently. Change the pattern and observe it. Think about what you would like to gain by changing the ritual. When you have designed a new ritual of behavior, rehearse it in your mind daily, until your low self has become proficient. Then just allow it to happen naturally in your life.

A ritual that is performed daily will become more powerful if it is done with intense desire and feeling. A perfunctory performance has no energy in it, no power at all. So your desire to achieve results with your ritual must be a major part of the ritual itself. Put a lot of feeling into it, join with your low self in performing the ritual until you can do it skillfully, and you will begin to see results.

The low self's belief in the effectiveness of a ritual is essential to its success. We use the word "half-hearted" to denote an action in which the low self is only partly involved. It is well known that half-hearted actions don't have much force. Explain literally what it is you want to accomplish, arouse enthusiasm in your low self for the goal you envision. Check your low self's feelings about the ritual, and revise it if necessary, until you get "whole-hearted" support.

Since most skills are performed ritually, that is, in a certain sequential pattern that brings success, we can perfect our skills by using this same method. A friend who plays the piano was unable to master a particular fingering technique. Physical practice wasn't achieving his aim of a smooth performance, so he sat down and reviewed in his mind each step in the process he wanted to learn. In his imagination, he slowly did each step in sequence, repeating and repeating, until he could do it in his mind at the speed he wanted to be able to play it on the piano. It worked! When he tried the technique at the piano, his fingers performed nimbly.

In an experiment, twenty men were taught to play golf. Ten practiced on the links for a week, and ten practiced in their minds. The result was that all developed approximately the same degree of skill. I practice many things in my mind, and have found it saves me much time and effort.

You can use ritual if you desire to make astral journeys, or trips out of your body. First, create in your imagination a moving image of a trip out of your body, around the room, and back in again. List the steps.

My ritual went like this: first, an image of me rising out of my head and dropping gently to the floor. Next, I go to the bookcase, then to the lamp, then to the desk, then to the telephone. Last, an image of me rising up in the air and descending gently into my body through my head.

I sat and practiced this in my mind until the routine was memorized. I got so I could do it in my imagination clearly and quickly, without forgetting any of the steps. I had established it as a pleasant ritual by doing it every evening before I retired. Then I chose a night that seemed propitious for a real out-of-body experience and got fully ready for bed before performing the ritual.

I sat down and imagined myself floating up and out of my body, landing on the floor, then going first to the bookcase, and then to the lamp. But here I stopped, opened my eyes and went to bed without finishing the ritual.

The natural, ritualistic low self was startled. Still moving irresistibly along the lines of established ritual, it pushed me to continue until the end. In order to do this, I got out of my body and proceeded along the route I had designed, finishing the ritual.

When facing a new situation, I have found that it helps greatly to deliberately rehearse in my mind how to deal with it successfully, programming my low self for the type of behavior I want. This has replaced a habit I used to have of imagining all the horrible things I feared would occur.

Franklin D. Roosevelt said, "The only thing we have to fear is fear itself." We think that if we accustom our selves to the worst there will be no shock when it happens. Shocks, of course, threaten our survival, but by trying to avoid them we may be programming our lives for the worst rather than for the best.

Using our new knowledge of the low self, we can begin to develop patterns of behavior that have built-in expectations of success. Thus we can create our own reality in a new design of greater achievement.

The low self is the guardian of our physical well-being and survival. It will send hunger pangs when it needs food and show its preferences for the foods it needs. It will attract our attention to anything endangering our existence and holds the power to keep us well and healthy or can create a climate for illness and injury. What is often considered a distraction by uhane is an attraction to unihipili. The low self will attempt to let uhane know why it is attracted to something other than what uhane is paying attention to.

Unless we have a strong will to live in the physical body, unihipili will not make an all-out effort to keep it strong and healthy. Unless our feelings find expression in the outer world, they will be destructive in the frustration of their power to express themselves. Unless our thinking is positive and ambitious, the low self will not furnish the energy necessary to fulfill our goals. Unihipili directly reflects our will to live and be, to actualize our potential or not even try.

The inner self has power over the physical body, but we have powers we can exert on our low self. We can command it to give us the vitality to accomplish tasks. We can command it to heal us immediately. Not by being arrogant, but by playing the role of the wise parent. For within each human body there is a child who wants to live a good physical life, but still be protected and guided by its inner parent. When our feelings and thoughts are in unison and in agreement, unihipili has no choice but to obey. Like all wise parents, we sometimes find we must be firm in our resolve, and steadfast in our intention to get our inner child to do exactly what we want it to and know it can do. Huna teaches us that unihipili has the power to heal the body, and we can use that knowledge to begin to train unihipili to obey our commands to heal the body when all is well between uhane and unihipili.

Balance in all things is one built-in goal of every low self. This is reflected in the physical body which has everything needed to maintain complete balance. Every chemical produced in the brain is accompanied by another which inhibits production. Each chemical is the mirror-reflection of another. The word "homeostasis" was coined as a label for this biological fact.

The mind of unihipili contains the ability to compute mathematically all that is. Space is measured as well as time. Distances far and near and time past and present are clearly distinguished by the low self. It can deal with minute quantities of physical energy as well as large ones and minute quantities of hormones, chemicals and other substances produced by the body. It measures doorways and ducks automatically lest you strike your head on the lintel. It moves your body into a car without hitting anything and runs up stairs, automatically stopping when there are no more stairs! Its nature is to run the physical body in full health at top functioning power. Unihipili cannot speak words, it cannot move independently, but it can send you urges, hunger pangs, emotions, memories and messages from any survival-structure-belief system.

It uses the physical body as a storage for energy as well as a factory for the production of physical energy. It stores memory patterns in muscles and nerves so that autonomic functioning will be intelligent. Unihipili, under orders from uhane, sends energy to the voluntary muscles for instant action. The energy contains the information about what action is desired. As you consider this lightening-fast process, it makes you feel wonder and awe at the orderly laws that govern physical existance!

Most of our functions are involuntary—that is, performed by your low self. It breathes for you, digests your food, re-energizes you when the body tires, yawns to get more oxygen into the system. It also does much more. Think about some of the things you have always taken for granted. Isn't it wonderful?

Unihipili's nature is to function as simply and efficiently as possible. It will always perform actions in the easiest, most effortless way if given the opportunity. Taking that statement on faith, the Huna student begins a new approach toward awareness of physical being. Health is the word to describe the physical body that is run well, without interference from belief systems, negative thinking or destructive effects from the environment.

Many of our muscles are in constant tension, trying to *go* and *stop* at the same time. In the past they were instructed to go into action and immediately inhibited from performing that action, a constant tremor, so tiny it was usually below our awareness. If you touch one of these muscles, tremorous or tense, it feels rigid and stiff. A relaxed muscle is soft and pliable.

Wilhelm Reich called these immobilized muscles our body armor. His therapy was to knead these stiff muscles, releasing the energy caged within. Almost simultaneously his client would reexperience mentally the events that created the original pain which was often the root cause. By rising into awareness, we can deal with these past events and release them from our own low self.

We can resolve this kind of dysfunction ourselves with some Huna techniques. We can tune into our own muscles, experience their quivering, their connection with other muscles, and ask our inner self to present to our awareness the memories associated with that particular muscle tension. We may recall events when we felt weak or powerless. We wanted to act, but were not convinced we had the strength to. We were fearful our knees would collapse under us; we stiffened the muscles in back of the knees with the certain belief that was necessary to keep from collapsing. If uhane feels weak, unihipili will express that weakness in an appropriate muscle. To continue believing we are weak in some aspect of life reinforces the tension in those particular muscles.

Many of us are conditioned to believe that weakness is a fault. It is frowned on and disapproved. Many males have outthrusting, firm, tense jaws to hide former feelings of weakness. *To be strong is a virtue, to be weak a fault* is a belief ingrained in many people. Weakness becomes a threat to being loved, approved of and accepted. We deny our feelings of weakness and unihipili must store that unexpressed feeling somewhere.

As a Huna student, I began to question my self whenever the efficient functioning of my physical body was disturbed. Instead of looking outward for answers, I went to my own self to find out why the normal process had changed. I began to get to know my inner self by getting to know my physical body much better.

My unexpressed feelings of the past were stored in my muscles, keeping them in a state of tension that resulted in stiff, aching areas which impeded my actions. I learned that it takes energy to keep this energy stored. That explained why I was tired so often. Unihipili has no choice but to store these old memories of unexpressed desires for action, inhibited feelings and suppressed ideas. I had sought help from others to relieve much of my physical distress, but now I am turning more and more to the one who knows all about it: unihipili.

If unihipili controls all physical functions, it controls all physical dysfunctions. We all know that doctors and nurses can aid us in our efforts to return to a state of health, but we also know that the healing process is an inner one. No one else can heal us. Only unihipili has that power.

To the Huna student, this is good news! We are well on our way to working *with* our own inner self. We are moving toward open communication wherein our self will inform us about the causes of our physical problems. By learning techniques of leading and teaching our own self, we will be able to oversee the healing process.

As long as our inner self is busy expending energy to hold many muscles in tension, it will be hard to get it to divert energy for other purposes. So let's get involved in some processes to release that muscle tension and learn more about ourselves.

Just as uhane needs the love and approval of other human beings, unihipili also needs love and approval. You can give your self your full love, approval and acceptance while still retaining the role of guardian and parent to it. Know that your low self will do your bidding and reflect exactly what your thoughts and feelings convey. It has a body image, and it loves or hates each separate part in mimicry of your loves and hates for each part.

Unihipili has a body-image that reflects what you feel and think about your physical body. It has created a state of tension in various muscles that reflect your desire for action and the inhibition of that action or expression. As we work with the following technique, we will discover that uhane's relationship of love/hate will be experienced as aliveness or numbness. We are alive and in connection with what we love. What we hate is dead to us. Any part we despise will seem numb. It will be difficult to reestablish our perception and experience of it if we refuse to admit into our consciousness memories of the old dislikes and fears of certain parts of our own bodies. As we pursue the technique to determine our love-hate relationship, we will also discover and experience many of the muscles in tension which are holding our unexpressed feelings and using up so much of unihipili's attention and energy.

The goal of this technique is to reestablish our initial love for our whole body and to eliminate unnecessary tension developed in the past. We can then free our energies so that we may be more fully alive and active in our pursuit of our purposes.

Find a period of time, at least an hour, when you will be undisturbed and are free to work with this technique. Sit in a comfortable chair, loosening any restrictive clothing and get into a very comfortable position. Close your eyes.

Start with your toes. Focus your attention on one big toe until you are in tune with its sensations. Blood is pulsing, nerves are giving it the perception of touch with the sock or shoe or slipper touching it. Share that touching experience, that feeling of being alive and pulsing. Be one with your big toe. If you experience a dull ache or a sharp twinge, focus your attention on dispelling the imbalance. A dull ache needs mana brought to the area to heal it. A sharp twinge will indicate crystallized energy which needs to be dissolved. Use your imagination to see either of these conditions alleviated. Stay with your big toe long enough to communicate your love and acceptance and gratitude of it. Recognize the vital part your big toe plays in your well-being.

Move to the next toe and repeat the procedure. Continue on, covering every part of your foot. Use your imagination to correct any discomfort or pain. Think love and acceptance continually. See each part in its unique beauty and form. The more you do this exercise, the more you will find the intimate relationships between various parts of your body. Eventually you will be able to experience your whole foot in one moment.

As you come across muscles in tremor or tension, recognize the stop/go syndrome there. Be open to memories of how this condition first established itself. Get deeply into the tremor until you are swinging back and forth with it. Feel it, experience it and reexperience the feelings that are bound up in it. As you become aware of these feelings, the energy will move out of the muscle and into your awareness to be dissipated by your understanding.

Continue on up through your ankle, calf, knee and thigh. Then move to your other leg. Start with the big toe and move along your toes into the ball of your foot, into the under-arch and then the top of your foot. Tune into your heel, the muscle in back of your ankle and then into the ankle. When you have finished both legs, they will tingle and feel alive. Your perception of them will be that they are larger than they were before. Stay with this experience of being at one with both your legs. Feel their unity and also any differences between them. Let your imagination inform you of any differences in size, aliveness or strength. Learn to know your legs intimately.

When you begin on your torso start with the genitals, an area usually fairly numb to the average person. Our society has so many taboos against touching or being aware of this area that most of us are conditioned to feel guilty if our genitals are truly alive and sensitive. Many of us find intimate contact with them difficult and discover a numbness there that can seem inexplicable. The first time you use this technique you will not be able to restore aliveness to every part of your body, so after a period of exploration, move on until you have completed your contact with each part of your body for the first time. It will give you a mental chart of your past experience of your body and your relationship to each part. Be determined to work with this technique until you have restored a close relationship with every part.

This target will bring to you the experience of being aware of your whole body in one moment. An experience of simultaneous relationship with every part of it will result. With each session, release a little more stored up muscle energy. Relive more and more of past experiences that locked up potential power within them.

There are so many secrets hidden within our physical bodies. Unihipili holds many more secrets. Your low self holds all the things we did not experience consciously and many things we did and have forgotten. The record of our feeling-thinking-experiencing life resides in the mind and bodies of the low self. Therefore, it is to the low self and our physical body that we must go to retrieve them.

You may find you cannot complete your whole body in one experiment. If not, begin where you left off the next time. Each time you will become more and more aware of what thoughts and feelings have been stored away and feel more complete as a person. Through unihipili, you can change any condition in your body that is below par to ultimate health and vitality. Through your low self you can correct all dysfunctions. Love is the key. Love each and every part of your being, and that force will transmute deadness to aliveness. Love is life and love is the healing force.

The physical body is a miracle in itself, and nothing our technology has ever accomplished can equal the wonders of our own biological form and function, and the processes that control and maintain it.

3

Uhane

Uhane is the Hawaiian term for the middle self or the human spirit that resides in a physical body controlled by a nature spirit, unihipili. Uhane speaks, reasons, controls voluntary actions and uses intuition to know. Uhane also feels alive and has a constant flow of *experiencing* which is the essence of being human.

Uhane is the middle self within which you are conscious. It is the self you merge with during waking hours, using the neo-cortex part of the brain to deal with daily concerns. It is divided into two separate and independent functional parts. On the right side lies our intuition and on the left our reason. Uhane is also a dual self. It requires energy to keep both sides of the neo-cortex functioning properly. They function simultaneously, but we are quite clear about the difference between what we feel and what we think.

Uhane is the self in which we embody our intentions, our initiative and our choices. Here is where we decide on targets or goals to accomplish. Causes initiated in uhane are then carried out by unihipili. Everything we think or feel flows down as cause to our low self, to be completed there. It is with uhane that we begin all that occurs to us in our life. We think, we plan, we act, and we speak. We analyze and come to decisions. Uhane is the evaluator for the whole being. It accepts or rejects the social morals and values that are presented to it. Uhane is unihipili's boss, parent, leader, authority and "self-in-charge."

The chart on the next page explains the dualistic qualities of uhane. They flow together to feed unihipili information in order that a single *gestalt* or whole can be organized as a basis for fulfilling and completing all that begins with uhane.

UHANE
Cause
Initiator
Intentional
Choice maker, goal setter
Decision maker
Chooser
Planner

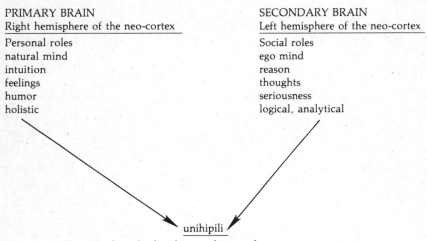

PRIMARY BRAIN
Right hemisphere of the neo-cortex
Personal roles
natural mind
intuition
feelings
humor
holistic

SECONDARY BRAIN
Left hemisphere of the neo-cortex
Social roles
ego mind
reason
thoughts
seriousness
logical, analytical

unihipili
Receives from both sides simultaneously
Organizes all material from uhane into a holistic pattern
Feeds back to uhane, memories, uncompleted emotions,
generates mana-mana for uhane to use as energy.

Our culture has developed an intellectual conceit about the method of thinking we call rational or deductive. We have been conditioned to start with a fact, add to that an observation, then draw a conclusion and gain some information. This is actually the more cumbersome approach. The primary brain with its intuitive process has been discredited in our culture.

We must take a good, long, hard look at the cultural belief-system about the two hemispheres uhane has to use. This means that although we continue developing our powers of reason, we also learn to ask questions of the intuitive side of our brain. Some people have actually considered the intuitive side as a higher consciousness, but in truth it is just a complementary side of the rational. Uhane should use both equally, each for the tasks they are best equipped to handle.

Most of us have overdeveloped the left side, particularly in its verbal skills. We now live in a world that holds for us a tape recorder that won't shut off. We have revered this verbal skill and that side of the brain has a puffed-up ego and dislikes shutting up, even when we order it to stop thinking. Uhane must develop more control over the left side and release some of the inhibited and frustrated powers of the right brain. Balance and harmony between these two will be reflected in our low self, who is fed by both. It holds the synergistic, or holistic memory of each hemispheric experience.

We must train our left hemisphere to be still and listen. The left brain has the capacity to be quiet and receptive, but this side of its talents has not been emphasized in our education or upbringing. We will have to do it ourselves. To shut off that tape recorder, that seemingly eternal inner dialogue, may take some time. It has developed power over a long period of conditioning.

The right hemisphere has been labelled the emotional, intuitive side of our nature and its receptivity is able to perceive the humor in situations, the inner feeling experiences within others and our own undeveloped potentials. This hemisphere dominates the left side of our physical body and is the part of us that draws into itself from the outer world things like inspiration, knowledge and reality.

The left hemisphere, governing the right side of our body, is the center for all voluntary expressions of our will. Our will to act, to speak, to do. The left designs the patterns by which we impose our choices on unihipili. The left hemisphere creates patterns or contexts within which it will be able to exert its will. It is here that the creation of a social self originates. This design is for our social survival and/or success. Since we must suppress many of our natural feelings in order to survive in society, the left ignores or refuses to act on these feelings and conflict between the two hemispheres results. *The right hand eventually becomes unaware of what the left hand is doing!*

Much unexpressed feeling is dissipated in the dreaming process where we can participate in the drama of our inner feelings, expressed symbolically (having been refused outer, active expression). Often the humor within our right hemisphere can be found in dreams.

Uhane has two aspects in its nature and these rest in the right and left hemispheres of the neo-cortex. We each can distinguish easily between what we feel and what we think. Unihipili responds to both. Many of us concentrate on "thinking," ignoring our feeling side. We develop our social self to an enlarged degree and that becomes the self we think we are. Feeling doesn't talk, it expresses through motion of some kind. Thinking expresses itself in words and willful action or voluntary action. Mana-mana should be evenly distributed to each side of the neo-cortex, but often these two sides of one life energy become unbalanced, with the thinking side demanding more than its share. An extreme case is that of an intellectual who displays little feeling.

If we consider that language is dual, with verbal skills expressing the intellect and body movements expressing our feeling nature, we see that each one of us is continually communicating in a dual manner. Those with restrained body language are obviously repressing some part of their feeling nature, and those who accompany speech with many hand gestures are endeavoring to express their feelings along with their words.

Our stiff muscles tell a big story in suppressed feeling-energy. Our limited repertoire of gestures shows our limited feeling response to life. When neither words nor gestures are expressed, we are not communicating to the outside world.

Uhane uses both foreground and background in its perceptive and projective skills. Uhane is aware of whatever is in the foreground; uhane is barely conscious of whatever is in the background. Most of us are unaware of the body language which we use constantly and with which we convey so much to others. Body language remains in the background, our own and that of others. We are so used to bringing words into the foreground of our consciousness, we need to expand our vision until we begin to perceive the tones and innuendos of voice expression, and the gestures that enhance or contradict the words.

Without lessening our intellectual powers we need to bring into our experience our own long-ignored feelings. Without losing the essence within the words of others, we need to become more observant of *how* they speak and what their body is telling us by the way it moves or does not move.

Unihipili is an holistic self. It is fully aware of how uhane divides its experience into foreground and background. What is attractive to unihipili in the background of our lives will prove to be a distraction to uhane as unihipili endeavors to draw uhane's attention toward it. By recognizing that uhane's distraction is unihipili's attraction, we can get to know our selves even better.

Uhane experiences time in different ways. The conscious, rational side perceives time as past, present or future, neatly dividing every event into one of these three categories. In our feeling, intuitional side, it is always now. "Now" includes the relationship between past and future, making them one. It connects all the parts that the other hemisphere considers in logical sequences.

Uhane has the privilege of making choices. Through uhane, you can allow your feelings to rule your life, or you can be the creator of opportunity for them to express themselves in a constructive way. You can choose to suppress your feelings until they become potentially explosive. Most of us have experienced the explosion of some feelings long held in check. Long suppressed anger can explode in a raging temper tantrum. We actually see a red haze in our own aura and perceive our world through that red haze. Some of us have seen the world through rose-colored glasses, often when love overwhelms our reason and the object of our affections is unrealistic.

It is the nature of both uhane and unihipili to love and respond to all others with love and caring concern for their welfare. When this is frustrated through social custom or some other condition, the love energy transmutes into a lower dimension, becoming anger or hate. We begin to despise the world that does not satisfy our needs.

Centering in the left hemisphere is a human tendency, channeled outward in logical and accepted ways into our world. Although we must control expression of our feeling, we often *suppress* feelings instead of *expressing* them. They all need an outlet into expression. With Huna we now seek ways in which this can be done safely.

When we feel good about our choices, when we feel enthusiastic about our activities, we can know that a full supply of mana-mana will be used by the whole neo-cortex. When both sides are in agreement, there is no conflict within uhane itself, and our endeavors are successful. They are so often in conflict, our feelings do not coincide with what we think we ought to do. Working with Huna, we can help to uncover some of our uhane's complexes, and dissolve them.

The downward flow of our thoughts and feelings to unihipili, who registers them, organizes them and makes a coherent pattern of them, brings a flow of vitality up to uhane in response. Unihipili has a perfect reflection with no distortion of the combinations sent to it. When we are not aware of the feelings that flow, a strange and distorted version of ourselves is created.

Gestalt psychology teaches us that these two hemispheres work together to produce a picture of our world at every moment, consisting of a foreground and a background. When we focus on the background from the left hemisphere, the right is observing the entire background within its perception. If there is something in that background that interests our personal feelings, the right hemisphere attracts our focus of attention to it. It is always something that relates to our personal desires, wishes and needs. If we do not pay attention to these "distractions" to our conscious focus, the information goes down to unihipili for storage.

Because the right hemisphere is holistic, it is the best part of us to perform any skill that involves the whole body, including dancing, sports of all kinds, driving a car, and other whole-body activities. The left hemisphere is best in performing skills that require just one part of the body, like reading, writing and typing. Speaking, which uses a tiny muscle structure, is controlled by the left hemisphere. Delicate hand skills reside in the left hemisphere too. All gross muscle movement is best performed by the right hemisphere.

Each hemisphere is like a bio-computer that develops physical skill programs that become automatic. These separate functions are now known about through brain research which has been able to examine individuals whose hemispeheres have been separated in accidents. This brain research is of great help in understanding Huna even better than we did before these discoveries were made. These discoveries about the brain have validated the Huna concept and clarified many of the obscure points and details that are not included in the basic Huna concept.

You are programming your own neo-cortex every time you think or feel. But you, who use your brain, may choose at each moment what to do. You can create programs within your brain that will be keyed off by a flow of mana to them that is beneficial to your keeping control over your life and living it in a self-actualizing way. Or, you can reinforce strong programs of negativity that will control you. Unihipili has no choice but to obey you when mana is sent to the brain. It also has no choice but to send mana to the brain when a specific brain program is triggered.

The middle self sleeps and dreams, but unihipili is busy regenerating and balancing all bodily functions. It is aware during sleep, guarding you and watching out for you. It is aware during anesthesia. There it does not have your protection, no logic or intuition to translate for it. So whatever the environment furnishes will be translated into unihipili in a very literal way. This is an important aspect of knowledge, for it affords parents of children to literally program their own children with thoughts and feelings of love during their sleep.

Unihipili is called "suggestible" for it takes any suggestion literally, and as an order from those in authority over it. You can be that boss and make sure your own unihipili does not accept suggestions from anyone but yourself. Tell your own low self, that you are its parent, boss and authority, and all suggestions must be acceptable to you before being accepted by it.

In working with a hypnotist always create the program of suggestions that the hypnotist will give your unihipili. Make sure they are in accord with your will, feelings and thoughts on the subject. Never allow another to contradict your belief in your own goodness and worth. Never allow negative suggestions to lodge within your unihipili that might rise up and influence your decisions. When communicating directly with another's low self, never try to influence another against what may be their will. It can only rebound and harm you.

When undergoing surgery or any process which entails anesthesia and unconsciousness of the middle self, speak with all persons involved and assure them that you will be aware—deep within—of every thought, feeling and speech that comes from them during your period of consciousness. If you believe that some damage has been done to your unihipili during unconsciousness, go to a good hypnotist and investigate what unihipili experienced during that period. It is difficult to work on your own for such deep-seated knowledge. Most people need the assistance of another. You can try the aforementioned exercise of contacting your low self and endeavor to find out for yourself, but usually a more thorough picture will emerge with another assisting you.

When speaking to yourself, always speak absolutely, literally, and accompany each literal statement with an image or picture of what the speech contains. Symbols may be used if your low self fully understands what the symbol means. This can be verified with the pendulum. The word "heal" has no image, so when you want the low self to heal the body you must give it images of what you want achieved. You must include a time limit within which you want it done. Create a movie within your mind of the changes you want accomplished to bring your body back into perfect health and vigor.

Both selves have extra-sensory perceptions that can be developed. The middle self can be receptive through its intuition, and the low self can reach out and gather much information about people and the world of nature. The natural self can touch on and communicate with all other natural selves, as well as with animals and other animate beings. It can explore within the earth and on top of the earth. You can send it on many errands to bring information back to you. Its sixth sense for danger is already highly developed, which is one reason for making a closer connection with your own low self. First, you must instill in the low self the belief that it can do what you want it to. Then you must help it develop skills from dormant talents. After that, it just takes practice to perfect the skills you have chosen.

As middle selves, the first selves we are obliged to love are our own low selves. Start loving your own right now. Admire it, approve of it and accept it unconditionally. You are the most important self in the world to your low self, and your approval and love mean more than anyone else's. With your unconditional love it will respond and mature, enabling you to become co-workers.

It begins with you as parent and guardian. Teaching your low self skills and control. As "top dog" you are responsible for training it in socially acceptable ways, for channeling your forces in constructive and satisfying ways. It will remember, long after we forget, what is forbidden. In some cases, we suppress so much that the low self becomes very inhibited and restricted. Much of its potential can be lost to us.

When you assume the role of parent to your unihipili, you begin to assert control over your own life and take responsibility for it. This can be a step toward freedom from others' control, freedom from the oppressive authority you may have been functioning under in the past.

Accepting responsibility for your life begins with giving up the hope that someone else will care for you and protect you. Many unihipili have looked outside for this and not to you. And if that is where you look, at least you are together in this fruitless quest.

Most of us had, and have been, parents who were not experienced enough to give the caring and protection that was "just right" for growing children. So most of us have never received the kind of care, nurture and protection that you should give to your own self. Most parents are not ready, at the age when their children are young, to take full responsibility for themselves. They often blame their children for errors they commit themselves. We continue this pattern.

You have the power and the strength right now to take charge of your own life, your own inner self and your own actions. It just takes a realization that it is so. The realization comes through understanding. Even if you only pretend it is so, be a hypocrite and pretend. Pretend it is so until it becomes your nature to make it truly so. It is well worth the gamble, for if you are not running your own life, supervising and controlling your own selves, who is? And do you want them to?

Is your life someone else's responsibility? Are you the way you are because of what others have done to you? Actually not, but it is difficult to comprehend if you are in the habit of thinking you are a puppet who only moves when your strings are tugged by something other than yourself. Do you believe that others know what is best for you, or do you feel that what is best for you can be found within your own being?

To be responsible for your own life will give you a heady sense of power. When you finally realize you are the cause of everything in your life, you begin to know that as the cause, you can create what you want. You can control the events that happen to you because you are respnsible for creating the context within which they occur. Power and responsibility go hand in hand. You cannot have one without taking the other!

If you take responsibility for your own life and all your actions and decisions, no matter what the results may be, there is nothing to be ashamed of or blame yourself for.

Can you believe that? Think back to some of your experiences in making decisions that turned out badly. This review may help you to realize how these kinds of feelings, which are extremely painful, may have affected your ability to take responsibility, to try out new ventures, to reach for new goals.

To the degree that you are hooked into the "shame-blame" game, you are controlled by your social programming. Close your eyes and remember how, as a child, you saw someone pointing one finger and stroking it with another finger, crying "Shame, shame, you're to blame." That is an old childhood behavior I experienced. In many subtle ways you have been convinced that you should feel guilty, that it's your *fault*, that you are to blame and should feel ashamed of yourself!

Shame and blame are other names for guilt. And guilt has no survival value to you anymore. It is a marvelous way to control people who have been conditioned to this belief system. So, for your first effort, begin not to blame anyone else for anything. Never try to make anyone feel ashamed, ever again. Not your children, nor any adult you know. First you must eliminate the shame-blame game from your attitudes toward others. Then you can dissolve that program in your own low self. The truth is that there is no such animal as shame or blame. It is a social concept, grounded in social control. Others distrust is reflected in you as you absorb the mighty social structure that has been built by those in precarious power. They will fear losing their power unless they can lower others to a level that makes them appear high.

Putting others down is a way of creating an illusion that you are up, but of course that is a relative position. Others are bound to rise up so that you are caught in a game in which you must continue to put others down in order to feel good about yourself. When we continue to put others down, we don't move anywhere. All our energy is devoted to that task, and none is left to really move up, to really advance and become what we potentially can be. If your experience is of being put down and experiencing that as true, realize now the fallacy of it. Realize how inauthentic and ephemeral it really is. Most people will relate how someone got them "down," "But I didn't stay down long!" You can't keep a good person down! True.

Symbolically, you lie in a submissive position and allow others to place one foot on your neck and crow like a rooster, a cry of victory. Picture that and associate with it. Which one are you? The submissive person lying down or the crowing victorious one with one foot on the neck of the victim? Decide now whether you really benefit or grow from either of these types of experience. Of what value are they to either party?

I have known people who very quickly admit it is their fault when anything goes wrong. They would rather blame themselves. They feel it is less hurtful than having someone else direct the blame directly to them. A quick "I'm sorry, its all my fault" is a device to avoid having anyone else say it. But, the effects on your unihipili can be disastrous. The unihipili takes everything you say as "Gospel truth." You programmed your low self to feel ashamed, to feel at blame for anything that might go wrong. Decide that the shame-blame game does not pay off in self-growth or control. Stop playing it. It is not as hard as you may think. Just the decision to do it, and a firm intention to keep that decision intact will accomplish it.

So many people use the word love in so many ways, and in our dual world love and hate are the opposite faces of one emotion. We are told to love one another, and we do to a great extent, but without really caring. When we love someone we are looking for results, we are looking to see that love reflected back to us as if the other were a mirror in which we perceive our own emotion. If the other reflects our love back to us, we feel successful, and success is highly rated by most of us. Who would want to love anything unless there is some return?

Let's not use the word love at all. It's become useless to accomplish what it is supposed to. Let's substitute caring. It has no polar opposite. It's either caring or its not there at all. Buddha did not like the way love had been interpreted either. He used the word compassion as a better word.

Really caring goes right to the center of the thing cared for. It penetrates because it has no fixed boundaries, no ifs and buts, no conditions imposed. The power of really caring abut someone else's experience carries you into that experience and helps you to know that experience as much as if it were your own. Through that experience of caring and the information you have gotten from it, you can use your innate wisdom to help you find the forms and forces that will change that experience to a higher level, a happier level, a healthier level.

You don't even have to know the conditions of another's experience to send a caring response to another. Along the aka threads connecting you to any person can flow your caring concern for their happiness and health. Sit down and contemplate how you really feel about other people. Would you really be overjoyed if they were healthy, happy and successful, or would you be envious and jealous? They say misery loves company. If you have chosen misery for your life companion, perhaps that is true for you.

We all have parts of ourselves we admire, and parts we despise. Our hate and love is divided in different measure for the parts of our body, for different behaviors, for different effects we create and pride or disgust for the thoughts we think and the emotions we feel. Make a list of the things you love about yourself and the things you hate. Take that list and check it out with unihipili. Find out whether unihipili agrees with you. Get unihipili to measure the amount of hate or love you have for each item.

We are all pretty mixed up people. We feel a bit helpless because we have already set some pretty firm standards for ourselves, and habitual attitudes toward many of our acts are integrated completely into our self image. Now, instead of trying to redress the balance, change hate into love, and all that complex work that needs to be done, we can do something that overrides all love and hate, all the positive versus negative emotions we feel about ourselves.

We will begin to care about ourselves, the whole person, all the selves, every body, every part. We fully care for the whole of us. Use a new affirmation. *I really care about all of myself. All parts of me. I really care about them and their well being, their success, their happiness and good health.*

Practice this like an actor or actress in a new role. Say it with vehemence. Say it one way and then another. Keep repeating it, even though you do not understand what you are saying or why. Just keep saying it as strongly as you can. At some point you will suddenly realize you really do care about all of you, about every single bit of you. This discovery will make you realize you cared deeply all along, but that care was unconscious. And, in your own way, you have tried to express it in all you have done, even though those things may look peculiar in the light in which you now view them. Bringing this true caring into awareness allows you to put it into *effect*—to give it form and substance. It will dispel all the petty little hates and loves you've held in the past.

As you develop this self-caring for the whole person that is you and realize every part is included in your caring, a new factor intrudes into your awareness. You also care about the relationship between every part and every other part. You really care that they love one another and that they all derive happiness from their relationship with other parts. For example your toes should love every other part of your physical body and gladly play their part and function well for the happiness of the whole body.

Now you can start to realize the changing relationships that exist from day to day in your experience. You will recognize the withdrawal of some part of your body or non-participation because it does not feel recognized or loved. Each part of your being is as important as every other part and most important of all is the relationship each part has with every other part.

This seems like a large task, but it isn't. We start with the whole and work on the whole by just caring about it. When we do, any part, any relationship that is not working well will immediately draw our attention for a little extra care that it feels it needs. It will be one step at a time. It will occur naturally as some part of you or another finds dissatisfaction in its work.

Dis-ease is a lack of ease. Now your caring that all of you feel at ease will pinpoint any area that is uncomfortable or uneasy. It will stick out like a sore thumb. It will attract your attention and demand its share of ease and comfort. Like a pinched foot from a shoe too tight, it will silently demand attention. This sounds like you might be overwhelmed by so many parts who have not had their share of care in the past, but your unihipili will take care of you. It will allow only one thought to enter your mind at any one moment. We only have one thought at any one moment. We are never overwhelmed by two at once. Perhaps when our programmed brain gets overworked the thoughts come too fast for comfort, but usually, the system works rather well. Once you have experienced true caring for your whole self, you can begin to really care about others. You can reread this chapter and apply what has been said to your feelings about others. Rise above any hatred for others by using the same affirmation, but word it the way you would like it to work for you in your relationships with other people. All of your past bias and judgements about others are irrelevant. Practice a new role. A role in which you care above all else that others may be happy, whole and harmoniously working to evolve their own potential. They should not be defined or restricted by what *you* feel their potential should be, but rather, they should realize what their potential is.

As you begin to care, a tremendous burden will fall from your shoulders. All your social conditioning about what you should admire or despise, all the mistakes that require blaming and the successes that should be praised fall away as inconsequential to the reality of life itself. The life force is a *caring force.* It is the most powerful force toward wholeness that exists. Life tends to create wholes and tries to perfect every part within each whole. You will be swimming in the current of life itself as you begin to do what life does. Your direction will be the same, your intentions identical.

But you must start with yourself. Until that is accomplished there is no potential to developing true caring for another. You need the personal experience of loving your own being whole-heartedly before you even know what caring is all about. Once you truly love yourself, all of you, you are then capable of fully accepting another, exactly as they are. Full caring is full acceptance.

When you accept all you are, you are ready to accept others. It has been said, "As you judge, so shall you be judged." Another statement I have heard is, "Your judgements of yourself will be accepted by others and reflected back to you." We have been projecting a self-image that has been intensified and returned to us. The vicious circle has been going on for too long.

As uhane, we are constantly reacting or responding to our changing environment. Learning to know the difference between reaction and response can be very helpful to the Huna student. Response and reaction are quite different. We can choose, at any given time, between reacting or responding to an event. However, many of us are not aware of having a choice. A very common remark is "I couldn't help myself!" That means there was no opportunity for choice.

A response is an action dictated by the conditions out there, while a reaction is dictated by conditions within oneself.

When we respond to what is happening in our environment, without comparing that event with any other, without recognizing its relationship with any past personal event, we perceive that happening as it is in itself. Usually, our response is appropriate to the event. When we react, we are moving from an inner state of personal beliefs or emotions developed through past experience. A reaction is based on our personal past. A response is based on the present situation.

As I mentioned earlier, Huna tells us that our thoughts and experiences are like bunches of grapes, clustered around a common stem. Each grape is associated in some way with every other grape in its group. Again, the word-association test is an outward illustration of this part of our nature. One stimulated grape arouses all the rest in the bunch! It happens one by one of course, but leads to a stimulus of a specific kind of action.

Reaction results from an inner event; response results from our focus on an outer event. To respond, it is necessary to recognize that no event is a duplication of another. Each event is new and current. Every event has its appropriate response from every participant. Reaction comes from the past, response from the present.

All of us do both. We react to some things, respond to others. Some of us could be generally classified as responsive or reactive individuals. Which classification would you put yourself into? How about your relatives and friends? Do this, see if it gives you further understanding of the differences inherent in reaction and response.

A response is never repeated, for no event ever occurs twice. Reactions are repeated, over and over, until many become automatic and under the control of unihipili. It holds the memory bank and acts under your instruction. Your low self is quick to learn how you like to act. If you keep repeating any action, unihipili will accept that as your desire, learn it and take over for you. It is your servant and does not evaluate the wisdom of your choice, only knows that is your choice and it is to be obeyed.

Some people repeat certain reactions so often that others observe and learn to expect them. Others can predict what that individual will do under any given circumstance. The other person begins to use the stimuli that will provoke a specific expected reaction. Our reactions, particularly the ingrained ones, are the choices we make to abdicate responsibility for our choices and place that on the shoulders of others who provoke our reactions to control us.

In the book *Games People Play* there are many cases of predictable reactions being repeated over and over. Each participant reacts according to past performance in exactly the same predictable way, keeping the game going. With Huna, you can learn how to "change the game," abdicating the usual role and becoming the director of life games instead of the puppet participant.

I don't remember when it started, but I do recall reacting strongly to the words "You are stupid" as a very young girl. I would scream "I am not! I am not!"—even when I was aware the other person was deliberately doing it to make me mad—answering, but still simmering angrily inside at the remark. Much later I found myself in a rage whenever the word "stupid" was used in reference to me. After getting into a study of Huna, I took responsibility for that rage and developed a new way of coping with the word "stupid." Finally, one day I was able to say quite unemotionally, "Everyone is entitled to their opinion, and I am delighted that I do not share yours." Now I hardly even hear the word. I consider it an ineffectual display of a shaky ego.

What words make you mad? What statements get an immediate denial from you? Sit down and think over the past. Remember certain actions you repeat many times that are stimulated by similar circumstances. These are your reactive patterns. Have any become automatic for you? Are there any you would like to see change?

One day two young women, sisters, were sunning on a beach. Alerted to a disturbance at the water's edge, they stood up to see a man lying prone and apparently unconscious. A few people were milling around him, chattering excitedly. Both sisters acted. One ran to the unconscious man and began to apply artifical respiration. The other sister ran in the opposite direction, as fast as her legs could carry her. Which one reacted and which one responded? Can you tell the difference?

By repeated reactions we become predictable to those who know us. When we become predictable, we are at the mercy of those who would manipulate us. They hold the power to make us angry, sad, happy and unhappy. They know all the "cues."

At this point you may agree with me intellectually, but feel that changing from a reactive person into a responsive individual would be a difficult process. In actuality it may be one of the easiest transformations.

You begin by clearly understanding the difference between a response and a reaction. Using your ability to observe and analyze behaviors, start classifying (without judgements) all actions, your own and those of others. Observe what happens. Notice the events following a reaction and compare these to the events following a response. The slow realization that you and others choose to react or respond will hit you. This realization will stir your desire to make choices for yourself. The changeover will occur effortlessly and painlessly. Our nature is to choose what works best for us and contributes the most to our own well-being. Paradoxically, what gives us the most personal happiness will eventually provide happiness for others.

Both response and reaction result from the stimuli arising in our environment. We need the stimulus and thrive on it. But developing fixed, specific patterns of reaction to similar stimuli and repeating them often makes life predictable and dull. It seems the same old things keep happening to us. Many of us feel that we can predict the future based on that sameness. I have stressed the importance of choosing the action we will take on being stimulated by events outside ourselves. We can also learn to moderate the amount of stimulation we will accept from any given situation and the type of response we will give to it.

Many of us are in a perpetual state of discontent over the tremendous extent of power others hold over us. We feel like puppets or people who are always dancing to another's tune. We resent this lack of freedom and often feel fate has been very unkind.

Of course it is mean of someone to do what they know perfectly well gets a reaction from us, but we should not allow them to continue to do this. As long as we keep our fixed reactions, others will activate them to keep the game going. Change the game! Others may not like it, but it will put you in the driver's seat. "Games People Play" is the theme of transactional analysis in which the therapist finds repetitive, destructive behavior between two or more people. The therapist converts that into a game structure giving each player a role in the game; victim and victimizer, powerless dominated by the powerful, the defenseless and the bully and the weak dependent on the strong. Make a list of the games you know people play and the roles they take on. Make a list of your roles and your games. Check out these roles with your low self using any applicable Huna technique. We all play many roles. Some we should develop further, others we should eliminate. Start making choices!

We all have a drive for power and most of us focus that drive on power over others rather than power over our own life circumstances. You can divert your drive for power into a constructive growth pattern of responsibility for your own choices and elimination of habitual responses to others.

If you desire to work with a change in your reaction/response balance, ask your High Self for help and begin to change your world view. Talk to your low self to get information about the past and work for its cooperation in reaching this particular goal. The three of your selves, united in feeling, can become an unbeatable team.

4

Aumakua

Aumakua is the third and most intelligent self of your three selves. It can be called your super-conscious, your super-natural self or the deepest consciousness level of your being. It can be called your divine potential because "akau" means "possessing the attributes of a god." It is the self that is totally aware of both unihipili and uhane. Its meaning for being is the assistance of these two selves in their growth and development along the path from ignorance to wisdom through experience.

Aumakua is also called "The Great Parent." It epitomizes the wisest parent that could possibly be. Each Aumakua is a member of "The Great Poe Aumakua," the family of High Selves who are in constant communion with each other. Each watches over and helps guide their own two selves.

There are other beings whose title includes the word akua. You may have with you for instance, an akuanoho. It's a guardian angel who dwells near you and aides your progress. It protects you from harm. This being can aid your Aumakua in its efforts to help you.

Your own Aumakua is connected to your subtle bodies by a cord of aka substance and its kino-aka body interpenetrates the other two kino-aka bodies. Its center of consciousness lies within its own kino-aka body, slightly above your physical head. It acts as your parent, your guide and your lover. The Aumakua is neither male nor female. It unites the masculine and feminine forces into one great power.

It plays the role of parent, but in such a wise way it is hard to understand how it functions. It never interferes unless it is truly needed and asked. It knows you can only truly grow through your own experiences. It would never deprive you of any event that holds the possibility of growth and understanding for you. Through Huna we can learn that the path to the Aumakua is through the low self.

It may seem hard to understand, but if we realize that uhane lives in the upperworld—the world of society and other human beings with their egos, heroes and authorities—leading the life of the "top dog" of the three selves, it becomes clearer.

Just below, in the underground, lives unihipili. It lives in what we call our subconscious, as if we relegate it to the basement of our life structure! The upperworld is ruled by embodied human beings. The underground is ruled by Mother Nature and all natural forces. It is our biological world, the world of animated beings and nature spirits. This second realm lies just below waking awareness. The underworld, sometimes called the "world of souls," holds all the so-called dead. Ruled by Hermes, God of Wisdom, it is the realm of our deepest level of consciousness. It is to the underworld that we go when we sleep, to experience the dreams created for our benefit. *The Great Poe Aumakua* are at two or three realms of consciousness simultaneously. The three selves, with their three forms of life vitality, live in three realms of reality. Unique and different from each other, they each have very specific functions to perform in your further growth and development. The Hawaiians felt one god was so far from our comprehension, we would do well to contact and work with the divine self closest to our understanding. Their advice was to pray to and work with our own High Self and its qualities that "resemble God-like qualities."

We now have a clear idea of why we must begin in uhane and go through unihipili to reach our High Self. We sit in the head, center of uhane consciousness, using the physical brain as a tool for manifesting, and are assisted by unihipili from the world of nature in using our natural body and its talents. Below that, the super-natural realm contains help for us in what is beyond human or natural and deep in the universal consciousness itself. In the underworld is eternal life that never ceases.

Just as there are three levels of consciousness in each being, there are three levels of needs. The low self has natural needs, physical needs and the need to survive as the prime need. It controls our needs for food, water, protection from the elements and sex. The physical reactions that cause action and rest, tension and relaxation are under the care of unihipili.

Uhane has personal and social needs, ego needs, the need to be recognized, the need to be respected and to be paid attention. Uhane needs to be admired, succeed in the eyes of others and to be thought of well. Uhane also needs relationships with others of its own kind. All these social needs must be fulfilled before uhane is willing to consider any higher level of needs.

Abraham Maslow gave a name to High Self needs. He called them meta needs. He said they are needs that go beyond physical, personal and social needs. Meta needs include the need for truth, beauty, justice, wisdom, and humor. When these needs are satisfied, we are able to perceive a higher justice than social justice, a wisdom which goes beyond knowledge and a love that moves from conditional to unconditional caring. The need and satisfaction for humor enables us to perceive paradox and higher thought forms. Take any list of divine attributes and you will find the qualities of the High Selves that give birth to these needs.

Physical survival comes first. Then, social survival must be assured. We all need a healthy ego and economic independence in order to be free to fulfill our potential. A healthy body with a healthy ego is well equipped to serve the High Self by seeking satisfactions for its meta needs. As your High Self's needs are met, you will be the beneficiary.

Emulating your vision of your High Self can bring you closer to understanding it. Communion with it becomes closer. Fulfilling its needs brings it closer still and makes it more active in your life. Its powers and forces begin to move with your goals and ambitions to make the path straight and wide. Its magnetism will bring to you opportunity and its creative powers will design contexts within which even greater opportunities will be presented to you.

Your low self is the channel through which you communicate and give to your High Self. The low self is also the channel through which you receive from your high self. Without the low self as intermediary, you cannot work closely or benefit from forces of the High Self.

This is the reason I emphasize beginning your Huna work with your low self. It is your gateway to your Higher Self. All the blocks and fixations in your low self are dark obstructions in the pathway. The path must be cleared, as one would weed a path through a dense wood. If you sincerely and deeply want a clear channel, your High Self will respond with all the help it can give, although you will have to do most of the work.

Clearing and cleansing are the two methods used for creating an open channel. Clearing away debris is ridding the low self of guilt, conflict and feelings of inferiority. As it becomes convinced you love it, the low self will be capable of accepting the love of the High Self. When it feels clean, it will be clean. Until then it will have a dark and heavy kino-aka body, filled with dark thoughts that keep the light from penetrating. When we dissolve the dark thoughts, the light of the High Self will be able to shine through.

Keeping in mind our goal of communication with our High Self and the sending of prayers to it for help in accomplishing our goals, we begin by using learning techniques and cleansing the low self of all guilt, fixations and blocks.

"Kala" means "restoring the light." It is used to dissolve the dark thoughts embedded in the kino-aka body of our low self. Particularly thoughts of guilt, blame, shame and regret. The low self needs to feel clean, feel guiltless, feel worthy and be willing to be a channel for the High Self's transmission and reception of communication.

To our High Selves, we are perfect the way we are. Uhane can begin to emulate the High Self by developing an unconditional love for its own low self, assuring it that it is perfect, acceptable, lovable and admirable in the view of uhane. With every word, every thought, keep reinforcing this view until the repetition takes hold as a powerful suggestion. Be a model for your own low self by eliminating worry, doubt and negative attitudes.

The kala-cleansing rites are wonderful to use for any low self who is clinging to emotional patterns of guilt or fear. It cannot rationalize these away like uhane can and they act like "ghosts in the machine," haunting our lives and creating problems and barriers for us. Any cleansing ritual is as effective as the strength of suggestion given to the low self. If it is greatly impressed by your ritual, and feels cleansed and full of light, then it will be galvanized into action in passing on any communication to the High Self.

The low self is particularly impressed by anything it can perceive factually through the physical senses. Because of its power to associate an object with its use and other functions, we use objects which clearly symbolize, through their ordinary, everyday function, what we want to accomplish on a higher level. If water can cleanse the physical body, we know we can use it as a symbol of cleansing other things. We can use water to carry the message of cleansing the kino-aka bodies and purifing them. Fire cleanses by destroying that which it burns. So with fire we can burn words written on a paper, demonstrating our desire that the meaning within the words should be destroyed. A vacuum cleaner is a well-known, common symbol of cleansing. It draws to itself the dirt that accumulates in our homes. Burning candles have the power to cleanse the atmosphere of a room. We can use them as symbols of cleansing our own personal atmosphere of negative emotions or influences. You can think of many symbols that are meaningful to you that you can use in creating cleansing and clearing rites.

The first technique for cleansing involves your imagination and requires a time alone, reclining on the floor or a bed. Find your place and the time, and then proceed to relax and get comfortable. Lay down and stretch your arms out wide. Tense them before returning them to your sides. You may want to stretch your legs out and up. Hold them as high as you can before letting them move into a comfortable position. Roll your head around. Stretch your neck until both head and neck are at ease. Now close your eyes.

Visualize your low self's kino-aka body as a dark blue substance pervading your whole physical body. Then perform the technique I call "roll back the blue." You know aka is sticky, flexible and versatile. Now, picture it as rolling toward the center from all extensions of your body. It is rolling up on itself, rolling toward the solar plexus. Simultaneously, there is a lovely, clear, transluscent pink filling all the empty space the rolled back blue has left. Keep this moving, the blue rolling to a center, the pink flowing and filling your whole body. When you feel all the blue is now a ball in the center of your torso and your body is filled with a pulsating pale pink, imagine a flow of pale yellow, shining and bright, flowing down from the center of your high-self consciousness. It fills the interior of your skull where your brain is. Imagine that golden yellow as cleansing and purifying the brain cells. Lay quietly filled with pink radiance, accepting the flow of pale gold beginning to circulate within the whole, changing in appearance to a beautiful peach color throughout your whole body. These two powerful colors do not really merge, but vibrating in unison they appear to.

Now, remembering the rolled-up ball of blue, do not move any physical muscle and imagine your subtle arms and hands reaching and cupping the ball of blue. Raise up your hands holding the blue and ask that it be cleansed of all negative and destructive patterns within it by the powerful ultraviolet light. Hold it just above you (in your imagination) as you visualize a vivid, deep violet ray of color penetrating the blue ball, disintegrating and dissolving all forms that limit you and obstruct your freedom to live fully and lovingly.

Next, in your imagination, draw those hands back and within your physical body, allow the blue radiance, now cleansed, to flow freely until your body is filled with a three-fold vibrating essence. Think of it as the pure-substance duplicate of your High Self. Pink epitomizes the High Self's love for you, the blue holds the divine pattern of your unique basic form, and the gold contains the powerful light of enlightened will.

This technique, repeated, will eventuate in experiences of great peace and tranquility. Enjoy this every time you do it. Lie still after doing it and enjoy feeling cleaner, purer and more related to your own basic pattern. End the session by stretching like a cat, or take a nap.

A second technique is done while you are taking a bath. Sitting in the tub, imagine that all dark, dirty and negative patterns in your subtle bodies are flowing out through your pores and going into the bath water. Affirm that all will remain in the water and go down the drain with it when you unplug the tub. While visualizing this, begin breathing deeply and visualize pure, clear light coming into you with each inhalation.

As you exhale, let out all the tension, worry, doubt and fear that you have been holding. Let it dissipate in the air around you. Visualize the incoming breath as pure light, the outgoing as having whatever color your imagination gives it.

If you have said something you feel badly about, cleanse the words from your system by pouring yourself a glass of water, filling your mouth with some while imagining you are putting those words into that water. Now spew out the water that contains the words that have persistently bothered you. They leave with the water and flow down the drain.

The symbol for mana is water. New life forces displace old ones and enter with a cleansing action. They renew and reinvigorate us. Mana is not water but water's nature is close to the nature of mana. Mana functions the way water does. It rises and falls, flows with great power, changes from a liquid to a gas to a vapor.

In nature we see the sky grow dark before a storm. Just as the atmosphere of our sky becomes dark, so too can our own personal atmosphere have dark clouds hovering over our heads. Psychics have seen these dark clouds over the heads of individuals who are full of negative thoughts. When the clouds in our sky release the water held in them, it pours down on earth as healing and refreshing rain. The rain nurtures the earth and light returns to our sky.

Use this imagery to picture your own low self sending all its doubts and worries and fears up to the High Self, releasing them to its care. Visualize this process and continue the scenario as the mana is transformed to mana-loa and pours down upon you in a sparkling shower of mana. Send it up, see it transformed and experience the downpour of grace which is the love your High Self is showering upon you. I call this rite "showers of blessings."

Using these examples, create some rituals that are meaningful to you and that will be effective in ridding yourself of unwanted thoughts, ideas, attitudes, beliefs, fixations and conflicts. Then you will be ready for communion with your High Self.

Dialogues and conversations are possible between middle and High Selves. Your low self can take place in meditation, at the typewriter, or using a tape recorder. Basic to the process is a complete understanding of what dialogue or conversation is. It takes place between beings, usually just two.

The two conversing take turns being transmitter and receiver, talker and listener. If it initiates with you, consider that you must be skilled at both transmitting accurately what you want to convey and being receptive to the response that comes. This may take practice. Many of us are poor listeners. We are so busy thinking about what we will say next, that we don't really hear much of what is said! Being a good communicator requires that you listen while the other being speaks.

When communicating with your High Self, keep in mind that the High Self's thoughts, ways and nature are far different from yours. You must be filled with an open, unbiased receptive attitude. No expectations, no previous concepts about how or what will transpire must affect your communications. The High Self is as different from you, as your rational, intuitive mind is from the elemental consciousness of your low self.

Precede any conversation by being curious about the nature and purpose of your own High Self. You will be energizing a force that brings about completion of your desires. Not greed, nor expectations, just a desire to *know*. Compare this to your own experience of meeting a stranger and suddenly experiencing a desire to know this stranger better. Remember your eager questioning? Your attempts to act so this stranger would respond to you with the information you desire?

When in dialogue with anyone, low self, High Self, or a friend, try to drop all preconceptions about the individual. They get in the way and are barriers. Forget to whom you are talking and listening. Concentrate on what is being transmitted. Often we hear a famous person speak and we get so carried away with the fact of *who* is speaking. We don't hear *what* is said. Many highly-respected people speak garbage and the listeners don't use their natural ability to discriminate, but tend to swallow whole what the "authority" says.

The value in any dialogue is the quality of it, not the source. I've often said that wisdom could issue from a drunk in the gutter, but we would not hear. We are eager to listen to any person for whom we hold high regard, but we forget to listen to what they say. Often there is no wisdom at all coming from so-called wise men, and so much wisdom from ordinary people. So, forget your awe of a higher consciousness and rest assured that if the person is wise he or she will not speak "over your head."

Sit at your typewriter and type what you would say to initiate a conversation with your High Self. Address your High Self in words as you begin. Then, pause, wait, sit receptively and be quiet for a moment, then when something comes into your awareness, begin typing it. When it becomes garbled, stop. Start again by clarifying your own part in this conversation. Type that. Wait quietly once more for something to enter your awareness and translate that to words on the typewritten page. You can do the same with a pencil. Keep a notebook for these practice sessions. That's all they will be at first. You have not yet developed the needed skills for this kind of communication.

Try a tape recorder. Clearly state your purpose in taping. Pose a question on a subject you would like to converse about, and then be quiet. Let the recorder run silently until some idea comes into your head and there is something you can relate into the recorder about what you are experiencing. Describe any physical sensations, feelings or thoughts that flow into your awareness. Keep the dialogue going back and forth. Equal time is the rule!

At various times in my life I have been urged to pray, but until I discovered Huna I did not know how. No one ever told me very much about the process. What they did tell me proved worthless. The usual advice was, "Just pray!" I knew through my studies that people have prayed successfully. Literature through the ages testifies to that. It seemed to me, though, that it was often a hit-or-miss proposition.

The first time I ever really prayed was when my baby was dying. I promised God all kinds of things if He would spare my baby's life. The baby died. So my experience was that if prayer worked, I certainly did not know *how to make it work*. Isn't it easy to understand something when we are looking back, but so difficult when we're right in the middle of it!

The High Self is well-qualified to assist us in our task of acquiring the abilities of a Kahuna. It can use its greater powers of creativity or destruction. We can best understand the High Self by thinking about its divine qualities of total acceptance and unconditional love, its powerful will and its great wisdom. To our low selves, Aumakua is a god because a god is one who can bestow or withhold favors. Will you go it alone or ask your High Self to help you? The decision rests with uhane. Free will, the power of choosing is yours.

The symbol of a High Self is wings. In nearly every culture some symbol is used to depict the High Self with wings. In Mexico we find the winged serpent, in Christianity we find winged angels, in the Tarot deck the High Self is a face with wings. This is an archetype symbol that has influenced mankind throughout history all over the globe. While the unihipili is ruled by Mother Nature and uhane is ruled by the upper world of living beings (society, culture), Aumakua is ruled by Hermes, God of Wisdom.

Telepathy is the means of communication with our High Self. It is silent and its presence is silence. Each presence is the "living silence" within the forcefield of that being. This living silence pulsates powerfully. Most of us never perceive silence, or the silence-pulsation within any being. To make contact with the pulsing center of any being is to contact that silence. Think of the great silence as the parent of all vibrations, whether they be perceived as color or sound. And then, bring that concept down into microscopic form and consider that within each being is a small portion of silence. In pulsation it produces the vibrations of the particular pattern of that being.

You have heard "silence is golden," and probably read of "entering into the silence." Let us just conclude that within our High Self there is a center of silence that we can touch and experience by focussing our listening ability into silence rather than sound. Our High Self has a presence, a small portion of silence that radiates its unique pattern. Think of silence and

presence being one and the same thing, and you will know you have
experienced it many times. Each person you contact has some presence that
can be felt. It is silent, for we never relate sound to the "presence" of another
person. It is hard to define, but you do evaluate how much presence each
person emanates. In some gatherings, you will feel the presence of one
stronger than some of the others. Some people have so little strength in their
"presence" it is hard to remember they were there!

Along this line, because we cannot experience the presence of a High
Self, we decide it is not real. The block is with us and interferes with our
ability to tune into the silence or presence. Prayer is channeled through
your own presence, your own center of silence. To become one with that,
you can practice techniques that will bring you closer to your own presence,
or into it. All techniques to achieve this require the focussing of your
attention on silence. Listen for it. Look for it.

Unihipili is silent; it has a tiny presence of its own. Aumakua is
silent, with a presence of its own. Uhane has a silent center of its own that
you can move to and become one with. It may only start with a wish, but
you can begin to desire it more strongly and it will eventually become your
"will" that you achieve this goal or target. This will make your prayer more
effective than if it comes from the surface of your being.

For now, your prayers will be channeled through your unihipili
unless there exist barriers to its transmission. You design and choose the
prayer. You create the "blueprint" of it with words, ideas and images.
Intention, a minor form of will, must be inherent in the prayer. The end
comes first. The target is like the seed which will grow to maturity having
come from the fully grown plant. Your prayer is in the design of the full-
grown goal, which will be condensed into a seed by unihipili and sent to
your High Self. You create the finish, and allow unihipili to shrink it down
into minute size before releasing it to the High Self.

The first task then is the creating or composition of the prayer. There
are a few guidelines that are helpful to follow. First, any prayer that hurts
none and helps many, has more chance of becoming reality than any other
prayer for it abides by the High Self's ethic. All High Selves work with
"harm to none, service to many" as their prime commandment. In Huna
you are free to pray for anything you desire, and you will get it if you are
ready to be responsible for its outcome. So be careful!

It will be the low self's job to send the prayer to the High Self, so we
must make the prayer intelligible to the low self. We already know that the

low self has a literal mind, is very sensitive to suggestion and understands pictures and images clearly. So we need specific precise words with meanings known to our low self and a clear picture of the result asked for by the prayer.

Symbol-pictures may be used if the low self clearly understands it is a symbol and the meaning of it. If it is appropriate that you be in the pictured result, put your person in. If you don't include yourself in the picture, you may see the prayer come true without you in it! That's how literal your low self is.

Write down your prayer first and go over it carefully. Make up two columns headed by "will help" and "will hurt." Divide all elements into these two columns and revise your prayer structure so that you can eliminate all those people who would be hurt, harmed or in any way be deprived by your getting what you pray for. If you can't eliminate everyone in that column, add methods to make amends for these hurts. Now list all of what you must be responsible for when the prayer is answered and comes to pass. Are you willing to mow the lawn of that house you want? Pay the mortgage? Keep it in repair? You may find you have asked for more than you want to be responsible for and you may revise your prayer. Do it now. Have your prayer as clearly stated as possible before you begin transmission.

The next step is to find out how your low self feels about this prayer. Is it enthusiastic about it? Any fixation contrary to this prayer will block its transmission to the High Self. If there is a fixation in your low self, you have work to do. It will be a fixation that has some association to this particular request of yours.

Be sensitive to emotions arising from within. Use whatever method you want to clear the way for the prayer. When you are assured the low self is willing and clear, proceed with a prayer rite to do the actual sending. The rite can vary according to your taste, as long as it includes the essential ingredients. There must be the action of sending mana to the High Self for conversion to mana-loa for the carrying out of the prayer. Also, you must release this mana to the High Self before it can go to work. The clearly formed prayer and your sacrifice of mana are all that are needed. Remember once more, before you begin, if you pray correctly you will surely get what you pray for!

Before you begin, look in Chapter 7 for the section on mana and find a technique for developing a charge of mana to use in the prayer rite. When you have chosen one, get comfortable and relax with your favorite method. It is usually most effective in the following rite to do this standing in a relaxed and composed stance. This technique is called *The Fountain Rite* and was recommended by Max Freedom Long.

Stand quietly and read aloud or recite from memorization the quote below. Feel each word and put that feeling into the tonal quality of your recitation for added power. Speak from within, using your diaphragm, slowly and fully aware of the meaning of each word. If you want to rephrase this to make it more authentic for you do it before you begin!

> We are now reaching out and making contact with our loving and utterly trustworthy father-mother-parental spirit. We are sending a large part of this extra mana along to it by way of the aka cord. We offer it as a perfect sacrifice to be used for the good of all of us or as may seem fit.

Give the prayer for your low self to send. Pause quietly and then say: "The flow stops, the action is finished. Let the rain of blessings fall. *Au-ma-ma* (for Amen)."

After you have made your prayer, sit quietly and relax a while so that your low self can complete the action.

In your prayer efforts, it will help to become aware of the center of consciousness in your solar plexus. After reading this book I'm sure you will be much more aware of that center than you were before.

While you are reciting the prepared prayer, the low self will be carrying the prayer picture with its full meaning along the aka cord with a flow of mana. Or, it may do the work later. Praying is like planting a seed in fertile ground. And, like planting a seed, we know that during its gestation stage, we must leave it alone. To dig up a seed before it is above ground is to destroy its possibilities for life. Give your prayer, like a seed to the High Self, and then leave it alone. Don't drag it back into your mind and consciousness to examine it or reconsider it. Just leave it alone, confident in the wisdom of the High Self to bring to pass results that will delight you.

Praying is a skill and every skill takes practice. Be patient with yourself, and be optimistic, for optimism warms your self and encourages unihipili to keep trying. Let your self know of your confidence in its ability to perform its part in the prayer rite efficiently. Perfect your ability to create good prayers by spending time and effort on each one you create.

5

Communication Between Uhane and Unihipili

As stated before, naming the low self is the first step in communicating with it. The second is teaching it a simple language or code, so that communication can take place. The third step, which we will come to later, is communicating directly without a code.

My students and I have found that the fastest, easiest code to learn, to teach and to use is the pendulum code, which is part of the science of radiesthesia and one of the tools used in dowsing. Perhaps you are already using some method of direct communication with your low self. If so, good. Still, I recommend learning to use the pendulum because it has many other uses as a tool for obtaining information.

We will start our practice with the pendulum by learning techniques that will obtain information from the low self about its attitudes and beliefs.

Basically, a pendulum is an object weighing approximately two ounces (about the weight of a half dollar) suspended from a seven- to ten-inch length of thread, string, or chain. The object can be almost anything, including a ring, pendant, bead, or button. It can be made of metal, wood, glass, or any other material that is not a conductor of electricity. The better balanced the pendulum is, the easier to work with it will be.

You may find a pendulum for sale in a shop or occult supply house. I have quite a collection of purchased pendulums that I use frequently, but I prefer the ones I've made myself. If you would like to make your own, here is a suggestion.

Take a piece of sealing wax about three quarters of an inch long and fasten to one end of it a ten-inch piece of light string or heavy thread. This is done by heating the wax over a flame, taking care not to set it on fire. When it has softened, use a match to push the end of the string down into the softened wax. Then squeeze the wax up around the string to hold it firmly. As soon as it cools, your pendulum is ready. If you would like your pendulum to be pointed on the bottom, soften it with heat again and pinch it until you have a pointed tip.

Now that you have your pendulum, let's experiment with it before we start learning to communicate. We'll become familiar with some of its characteristics and have some fun, too.

Hold the string in whichever hand is most comfortable for you, and arch your wrist so that the pendulum can hang freely. Extend and separate the unused three fingers for better balance. They may also act as antennas for you. Support your elbow on a solid surface, or your arm will get tired and start to tremble.

You have probably been holding your pendulum by pinching the string between your thumb and index finger about seven to ten inches above the bob. Here are some suggestions that should make your pendulum more comfortable to use. You may attach the string to one end of a four-inch stick and hold it between the thumb and forefinger with the end of the stick near the root of the little finger for easier manipulation.

The physical body has an electrical field that emanates both a positive and a negative charge. Usually the positive electrical charge is on the right side of the body and the negative electrical charge is on the left. When the pendulum is held over a positive electrical field, it swings in a clockwise circle, usually indicating the strength of the field by the size of the circle. Over a negative electrical field the pendulum swings counterclockwise indicating the strength of the field by the size of the circle.

Right-handed people usually have the positive charge on their right side. Experiment and see which side of your body is positive and which is negative. To do this, sit down, spread your knees apart and hold the pendulum about two inches above one knee. Watch which way it gyrates. Then hold it over the other knee and watch which way it gyrates on that side. Now hold it in the neutral space between the knees. It will probably swing back and forth in that area.

We must teach the low self the code we want to use in communicating with it. The code swing for *Yes* is like an affirmative nod of the head. The pendulum swings away from the body and toward it again, back and forth. To teach it the code, swing the pendulum that way, telling your low self that is the code for *Yes*. Then stop the swing with the other hand, saying aloud, "Stop." Repeat this until you feel that your low self would like to try it. Then sit still, hold the pendulum, and watch for any movement.

As soon as it moves, no matter how, start encouraging your low self. This is a new skill. By nature the low self likes to cling to the old and is often reluctant to attempt the new. Use praise, admiration, and any other reinforcing encouragment you can think of. Don't try to kid your own self, that is impossible. Be sincere. It probably will not be hard. You won't feel a single muscle move, but will notice that the pendulum moves with no perceptible force pushing it.

As soon as you have taught your self to swing *Yes* and to stop the swing on a verbal command, go on with the rest of the code. *No* is like the sideways shake of the head that we use in conversation to indicate *No*. Swing the pendulum from side to side in front of you, stopping it with your free hand as you utter the word "Stop." Keep this up until you feel that your low self would like to try it. Then watch its efforts.

What you say at this time may be crucial. Encourage and praise its efforts. Be patient and courteous, and probably in a short time your low self will be merrily swinging the pendulum. Through repetition and practice, your low self will become more confident, and as the skill becomes familiar it will enjoy showing off its dexterity.

The next code word is *Maybe*. Tell your self to swing the pendulum diagonally, between yes and no.

Then go on to the code words *Good* and *Bad*. We use a clockwise gyration for *Good* and a counter-clockwise gyration for *Bad*. My Junior uses good and bad to let me know whether or not I have phrased my question well. That is a common difficulty. Bad and good can also be used to detect spoiled food or to determine what vitamins are needed by the low self to maintain the physical body. You'll think of other applications as time goes on.

For the moment consider that you are a teacher and your low self is a pupil. What teaching methods are best and most effective? The best reinforcers are repetition, firm conscious will and clear instructions. Combine these with praise and credit for each of the low self's attempts to comply. The most productive techniques with my low self are appreciation, warmth, and approval as I tell my self how much I love it above all other selves.

Now you are ready for communication. Begin with questions that can be answered *Yes* or *No*. Don't insult your self by asking silly questions like, "Am I twenty-eight years old?" The object here is to get acquainted, not to watch a performance.

Some of the answers you get may surprise you. Watch your comments! Don't say, "Oh, that's silly," or make any other belittling remark. Thank your self for every answer, no matter what it is. At first your self may lie to you. Why not? It's been conditioned to lie. Lying has saved it a lot of pain and trouble.

So, along with asking questions, keep reassuring your low self that you will accept the truth without getting angry or indignant. Let your low self know you are ready to accept it unconditionally and will never knowingly hurt its feelings again. It may be a very shy self, reluctant to come forward and be known. You may have to work hard to get to know your low self. It will be worth it.

You may want to keep a diary of questions and answers. It will be very interesting and helpful some day to look back on your early work.

Working with Huna means you must begin to ask many questions. Your attitude about asking questions is crucial here, as is your low self's attitude about asking questions. This first list of questions is to be answered by you before you ask your low self. Then compare the answers. This list uses "I" for you to answer the questions. When you are finished, convert the pronoun to "you" and ask your low self the same questions. Use the pendulum code to set the low self's answers. Work with these two sets of answers to clear up any blocks to asking questions.

Do I fear asking what may be a stupid question?
Do I fear appearing ignorant by asking questions?
When I do not understand answers, is it because I am stupid?

Do I fear revealing my ignorance?
Do I fear getting information about my self?
Do I fear having my imperfection uncovered?
Do I fear asking questions of authorities like doctors or lawyers?
When asked a question, do I ever fear answering it?
When asked how I feel, do I reply truthfully?
Do I feel there is risk in asking questions?
Do I ask questions when I do not understand some statement?
Do I ask questions when I am ignorant of a subject?
Do I avoid reality by not asking questions?
When I do not understand a repair bill, do I ask questions about it?
When I feel confused, do I admit it?
Do I avoid asking questions, pretending to know more than I do?
Do I ask questions that will uncover my problems?
Do I ask to find out if I am correct or incorrect?
Do I fear hearing I have been wrong?
Do I fear finding out I have made a mistake?
Do I fear that questions mean I am ignorant?
Is it painful to ask and get an answer that hurts my pride?
Do I ask questions from my feeling of guilt?
Do I feel I have the right to ask any question of anyone?

Now re-phrase the questions and ask your low self to answer through pendulum and the yes/no code. Write down all the answers and then work them over until you have a clear picture of your attitudes about working with questions, both consciously and unconsciously.

We have all been programmed with social values and attitudes. We have adopted these convictions under the guise of "truth." It is important to realize these are "imported" into our system and did not originate there. Consequently they can be dispensed with if they prove to be barriers to a full and satisfying life. Here is a short list of some with which I am familiar. They can all be answered by a yes or no.

Do you have guilt feelings about_____? (Fill in appropriate word.)
Do you believe the saying, one pays for everything one gets?
Do you believe that a person's sins always catch up to him?
Do you enjoy having responsibility?
Is it wrong to want to be rich?

Are you afraid of physical death?
Does it hurt to be criticized?
Do you have feelings of anger you have not expressed?
Do you like to have goals to work for?
Do you ever feel inadequate to a task?
Is it difficult to behave as others expect us to?
Do you believe you have to work hard to keep friends?
Are you worried about economic security?
Is it a sin to tell a lie?
Is laziness a sin?
Do you feel you should make good use of free time?
Do you enjoy traveling away from home?
Do you resent being told what to do?
Are you proud of your achievements?
Do you believe you have ESP?
Do you like_____? (Fill in the name of a person.)
Do you have a strong urge to express yourself?

Now that your low self has mastered the skill of manipulating the pendulum, you can develop another use for it and move to another, more informative method of getting to know your own low self. We will measure attitudes.

For this, use a chart like the one shown in Figure 1 (on following page), with a scale in increments of 5 from N (neutral) to 30. This is an arbitrary scale. You may change it if you wish. Copy or create your own chart on cardboard or some other material that will wear well. You will use it often.

Now make up a set of index cards. Draw a line down the middle of each card, and on each half print one word of a pair of polarities (False/True, Bad/Good, Difficult/Easy, Hate/Love, No/Yes) as illustrated in Figure 2 (on following page). Make one card for each pair you want to use.

Avoid overworking your low self in your new enthusiasm for it will tire easily when first practicing a new skill. Ask frequently if it wants to continue. Stop if it indicates that it does not. If your low self is tired, further work will be fruitless for getting correct answers.

You are ready to begin when you have a pendulum with a pointed end, a chart, a set of cards and a list of attitudes on which to rate your self.

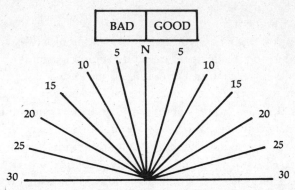

FIGURE 1: ATTITUDE SCALE. Place polarity card above scale as shown. The low self will use numbers on the left to indicate False, Bad, Difficult, Hate, No; numbers on right to indicate True, Good, Easy, Love, Yes.

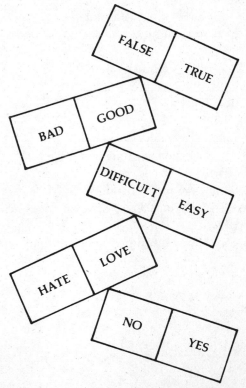

FIGURE 2. Polarity cards for attitude measurement. Notice that False, Bad, Difficult, Hate, and No go on the left sides of the cards.

Place your chart on a table, and put one card above the chart, clearly telling your self which one it is.

When you begin any work with the pendulum, always ask your self if it is willing to communicate with you through the pendulum at this time. If the answer is *No*, wait until a later time. If the answer is *Yes*, ask your self if it is willing to communicate about the subject on which you are seeking information. If it says *No*, ask about another area of questioning until you get an affirmative answer. When you get a *Yes*, proceed.

Holding the pendulum over the point on the chart from which all the lines radiate, ask clearly—aloud or silently—about the first item on your list. Wait patiently, without guiding the answer in your own mind. The pendulum indicates the strength of the attitude by swinging out toward a number. Give it time to become steady at one place on the scale. When you feel that your low self has answered, put down the pendulum and record the answer in your notebook.

On the following pages are lists of statements, you can ask your low self to react to each. Start with these and then ask your own.

Good or Bad

Asking someone else to do work you dislike.
Refusing an invitation.
Hurting someone's feelings.
Refusing to satisfy another person's desire.
Expecting another to give his or her time and attention.
Not loving someone who expects love.
Being too tired to do a favor for a friend.
Interrupting someone who is busy.
Not finishing a job.
Considering one's own happiness more important than another's.
Wasting time.
Working hard.
Being unfaithful to one's spouse.
Losing one's virginity.
Saying no to a request.
Feeling angry at someone.
Hating one's self.
Being exuberant.
Being reserved.

Being noisy.
Being quiet.
Getting good grades in school.
Obeying another person.
Resisting temptation.
Being daring.
Being aggressive.
Being hostile.
Winning.
Being active.
Exploring.
Being impulsive.
Getting angry when frustrated.
Being the center of attention.
Having a lot of children.
Smoking marijuana.

True or False

Females are inferior to males.
Females are inherently wicked.
A woman's place is in the home.
A person should get involved with "issues."
Men shouldn't cry.
A man should be the boss in his home.
Men are more capable in business than women.
One cannot control Fate.
Life is just a rat race.
Financial security is absolutely necessary.
It pays to be honest.
Politicians are crooked.
The country is in bad shape.
War is wrong.
We should all love one another.
Do unto others as they do unto you.
Children are naturally naughty.
All babies are beautiful.

Love or Hate

List your friends, relatives, co-workers, correspondents, etc. Ask your self to indicate its feelings for each one in turn. Then ask about each of these:

Being criticized.

Listening to others talk.

Reading books.

Going to the movies.

Watching TV.

Fulfilling job duties.

Fulfilling obligations.

Being right.

Being creative.

Working with the hands.

Learning new skills.

Sharing material possessions.

Being poor.

Being rich.

Staying home.

Solitude.

Physical comfort.

Crowds.

Excitement.

Novelty.

Peace.

Adventure.

Now make a list of your own questions.

Easy or Difficult

Studying.

Relaxing.

Going to sleep.

Refusing requests.

Accepting disappointment.

Dancing in public.

Waking up.

Doing physical work.

Releasing feelings.

Spending money.

Being lazy.
Fulfilling responsibilities.
Accepting blame.
Accepting compliments.
Facing the unknown.
Forgiving someone.
Holding resentment.
Forgetting an insult.
Blaming someone.
Being punctual.
Losing belongings.
Associating with ill people.
Being optimistic.
Being pessimistic.

Do you need to...

When using *Yes* and *No*, the pendulum will indicate the strength of a conviction, feeling, or fixed attitude, depending on the question. It is the most versatile of the pairs of polarities. Here are a few needs you might check. Do you need to...?
Feel safe.
Feel loved.
Be liked.
Be approved of.
Be punished.
Punish.
Suppress hostility.
Minister to others.
Serve others.
Be dignified.
Earn father's love.
Earn mother's love.
Get praise.
Be hurt.
Be respected.
Hurt others.
Have peace at any price.
Be alone often.

Have people around a lot.
Have one person to love.
Feel more worthy.
Be needed.
Feel useful.
Feel wanted.
Lose a bad habit.
Be protected.
Have decisions made by other people.
Feel virtuous.
Be successful.
Have self-esteem.
Travel.
Escape.
Be admired.
Be dominated.
Dominate.
Give.
Get.
Be forgiven.

These questions will give you a start. Not all of them will be useful to you, but they will suggest others that are.

Use the information you receive in any way you like. Usually the highest numbers indicate your most fixed attitudes and beliefs, which are probably the ones you will want to work on. Remember that these attitudes and beliefs were built through repetition, experience, and the voice of authority; you can change them by the same method. And, you can let some attitudes fade away through malnutrition by just not feeding them any more.

An important change in myself came about when I stopped saying "I hate my self" and began repeating "I love my self." When you first try to change a firmly-held attitude, your efforts will be very mechanical, and you will probably feel very foolish repeating words you do not mean. You just have to work through this period. Soon the new attitude, as it is absorbed, will be reflected back by your low self, and you will be able to say the words with sincerity.

Once I decided to change my attitude toward house plants. For years I had asserted that I wasn't good with plants. And it was true; they did not thrive under my care. Then I bought a small ivy with three leaves, placed it on my window sill, and spoke to it every day. "I love you, I think you are beautiful."

For about five days, I felt like a complete nut, grateful that no one could hear me. Then one day, as I was mechanically repeating these words, I became aware of a change in my feelings. I really meant them! Excitedly, I loudly exclaimed to the ivy, "I love you, I really do, and you *are* beautiful!" As I expected, the result of this exercise was a thriving ivy plant that grew more rapidly than any plant I had ever seen.

Winners and losers come from the same space, the same social program. Winning is good, losing is bad. Winning is a virtue, losing is a sin. Winners need losers, for without them they are not winners. Losers need winners, for without them they cannot lose.

Most of us have strongly-held attitudes about winning and losing. Our society is enamored of games and sports in which winning and losing are the two most important aspects. We get caught up in the winning and losing game so early in life that we believe the concept is universal and is a necessary part of growth and success.

Not so! Be not a loser or a winner in the game of life. Neither is virtuous nor sinful. Your investment in winning or losing can be withdrawn and placed in another category. Find out your underlying attitude about winning or losing. Make a chart with one on each side, and use your pendulum. Ask:

Am I a winner all of the time? Some of the time? Often? Infrequently?

Am I a loser all of the time? Often? Seldom? Sometimes?

You have probably already found out how little satisfaction there is in being either a winner or a loser. These estimates are always from the perception of others. Feeling like a winner is valueless unless it is validated by your experience with others. Being a loser, if that is what you feel you are, must be validated by others, must be verified by actually losing in the game of life.

There is an old saying that suggests "It is not whether you win or lose, but how you play the game." Yet we are programmed by our news reports about inter-country squabbles, about athletic teams, to put undue emphasis on winning and losing.

Anyone who is serious about winning or losing has been hooked. This is what our culture would like you to be serious about. Down deep, the culture believes that without the stimulus to win, you would never accomplish anything. Does that sound silly to you? Or do you believe it is true?

The game of life is one in which we are designed to function admirably. Our whole natural thrust is forward, flowing into the new now, facing new and novel circumstances and dealing with each in an original way. This is the evolution of a growing person. The results of living your life are not important at all, but are you participating? It is in living that we find enjoyment and pleasure.

Now you have learned how to get information from your own inner self, you now need to consider methods for you to communicate to your self. Self-suggestion or autosuggestion is one method. Repeating suggestions will cause the low self to integrate those suggestions into its framework of skills, habits and attitudes. Self-suggestion is the process by which uhane impresses on unihipili an idea tht will take root in the mind of unihipili and produce desired results. In actual fact, all our thoughts and feelings are suggestions that go into the organization of the mind of unihipili, but they lack the impact of what is repeated over and over.

The sound of your voice can implement the power of suggestion by injecting vital force into it. Feeling charges any suggestion and the tone of authority gives it power. Use of a tape recorder may lack some of the impact of the original spoken words, but the repetition will be effective. A simple idea, when filled with feeling and stated authoritatively and firmly, will cause unihipili to react in some way. Rebellion can be felt as well as agreement if you keep tuned to gut feelings.

To use self-suggestion, first relax your physical body, still the tape recorder of endless words running through your conscious mind and move into a state of non-action: no physical action, no emotional action, no mental action. Just be in a still, expectant, alert state. Instruct your low self to suspend all activity and be open to what you are about to do. Ask your self to be receptive to your wishes and desires. Unihipili takes the idea you have planted within, surrounds it in aka substance and fills it with mana.

Post-self-suggestion works because of the good comprehension the low self has of time and measurement. When a suggestion is given that an action will be performed at a future time—and perhaps place—it will remain aware of the passage of time and will react on schedule. You can instruct yourself what time you should be awakened in the morning or what exit you want to take off a turnpike.

The middle self has the ability to create images within its mind that can be used to impress the low self. This form of suggestion is very effective and becomes more and more effective as you use it. Be very clear about what you are doing. Recognize that each image is having an impact on your low self. From now on, be aware of the random images you create. Change them if they are undesirable to the kind you want your low self to get.

In using your imagination the energy required to hold an unmoving image is great, for the nature of images and energy is to flow. Trying to hold an unmoving image is tiring, unnatural and quickly uses up your vitality. Rhythm pulsing can be used if you want to stay with some image because it is a form of motion. Image it, let it fade, bring it up clearly again and let it fade in alternate cycles. It gives you a natural rhythm of come and go, come and go. Use this to charge up a specific image that needs its power increased. Each time it reappears you can charge it with more intention and feeling.

You can create a slow-motion sequence in your imagination. It must have a beginning, a middle and an end. This can be recalled and run through again to intensify it. Each repetition should be run through a little faster until you have it moving at normal or even faster than normal speed. Three repetitions should be sufficient.

Imagining the sensory qualities of touch, taste and smell is difficult for some students. The best recall includes sharp detail of that which was in the foreground of your consciousness. Practice recalling events during which you smelled something or ate something and evaluate your own ability to resee it, resmell it and retaste it. This practice will also clue you in to what you are most aware of in any event and what you often neglect to notice as you experience external events.

When you want to communicate a goal or a plan to your low self you must imbue it with will-force, or intention. Strong, firm intention on the part of the middle self makes a deep impression on the low self and obedience is a natural response to it. Let your low self know your specific purpose, your intention of what the outcome should be and how strongly you feel about the importance of what you are planning.

Determination is a force at the service of the middle self to use to influence the low self. Determined will-force applied to a plan or design will vitalize it so that it becomes reality. Will-force or power is not effort or trying. It is not curbing, attempting, restraining or controlling. It is a force that moves into and vitalizes any product of your mind, any thought form. Will power is similar to desire power but is the *force* added to desire in actuality.

The word for suggestion in Hawaiian is *kumumanao* and it is defined as an exchange of thoughts or seeds. The low self can be gotten to accept a suggestion from the middle self in exchange for one it will "trade off" to the middle self. The easiest trade-off is to ask your low self to respond with its feeling about what you are sending.

In the Hawaiian language we find that the word "seed" is a set of ideas, the likeness of a thing, a mold or shadowy thought form duplication. *Ano* means seed, but it also means "a sacred place of stillness" which gives us a clue as to how we should plant seeds in our low self. The low self should be tranquil and still, fully relaxed during the technique of planting seeds or ideas into it by suggestion, repetition or imagination. *Mano* or *nanao* means to think hard and to believe. If your middle self is fully convinced of the rightness of the goal to be achieved, it will have a greater impact on unihipili.

First, create a set of ideas. Second, charge it with mana- mana. Relax your low self and then impregante it with the seed and ask for its acceptance and a response signifying it has or has not accepted the seed.

Through the Hawaiian language we find the low self described as one who is slippery, hard to find and to hold once found. The low self can lead one astray, distract one and cause the middle self to turn aside from its purpose. The low self lives in the dark, unseen and silent. From the Hawaiian dictionary we know that once found, "the hand is thrust in to feed it, force-feeding if necessary."

Hahao means literal and direct suggestion but it also means to breathe hard. Breathing hard accumulates vital force. *Hahao* also means hard thinking which we would probably translate as firmly focussed attention. *Hao* means to place a little thing into a larger thing and obviously relates to the ability of the middle self to put small suggestions into unihipili's larger framework of ideas.

To get, and hold, the attention of your low self, take control of your breathing. As this is usually an autonomic function you will immediately attract the attention of your low self who breathes for you all the time. After you have taken control of your breathing, begin to breathe heavily in order to build up vital force. Pump your abdomen in and out in rhythm with your lung expansion. Keep on, breathing even more deeply. Start sounding *ha* when you exhale, visualizing all tension being released on that breath and in that sound. Between *ha*'s (outbreaths) visualize the suggestion you want implanted pulsing in rhythm with your breathing. Each *ha* will charge up the idea held in your mind during the inhalation. The HA exercise builds mental vitality or force called "will." This helps you to retain dominance over the low self.

When your low self relaxes, the physical body follows suit. We work to relax the low self which controls physical relaxation. From active to passive is the route we go. From an expanded state for action, we retract or contract away to the passive, receptive state. The low self stops producing energy for physical action and goes into a non-productive state, lowering the voltage it normally uses. This lowering of its own energy force allows the stronger voltage from the middle-self mind to enter into it without resistance. The sensation of tension reveals resistance to the penetrating power of planting of the suggestion. We need to move the low self from positive active to negative receptive, releasing energy for use of the middle self for the activity of "thinking hard."

Hoolulu means relax. You can use it as a code word, teaching your low self to automatically respond to it by relaxing. Sound it aloud, "who-loo-loo." This word also means to "sow or plant seeds" so you can see what the Kahuna did when they relaxed their low selves.

Sounded aloud hoolulu allows tense energy to be released with the sound. Also, you can add a command to your self to "relax your mind" or "relax your intestines" or "ease up on your activities." Any helpful suggestions are good.

If you find it hard to get your low self to relax, try this technique based on the knowledge that tiring the eyes uses up a lot of energy. Put your eyes under muscular strain by staring at a far corner of the room, or focussing on a whirling disc painted in a spiral line. This causes the eyes to close and your low self to relax. You can make one of these discs by cutting white cardboard to match your record player disc, painting the spirals on in black and white, and then using it instead of a record to help you relax. Put it on and set your record player at its lowest speed. Stare at it as you tell yourself to relax and let go. Allow your eyes to close, turn off the player and sit back for the process you intend to use at that time.

You may want to tire your low self so that you can go to sleep. Sleep uncouples the two selves or creates a change in their relationship. When you become physically inert, the low self may be active, churning up thoughts. To slow these down to a stop, increase your breathing rate, and hold a mental picture of drawing all the aka substance to the solar plexus and the mana from there up to the brain.

Tell your low self to take the mental image on which you have been working and care for it carefully because all things in it are going to be very helpful, delightful, useful, important and necessary. Command it to do all it can to bring about the desired condition. Promise that you will do all you can. Mean it sincerely and keep your promise. If you change your mind, recall it and cancel it—otherwise, you will have a "time bomb" which has been already set to go off.

After every session with the low self, end the session. Command it to return to its work of the day, refreshed, full of energy and enthusiastic. Whenever you end a session in any altered state of consciousness, make sure you return to everyday consciousness and be certain your low self has, too. Tell your self to transform from a passive, receptive condition to an active one. Use a count-up if necessary. Stretch your physical body and ease into a physically vital state.

When your two selves, middle and low, begin to think and act as one, then you *two* can be a Kahuna. That is my personal goal.

Setting goals is the job of the middle self, but carrying out these goals is largely the job of the low self. You must define your goals in literal terms, clearly and concisely, so the low self won't have any difficulty in knowing what you want to achieve. It can't reason through your vague daydreams or wishes and come to a rational conclusion about your desires. Keep the directions simple, clear, and literal.

Your low self understands pictures and symbols very well. Use this fact in setting your goals. Make a clear mental picture of attaining your goal and the circumstances that will surround it. Use symbols that you have clearly defined to the low self. Post these symbols around your home so the low self will see them often. Your self is always impressed most by information perceived through the five physical senses. Pictures are great! Your self also perceives the pictures you place on the screen of your imagination. They should be accompanied by a clear thought about the goal that you want to achieve.

Practice visualizing with your eyes closed and rolled slightly upward into your head. Pretend you are looking out through your forehead at a movie screen about three or four feet in front of you. That's your screen of imagination, on which you can visualize any picture you want. You can also look at its blank surface and ask your self to project a picture on it. That's another way of getting to know your self. Or ask your self a question and watch for the answer to appear on the screen. It is fun and usually quite enlightening.

I recommend Maxwell Maltz's book *The Magic Power of Self-Image Psychology*, for additional material about goal-setting. This book will enable you to understand the importance of setting goals and give you other useful ideas for finding out what your low self is like.

The low self is never happier than when it's working to achieve a goal. This statement is easily verified. Think of the people you know who are bored, depressed, unhappy or listless. Think about their goals. You'll find they don't have any beyond getting up in the morning! Now look at the people you know who are bright-eyed and bushy-tailed. You'll find that they have very definite goals that they are happily working on. Examine your own past for the times when you have worked for goals, large or small. Were your mood and outlook improved when you had concrete goals ahead of you? Were any past periods of depression and discouragement related to your goals? Perhaps your goals were unrealistic or seemed unattainable. Examine them closely.

What is a goal? A goal always applies to the future, even if it's only five minutes from now. Everyone has many goals, such as getting up in the morning, making purchases at a store, going to the bank, having a car repaired. You set all these goals, but you have to depend on your low self to remind you of the right time for acting on them. You can ask your low self (out loud, if you like) to remind you when it's time to take a certain action, and it will oblige very nicely.

I depend on my Junior as a reminder for many things. I program my low self very clearly and concisely, and Junior reminds me when to pick up my check, when my car payment is due and when I must pay my car insurance. These regular events in my life now run very smoothly because they are tied into my goal of simplifying my life through managing necessary details efficiently. If you would like to achieve this goal yourself, some understanding of the processes of memory, recall, and forgetting may help you.

The low self contains the memory bank from which it selects the data to send to you at every moment. It sends whatever it is programmed to send. For a long time I told my self that I just could not remember names. I was programming my self to forget names, and, of course, I did exactly that. Then I changed the program to, "I am constantly improving my ability to remember names and getting better at it every day." Now I am improving slowly, and I'm grateful to my low self for its cooperation.

If you ask your self to remind you of something, you must have faith that it will do so. Once you have programmed the reminder into it, you must drop the matter. For many years you've probably been asking your low self to do certain things for you and then not trusting it, worrying and fretting and keeping the idea in your conscious mind "for fear I'll forget." Trusting your low self may be difficult, but instilling your faith and trust is well worth a few failures.

One failure I experienced brings up a new point for consideration, that is, the wisdom of the low self. Once I programmed myself to get up in time for a 10:00 AM staff meeting. I included in the reminder instructions to leave plenty of time to get to the meeting room. Can you imagine my amazement when I awoke at 10:00 AM with thoughts of the staff meeting? Fifteen minutes later a co-worker called to inform me that the meeting had been cancelled!

I patted my tummy, thanking my self for saving me a lot of trouble. But such occurrences are infrequent. Now when I forget something I look for the cause within my low self so that I can root out the reasons why it does not want to remind me of something I've asked it to. I have also learned to forgive my self immediately when it forgets so that it feels no guilt. Only if I do that can I find out the true causes underlying the forgetfulness.

The low self likes long-range goals best. As an example, let's take your vacation that comes up about a year from now. You, the middle self, must decide where you will go and what you will do with all that free time. You may want to make notes or lists and plan what clothes to take. Have you ever thought of asking your low self how it feels about those plans? You may not consider that very important, but I've known people who didn't do so and should have. Apparently their low selves didn't like the vacation plans, because something came up to spoil their plans or ruin the vacation. Have you ever known someone who broke a leg just before going on a long-planned trip? That's the kind of occurrence I'm talking about.

We'll assume that you've planned exactly what you want to do on your vacation. If your low self is enthusiastic about your goal, it will work very hard to make it come true, usually with a few bonuses, the small miracles that appear to be chance or coincidence. From now on, you can make sure that chance and coincidence work in your favor.

Let's deal with the problem that occurs when the low self refuses to work for a goal you want to achieve. Why does this happen? The cause lies in a fixed attitude that is contrary to your goal.

A child is born with only a few fixed beliefs, which are holdovers from a previous life. How do new beliefs form? They are formed by conditioning, through constant repetition by selves external to the low self—parents, playmates, teachers, and, later on, the middle self. Anything you keep repeating to and about your self becomes a fixed belief in its mind. It learns from experience and registers the dictates of authority, even when that authority speaks only once. Experience, repetitive teaching and the voices of authority all combine to give the low self fixed opinions of good/bad, pain/pleasure, success/failure and so on.

The low self cannot reason as the middle self can and accepts literally whatever is heard or experienced. Anything it sees, hears, feels, tastes or smells makes an impression that is never forgotten. All perception is indelibly imprinted in the mind of the low self, a process that is called registration. After registering all incoming perception, the low self files this data away in the memory by a system of associations. That is the basis of the psychoanalytic technique of free association. Many different experiences can trigger many more memories associated with them.

What has all this to do with goals? It is very important to know which of your fixed attitudes will assist you in achieving a goal and which ones might prevent success. Let me give a few examples of attitudes that block the achievement of goals. All these examples are beliefs that result from conditioning about sins and "bad" things.

Some people believe it is a sin to be rich; some believe it is a sin to be poor. You may believe it is wrong to disobey your mother or father or that it is bad to rebel against society. Some believe it is bad to want what others have, that luxuries are sinful. I could go on and on, but it is your own beliefs that are important to you. The first task of each Huna student is to communicate with their own self and get to know its feelings and beliefs.

Where there is conflict between the two selves, the low self always wins. Think about that. Where have you been in conflict in the past? What beliefs have you changed your conscious mind about? Is your low self in opposition, stuck with a past belief? Do you still believe you should not displease your parents? That's such a common one, nearly everyone shares it.

In Huna there is only one sin: to hurt one's self or another's self. That's simple but it covers a lot of ground. The Polynesians felt that this sin was basic to the nature of the low self and that it applied whether the low self was conditioned to it or not. Perhaps it will help us to return to this simple concept of sin and dissolve some of the conditioning our low selves have received.

What is a sin to your low self now? Probably anything it has been conditioned to believe is bad. By its nature, the low self worships the gods and values whatever the gods decree to be good and desirable. By its nature, it works hard to achieve the good and avoid the bad. It has a sense of sin.

What does your self believe in regard to sin? What are your low self attitudes about bad and good? Were you taught in Sunday school about sin? Did your parents use that word at home? Re-examine your early training for these concepts. What have you been taught to think of as bad? The seat of the conscience, the sense of right and wrong, is the low self. You weren't born with a conscience, so where did it come from? Other people's beliefs.

Experience teaches us about many things that are bad or good for us. Many of these experiences are valuable because they help preserve physical life. After all, we are glad that our low selves have learned to avoid hot stoves, speeding cars and other threats to our well-being. But what of the other taboos? Are there some that were useful in childhood that are now outgrown and no longer useful? In fact, they may be now limiting you.

The low self naturally clings to whatever it possesses, whether it be a piece of property or a belief. It does not like change and will resist leaving a comfortable rut. This is a good trait when properly applied, but it limits us when our low self clings to what is no longer useful. Since the low self has this trait of clinging, it may be difficult to get it to give up some of its cherished beliefs. It is afraid to defy the gods! So sometimes it may be best to replace one belief with another belief.

Our first task is to find out what our low self's beliefs are. Let us return to our childhood and try to recall some of the ideas that were repeated over and over, engraving a deep groove in the middle of the low self. Here are some common ones:

Mind your brother, he's smarter than you.
Big boys don't cry.
Wear your rubbers or you'll catch a cold.

Behave yourself or no one will love you.
You'll come to no good end.
You'll never be a success.
Just like a girl.
Mother knows best.
It doesn't pay to be honest.
Why can't you be like other children?
Too bad you aren't good-looking.
If people knew what you're like inside.
You're always catching colds.
No wonder the other kids don't like you.
Naturally my child is superior to other children.
We're different, dear.
What will the neighbors think?
You'll never know a man as good as your father.

Make a list of the repeated ideas you remember, then pick up your pendulum and ask your self to indicate if it still believes those statements to be true. Even though the middle self changes its mind often, the low self does not change easily, so you may be surprised. Reason helps the middle self to realize that certain beliefs are outmoded and no longer needed, but the fixed opinions of the low self continue to affect our behavior.

We all behave automatically in many situations because the low self is constantly sending stimuli to the middle self to influence its choices. The stronger the belief, the stronger the stimuli. Usually the middle self responds with the appropriate action without even thinking about it. Examine some of your habitual behavior and see if you can perceive any low self beliefs manifesting themselves in this way.

What statements do you find yourself repeating, particularly about your self? Do you tell people you have no talent? Can't make decisions? Can't remember names? Awkward on a dance floor? Too nervous to drive?

Make a list of the statements you remember and check them with the pendulum. Maybe you are just responding to stimuli coming from the low self. It likes to have its beliefs confirmed! Our limitations are imposed on us when we are young and imposed by us when we are adult. But we don't have to preserve any limitations that have no value.

In his book, *The Center of the Cyclone,* Dr. John Lilly says "Whatever you believe is true becomes true," a statement that applies to the low self. I have found on occasion that I have one belief, my low self has another or the opposite belief and it turns out that what my low self believes comes true.

Here is an interesting true story of how people can hold contradictory beliefs. One day the father of one of my Huna students went to see Kathryn Kuhlman, the famous faith healer, perform. He observed two people, a woman and a man, who expressed different ideas about what they expected would happen. The woman believed totally in spiritual healing and urgently desired to be healed. The man, a reporter, scoffed at the whole idea and took notes during the service. Who was healed? The reporter. The woman departed, unhealed and disappointed. It is a very good example of how one's low and middle selves can hold opposite and contradictory beliefs. Perhaps this story will shed some light on events that have puzzled you in the past.

The only sin we should consider is the sin of hurting one's self or another's self. But what if you can't avoid hurting someone? Huna has a remedy for that. Whenever a sin has been committed, the low self develops a sense of guilt. This eats away at the low self and can easily manifest itself through illness. The sense of guilt can be dissolved only by making amends to the victim. The middle self must decide what the amends should be, consult the low self to see if it is satisfactory, and then proceed to carry it out. When the low self is content that amends have been made to cancel out the hurt, forgiveness is automatic and the feeling of guilt dissolves.

Everyone's long-range goals should include integration of personality and spiritual growth, as well as material success and achievement. In Huna there are no limitations imposed on the individual. All limitations are self-imposed through programming or allowing others to program us.

A wonderful book about attitudes toward money is Napoleon Hill's *Think and Grow Rich.* It can help you revise any restricting beliefs you may have acquired about this important subject.

In the next chapter, we exmaine another aspect of the low and middle selves, their wills. How are they different from each other, how do they function, and what are their purposes? Understanding them can lead to harmonizing them and gaining more power over the events in our lives. To become a Kahuna, we must be able to use each will to its greatest potential in order to be the captain of our own fate.

6

Will, Force and Other Powers

All three selves have a will. Just as the essence and nature of each self is unique, each will is different.

We often speak of a "will to": the will to live, the will to die, the will to do, the will to achieve, the will to dominate and so on. Let us keep the wills separate in our thinking, so that eventually we can harmonize them.

I believe the will to live and the will to die are basically attributes of the low self in regard to the physical body. But they are so related to the low self's will to express and create, and its will to destroy the body when frustrated, that we cannot isolate them as the survival instinct or death-wish.

The will to live undoubtedly drives the low self to heal the physical body when it is hurt or ill, but it does this so that it can continue to express its ability to create out of itself. When these desires are denied, the will to live or create is turned inward and becomes the will to die, the will to destroy one's own body or at least the lack of will to defend the body against invading germs. Denied expression will often manifest itself as illness or accident-proneness.

The low self's will serves as the director of energy for all its functions. There is a dynamic aspect to the way it uses force or energy. The force of the low self's will can sometimes arouse the middle self's courage to make a difficult choice. When we say that someone has "the courage of his convictions," it means that the middle self has the courage that the low self has given it because of a very strong fixed belief.

We all know the phrase "the will to get well," which is often applied to hospitalized patients. We also know how much the low self's will to get well is aroused by conditioning. The patient doesn't even have to be conscious in order to respond to repeated encouragements to "live for your loved ones" or the like.

When we say we have a free will, we are talking about the ability of the middle self to choose. Once a choice is made, the middle self's will comes into play. "I will stick to my diet." "I will refrain from criticizing." "I will stop smoking."

"Use your will power," we are told. But what we are being asked to do is to pit our middle self's will against our low self's will! It is our conscious will power that suppresses our low self's feelings and desires. We already know that this is not healthy or productive. The will to power is misdirected if it is turned toward attaining domination over the low self.

When the middle self chooses to act as directed by the will of the low self, there is no effort, no strain in the action. But if we choose to act against the will of the low self, it takes a tremendous amount of energy to enforce our will, and we can usually keep it up for only a short time. When we relax that effort, the low self takes over and has its own way. Witness what happens when the will to diet is relaxed!

The middle self's will can do almost anything with the cooperation of the low self's will. Your low self can help you get where you want to go, so if your low self's will is dormant, awaken it. Arouse those inner energies with goals that will bring satisfaction to you both.

The will of the conscious self should be used to find opportunities to express the talents and potentialities of the low self. You must guide that inner will and assist its drive for expression and achievement. Set goals for your self and then stimulate your self to achieve them.

The will to destroy should be directed toward destroying the limitations, the horrid fixations that bind—all the things that prevent happiness in the low self. Never let your will to destroy be directed toward any self. Do not use the biting edge of sarcasm to wound or the fire of anger to burn, at least against another self. Save those wonderful weapons for the destruction of all that prevents human beings from being happy, creative and free. There's plenty on which to vent your anger. Attack dirt and germs and bad smells and limiting conditions. But leave selves alone!

Use your pendulum to check the strength of your low self's will to express itself. Ask it to swing in a circle, to gyrate. Is the circle wide? Do you sense enthusiasm? Your low self may be low on vitality and unable to show you, now. In that case, try later. The pendulum may swing counterclockwise, indicating discouragement. Experiment with this and think about it. Communicate with your low self about it.

What happens when the two wills are in conflict? In the short run, the middle self can impose its will and get its way. For instance, if you decide to go somewhere even though the low self doesn't want to, you will probably get your way, but you may have to pay a penalty. Let me tell you about an experience of my own that illustrates this point rather clearly.

Last summer, toward the end of my vacation, I promised myself that I would take a few days off from the sewing I had been doing, making stuffed toys for a shop. Of course, my Junior had done all the physical work and deserved a rest. But two days before I was to return to my regular job, a former customer asked me to make up eight stuffed toys. I decided quickly that I could manage this and set to work sewing busily.

A little later, when I was getting into the car, I smashed my head against the upper frame instead of ducking. Since I had owned the car a year and a half, my low self was well trained in getting into it. So I immediately asked my self, "Why did you do that?" And the reply came loud and clear inside my head. "You broke your promise to me."

Dieting is a common example of conflict between the two wills. A woman who has weighed about 160 pounds for a long time suddenly decides to go on a diet and lose 30 pounds. Obviously the low self has set 160 pounds as the point of equilibrium, the right weight for that body. The woman decides to use her will power and go on a diet. She uses her reason, consults a doctor, and has a weight-reducing schedule planned for her.

Now the two wills go to work, each to achieve a different goal. The contest is on! The middle self is determined to reduce the body's weight to 130 pounds. It succeeds—for a few weeks. But the low self uses all its wiles to get back to its goal of 160 pounds. It sends up hunger pangs, haunts the mind with visions of food and delightful, fattening treats, constantly stimulating the conscious self. The effort to suppress these constant thoughts is so tiring that the middle self's will weakens. After imposing its will over the low self for a short time, the middle self gives in. Up comes the force of the suppressed desire, overpowering the middle self. Back to 160 pounds goes the body and there it stays.

Do you have a weight problem? Here is how you can settle this difference between you and your self. Inherent in the low self is a desire for balance and harmony in all things, a desire to reach the middle point of all dualities. This is a wonderful, essential drive that contributes to our well-being and helps us survive. Let us understand the wonder of this and cooperate with it rather than fight it. Let us find out where the individual differences in balance points come from.

The low self constantly seeks a point of equilibrium, or balance, between hot and cold, thin and fat, rich and poor, and many other dualities. It is interesting to find out what our own balance points are, and it is absolutely necessary to know them if we are going to change them.

Draw a diagram like the one in Figure 3. The greatest weight shown (on the right) should be about half again as much as you now weigh. The least weight shown (on the left) should be about half of your present weight. Your present weight will fall somewhere in the middle.

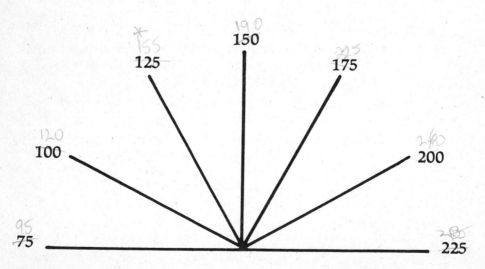

FIGURE 3: WEIGHT EQUILIBRIUM INDICATOR. This is drawn for a 150 pound person who wants to lose weight. A much larger person might need a scale going, say, from 150 to 250 pounds.

You can use this to find your weight equilibrium point. Hold your pendulum at the center of the radiating lines and ask your self to swing it outward, indicating the weight it considers ideal for this body. It will swing soon, telling you what you want to know.

Let's say it indicates 160 pounds, even though you think 130 pounds is an ideal weight for you. How do you go about changing the balance point?

First you should give a lot of serious thought to your desire to change your normal weight. Why do you want to change it? Are there good reasons that affect your happiness, or are you trying to satisfy someone else's desire? Consult the low self with the pendulum and try to find out why it has set your weight equilibrium at 160 pounds. Ask your self questions like: Is it because Mother weights 160 pounds? Is it because you feel you have to hide from other people? Are you afraid of being thinner? Are you afraid you will be cold without the weight you have?

If you are sure that a drop in weight is desirable, healthy, and wise, begin the process of changing the point of equilibrium by using suggestion, repetition, and the physical senses.

Firmly, clearly, and literally, tell your self that it is going to change its weight goal to 130 pounds. Close your eyes and visualize yourself as you are now. Put the words 160 pounds under the picture. Now, draw a big X across it. Let the whole picture fade away before you open your eyes, then sit quietly for a moment and tell your self it is going to see the ideal weight for this body. Close your eyes, visualize how you want to look, and write 130 pounds under it. Make the picture glow; see a happy smile on your face. Then open your eyes.

Now place some visual aids around the house, such as fancy posters with the message *130 pounds*. Put these where the low self will see them repeatedly. Tell your self of the rewards that will come with a reduction in weight, then let the low self achieve the goal you have set. Do not worry about whether it can achieve this, for that is a vote of no confidence. If you worry about it, the low self will become anxious, guilt will replace striving. Give your low self the job, relax and let it go to work.

Let's look at another kind of confict between the two selves involving a point of equilibrium. Many people have a conflict between the goal of being rich and the goal of being poor. Many children are taught at home to believe in working hard to acquire money and possessions. But they also go to Sunday school, where they learn that it is blessed to be poor and that the rich are greedy. Oh, the poor low selves! What can they do?

Your father says it's shameful to go on welfare, only lazy bums do it. Father has a lot of debts, perhaps thousands of dollars, but he says that's all right. People don't mind waiting for their money when they know they'll get it sometime. And your Mother buys a lot of things—why not, when Daddy is so cheerful about the bills? The child develops standards for being poor or rich from the parents, as well as from the church, which make him feel a little guilty about living in all that affluence. The child grows up and finally achieves his own balance, which is a little different from his parents. His debt limit is a few hundred dollars lower, and he lives in relative austerity because of previous guilt pangs. But sometimes he wonders why everyone else seems to get ahead. And he is very resentful of welfare recipients.

What is your financial point of equilibrium? To find out, use your pendulum and an Income Equilibrium Indicator. It will be just like the Weight Equilibrium Indicator, only the scale will be in dollars instead of pounds and will run from about half your present income or less on the left to about double it on the right, with your present income somewhere in the middle.

When you have found out, by means of your pendulum, what your equilibrium income is, you may decide you want to change it. It is possible to gain income by methods like those just outlined for losing weight. However, if your low self's attitudes toward money are firmly fixed, as attitudes toward money often are, you may need to get in touch with your low self and discover what its attitudes are and how it learned them before you can change them. To accomplish this, I, once again, recommend Napoleon Hill's *Think And Grow Rich*, the best book there is about attitudes that get in the way of financial success. By itself, Hill's book has done wonders for many people. Combined with the techniques in this book, especially the use of the pendulum for attitude-testing, it is unbeatable.

I have tried to outline this universal law of equilibrium as I perceive it so that you may better understand the wonderful self that lives in your body with you. The most important goal you will ever set is the goal of understanding that self. From that will come peace, tranquility and happiness, not only for you but for all those with whom you associate.

We have many other powers. Our feelings have power when channeled outward in specific form. Developed abilities of thinking give us power to change our lives. Desires impel us into action and have magnetic power to attract to us the fulfillment of those desires. The power of attraction/repulsion is a constant in each subtle body as well as our physical body.

Two great powers we all can use are *focussed attention* and *clear intention*. They both require skill and understanding to be effective, but each of us can develop them to a high skill level and comprehend their power through using them. Focussed attention creates a cord of mana extending from us to the object on which we focus. Along that cord flows power in the form of energy, which acts according to our intention. So these two powers are used together. Many stories of successful healings through the focussed attention and intent of healers abound throughout history and in every culture.

Intention and will power are often confused by us, and both lose power through this confusion. By separating the different powers we possess and utilizing each one appropriately we begin to have more control over the power we exert.

Frequently we state "I will" when we mean "I intend." Getting clear about this can simplify our lives. "I will" can cover many different shades and qualities of intention. We may be saying it to get another to stop pressuring us and have no intention of doing what we say. We may say "I will" without any inner certainty that we can do what we speak about. Perhaps we are sure it is something we are unable to do, and we speak the words with gritted teeth and clenched jaw.

Begin to use the words "I intend" instead. And, as you speak those words tune in to how strongly you do intend to do what you are speaking about. You may find you have no intention at all of fulfilling that commitment. For an intention is a commitment to act. "My intentions were good" we lament, as we survey the results of our actions. What exactly do we mean when we say that? Think about your intentions, for although uhane may be vague or confused about them, the low self has them fully rated, evaluated and classified. Intention is closely related to the feeling side of our nature, the side with which so many of us are out of touch. An intention holds only as much power as the feeling that accompanies it. Your low self can give you a pendulum rating of the power of any intention about which you would like to inquire.

When you set goals, plans or orders for the day sit down quietly and make sure they are what you really intend should be accomplished. When you have decided they are, communicate this to your low self. *This is what I want accomplished, and I firmly intend that this be so done!*

At all times be masterful with your low self. Be clear in your own mind and transfer that clarity to your low self. Leave no doubt as to your real intentions.

If you like to use the word "will," a good affirmation is:

MY WILL IS STRONG AND POWERFUL.
I AM THE CENTER OF FORCE.
I AM STRONG AND POWERFUL.
I AM THE MASTER OF MY FATE.
MY INTENTIONS ARE CLEAR.
MY GOALS WILL BE ACCOMPLISHED,
MY WILL BE DONE.

Your intentions should become the intentions of your low self. Your intentions should always be favorable to the well-being of your low self and never to its detriment. Use this as a guideline in investigating your intentions. If your intention is to use power to curb and inhibit natural desire, you are going to have the power of the low self pitted against you. Being telepathic, your self often knows of your intentions before you do. Uhane has a tendency to kid itself, thinking one thing and feeling another, saying one thing and intending another. "I'll go visit Mary and cheer her up" may mask an intention to make Mary feel worse than she does! And the low self knows that intention. Whatever you plan, delve into the intentions behind that action program.

The will of the High Self is not "instructions of what to do." It is a power that can be ours if we desire it, and know what it is. If we can accept the fact that we are perfect in the perception of our own High Self, and that it loves us without criticism, judgement or forgiveness, then we can move in this power and transmit it to others. We will then be able to accept others, knowing we have nothing to forgive them for and every reason to accept them in their totality, as we are accepted.

The middle self has feelings which become emotional patterns and thoughts which become thought patterns. These reside in the subconscious and direct our lives. We move and act from that base. Most middle selves become convinced of beliefs that they are unlovable, unforgivable, unacceptable. We have created these programs, and our lives manifest them. If we give them up what may appear to be a loss, becomes a gain. In giving them up, we can be receptive to the compassion and acceptance emanating from our High Selves.

We have patterned our lives from our thoughts and feelings. Our power has lain dormant. We mistake self-control for will power, which it is not. Self-control is the power to suppress the natural self, instead of guiding it into channels of appropriate expression which will not endanger our social or physical lives.

Because we say "I will" we think we have will power. However, what is meant, is "I intend" and these intentions have little power or duration. Our intentions fade quickly unless we add stubbornness or determination to them. Both qualities of middle self, human consciousness. This dogged determination or stubbornness, a mental attitude that works in place of real power will only last until we have relaxed our control and tension exerted over our natural state. Self-control is achieved through suppression and repression rather than will. Will has nothing to do with it. Will power comes from self-directional force based on being loved and knowing it. It never interferes in our freedom of choice, but only responds when we ask for help in what is beyond our powers to accomplish. High-self will could be called "grace," for it flows to us with such power when we open ourselves to it that we are flooded with a sense of well-being and strength.

There is a divine will power that can enter into us and become our power when our intentions are worthy of High Self help. My intention is my will. "I will do it" means "I intend to do it." My intentions can be weak or strong, firm or flimsy. The power, or will, any intention holds depends on the depth and sincerity of that intention.

We all have the power to resist. To refuse to comply or go along. That is often called will power. Use your will power to break a habit! Use your will power to resist eating! or smoking! or stop doing something that another wishes you to. It doesn't work and leads us to feel we are deficient in will power. Actually we have no intention of "not doing" whatever it is we are asked to stop doing.

The will to dominate others is the intention to do it. The will to power is the determination to gain power that is strong and unswerving. The will to achieve is the intention to achieve. Achievement cannot be gained unless one really intends to achieve.

When the intention of uhane is blocked by unihipili it could be called a conflict of will, but that is not very helpful. First uhane determines what he or she really intends should happen or plans a series of actions to fulfill an intention. Checking with the low self will find out if the intentions will gain support from it or will be resisted. If they both hold the same intent, deepen and strengthen it through action, it will move toward completion.

How many times have you said "I will do that tomorrow," fully aware you have no intention of doing it at all? Is that your will? How many other times have you said "I will do that" and meant it sincerely, only to find later that you just don't do it? No intention behind it to give it the power to happen! Stop and write out a list of your intentions for the following week. *I intend to clear up this problem, I intend to call so and so, I intend to be more prompt at work*, etc. etc. Take your time and try to dredge up all the intentions you have formulated recently for the near future. After each one use a numerical value. Ten will mean a very strong intention to actually do it, one an intention so weak that you already know you just won't "get to it." Revise your list and put it in numerical order.

Working through uhane begin to stop creating intentions you have no intention of fulfilling. Stop saying "I will" when you mean "I won't." Begin to observe what your intentions really are and put the power behind the ones about which you really are sincere. That is will power! "I should" means you are aware that something needs to be done to fulfill a social obligation you do not want to fulfill, but others want you to. Begin to apply your power more simply, to those things you really intend to do, want to do and are determined to do.

Stubbornness is a power many people have. That is the power to stay fixed and unmoving. We remain tied to something, good or bad, and are either liked for it or looked down on. "Sticking with it" is often an admirable trait. We have power not to change, and we have the power to change. It is a choice we can make. We can make choices of the way we use power and which of our powers we apply.

We have natural tendencies that tend to surface under certain circumstances. These are universal characteristics, like hope rising when the present does not contain the satisfactions we want. Hope is an expectation that the future will furnish what we need and a statement of our lack of satisfaction in the present. A hope for freedom implies a state of imprisonment. I hope for better things implies it's pretty bad now! This universal characteristic to hope is called the will to hope. Once again we have a misuse of the word will. For will is power, not an attitude or a characteristic.

The will to live has been created out of the natural tendency toward health and balance by a low self who is working forward in unison with uhane. When there is no meaning to one's life style, no gaining of satisfactions, this zest for life disappears, health is not maintained, there is little production of mana and we label this condition "the will to die."

Never give your low self permission to act in opposition to your intention. Your intention must always happen because of automatic function. The low self reflects your intention, but so few of us know what our real intentions are! We say something, intending to convey love, and the reverse happens. Our underlying intention was to hurt, but we were unaware of it. Huna can help us to become very clear about our intentions. We can work backward, assuming that every event happens as a result of our intention, conscious or unconscious. If we are late, we will realize that was intentional and was part of our "will to be late." Ask your low self why and you can get information about that puzzling intention.

7

Kino-aka and Mana

The aka body of the low self holds the "blueprint" for the physical body. Knowing this, the Kahuna of old were able to dematerialize a damaged portion of the physical body, reorganize it, and rematerialize it. An illustration of this is the story of the miraculous healing of a broken leg in Long's *The Secret Science Behind Miracles.* The healing is explained as a process of dematerializing the broken fragments and rematerializing the bones in the pattern held in the aka body of a whole, healthy leg.

Huna tells us that we are enmeshed in a web of aka threads drawn out of our kino-aka bodies whenever we touch anything with any part of our body or with a glance. Our eyes extend a "finger of aka," which touches and sticks to anything we look at. As energy follows attention, it strengthens that finger of aka to the degree that we are aware of what we are perceiving. This ability of the eyes to project a thread or finger of aka has been demonstrated in photographs taken of Nina Kulagina, a Russian sensitive who moves objects by staring at them. These pictures show rays of luminescence shooting out of her eyes.

Dr. John Pierrakos, a Greek-born psychiatrist, showed detailed drawings of the three aka bodies at a lecture in New York City's Town Hall in February of 1973. From his work, we learn what these bodies look like to those with extended vision. They are seen as layers around the physical body, the closest being a dark band one-sixteenth to one-eighth of an inch thick, with a transparent crystalline structure. The second, a broader dark blue layer resembling a cluster of iron filings, appears ovoid from the front. The third layer is a light blue haze of radiant energy that extends several feet from the body when the person is in good health and high spirits. The number of pulsations per minute gives information about the person's internal state.

The direction of the flow of *mana* (energy) through the aka bodies is from the solar plexus, the center of consciousness for the low self, downward in a curving L-shape toward one of the legs and upward in an inverted L to the opposite shoulder. The flow then reverses on the back side of the body. This results in a pattern resembling a figure eight or the sign for infinity.

The ten elements of the Huna concept of a human being are: the three selves, *Aumakua* (High Self), *uhane* (middle self), and *unihipili* (low self); the three invisible bodies, all called *kino-aka* bodies with different densities (High Self body is least dense, middle self body is more dense, and low self body the most dense); and the three voltages of *mana* used by all three selves, generated originally by the low self and sent to the other selves according to need. The tenth element is the physical body in which the selves reside during their terrestrial existence.

Mana is life energy. Other words for mana are: vital force, orgone, odyle, psychic energy, and *prana.* In Huna, as in many other philosophies, water is used as a metaphor for mana. It flows, it has waves, it permeates substances, and it brings life. In the Hawaiian language, the word *wai-pa* "to pray," also means "to divide the waters." It refers to the practice of sending mana to the High Self for its use in manifesting the answer to prayer. In other words, you divide the mana you have and send a portion to the High Self. Another interesting Hawaiian word is *mana-o,* "to think." This tells us that the low self must furnish mana to the middle self in order that it may think.

According to Huna, the low self controls the supply and use of mana. When the middle self requires energy to think, it calls on the low self for a supply of mana, which is then converted to *mana-mana* (a higher voltage) for middle self use.

If the two selves want the High Self to do something, they must send it a supply of *mana*. The High Self converts the voltage of this *mana* to a higher frequency. This higher energy is called *mana-loa*. This force is atom-smashing and can cause the dematerialization and rematerialization of matter.

When offering *mana* to the High Self, a person sacrifices some of his or her *mana* in order that the High Self may have enough for its work. This offering is essential to effective prayer.

So now we have three different voltages of energy or vital force for the three selves to use: *mana*, *mana-mana* and *mana-loa*. Because the low self controls energy, the middle self is quite dependent on the low self for its supply of this valuable stuff. What can we do about that? Is there a way for the middle self to get this psychic energy on request? Can we train the low self to generate a surcharge of energy on command? Yes, there is a Huna way, so let's begin learning these methods and teaching them to our low selves.

Let's start with a simple exercise. Sit down and relax. Tell your self to generate vital energy every time you draw a deep breath. This will be an extra supply, over and above the normal amount of energy generated. Realize that your physical body is surrounded by this energy in the atmosphere, and impress your low self with the reality of this.

Take three slow, deep breaths. Do this easily, not forcing them. Imagine the vital force coming into your body with each breath. Imagine it spreading all through your body. Hold each breath just slightly to fully imagine this, then let the air out of your lungs easily and smoothly, knowing that all the vital force is retained in your body.

This energy is wonderful stuff. It is the healing force used by the low self to mend broken bones, drive out invading germs, and do all kinds of repair jobs on the physical body.

Baron Eugene Ferson called this energy the "Universal Life Force," and he taught a method for getting a surcharge of it. His instructions were: Stand with feet wide apart and arms extended at shoulder level, palms angling slightly upward. Hold this position and say aloud something to this effect: "The Universal Life Force (or "energy" or "*mana*") is flowing into me now. I feel it." Repeat this about four times, slowly, breathing deeply, with a pause of about twenty seconds between repetitions. Expect to accumulate a surcharge and expect to feel a prickling in your palms or your wrists.

Electrical energy is manufactured by the low self from blood sugars in the body, using mana. The blood sugars are stored as fat and require oxygen in order to burn it into energy. That is why breathing is important in creating more physical energy. When exercising, we are inclined to breathe more heavily than usual, restoring energy as it is used up. Yoga practices that emphasize breathing usually result in renewed vigor and a feeling of well-being. Always have a plan of action in mind when you use a technique for getting a surcharge of energy.

The Kahuna of Hawaii were wise in the ways of gathering excess energy. They knew how to use mental pictures to assist their low selves in generating energy. One of these pictures is contained in a Hawaiian word that means "to rise up like water in a fountain until the water overflows." To use this mental picture, sit or stand, breathing deeply, and imagine a build-up of *mana* water, beginning at the feet and rising like a fountain through the body and up through the head in a beautiful fountain that overflows and showers you with energy/water. I usually use this picture when I desire to send energy to my High Self so that my High Self can manifest the answer to a prayer.

I have often experienced a tingling sensation around my head after doing the "fountain rite," as I call it. Sometimes it feels like a liquid dripping down my forehead. Once in a while it makes my eyebrows stand up, a really weird sensation. Now and then it feels like bugs crawling on my face, and I have to rub my hands across my face to stop the tickling sensation. I take all these sensations as a sign of successful practice.

Lyall Watson, in *The Romeo Error*, suggests that the body may have a fourth system that carries mana. The first three major systems are the cardiovascular, digestive and nervous systems. In *The Secret Life of Plants*, Tomkins and Bird speak of a fourth state of matter known in physics as plasma. Plasma is described as an electrically neutral, highly ionized gas compound of ions, electrons and neutral particles.

The term *bioplasma* was coined in 1944 by the Russian scientist V.S. Grishchenko. The bioplasma body has an energy pattern different from that of the physical body, yet it is a polarized, unified organism that gives off electromagnetic fields called biological fields. These fields are being photographed by a special device named after Semyon and Valentina Kirlian who invented it during the 1950s in Russia. The Kirlian device registers on film very interesting coronas that appear around the human body. In the U.S. today, excitement runs high because Dr. Thelma Moss, professor of neuropsychiatry at UCLA, is working with the Kirlian device, uncovering data that point toward a new method of diagnosing disease and perhaps detecting diseases before they affect the physical body.

Through my own research, I have concluded that mana is related to the electrical atmosphere that we breathe into our system along with air. Negative, positive and neutral ions in the air flow into us as we breathe and are conducted through our system. Air-conditioning taught me the importance of atmospheric electricity. Some of the earlier systems caused an illness called "air-conditioning sickness." I myself suffered from it on the job, experiencing a feeling of suffocation in a large room that had plenty of oxygen. When we tried to open the windows, we were told that they had to be closed so that the air-conditioning would be effective. Later, to our horror, the maintenance crew nailed our windows shut. During the short time I was there, I experienced depression, nausea and headaches almost constantly.

We can expect much research in this important field in the near future. There is a fast-growing, renewed interest in Wilhelm Reich's theories of orgone and negative and positive ions, and some very productive experiments are being conducted. Many individuals have built replicas of his famous orgone box, which collects and traps negative ions. They have found, as he claimed, that the boxes have tremendous potential.

To understand the effects of positive and negative ions, recall a summer thunderstorm. Recall the oppressively heavy atmosphere that preceded it, and recall your sad mood and lack of vitality. When the storm broke, lightning released tremendous charges of electricity from the atmosphere. After the storm, the air was refreshing, your spirits lifted; you felt light and energetic again. This is an example of the atmosphere changing its electrical polarity from positive (heavy, warm, oppressive) to negative (light, cool, refreshing). There is now a device on the market that, when plugged into an electric outlet, creates a miniature electrical storm in your room, generating many negative ions and refreshing the atmosphere.

Kahuna tradition holds that the three non-physical bodies, called kino-aka or aka bodies, are affected by magnetic fields. The low-self aka body is concentrated at hundreds of points, which are mapped along twelve meridians by the ancient Chinese system of acupuncture. Mana flows along the twelve meridians throughout the aka body of the low self. Imbalances in the mana flow are corrected by inserting needles at certain points, which have now been photographed by the Kirlian device. Also being observed by means of the luminous surrounds of aka bodies, are reactions to changes in planets, to moods and illnesses in other bodies, thoughts, emotions, sound, light, color, magnetic fields, the seasons, cycles of the moon, tides, strong winds, thunderstorms and even levels of noise.

The subtle bodies called kino-aka in Hawaiian have been recognized in many cultures throughout history. It is interesting to review some of the labels for these bodies and realize we are all talking about the same thing. In Tibet it is the bardo body; in Egypt it is called *ka* very much like the word aka; in Hindu, *pranamayakosha*; Roman is *larva*; Suk Shuma calls it *linga shirira*; Theosophy has its etheric double; the Rosicrucians use both somatic double and the vital body; and in France the *ame vital* means "vital soul." Leadbeater called it the health aura and Steiner "the body of formative forces." Gurdjieff named it the "kesdjun body," and it has been known also as the "vehicle of vitality" and the "electro-magnetic body."

Our planet Earth has subtle bodies, too. The macrocosmic subtle bodies compare to our individual microcosmic subtle bodies. In India they call Earth's subtle body *akasa* and claim this substance holds all planetary memories which they call "The Akashic Records." Through Huna we learn that unihipili stores all our personal memories in aka substance, in its etheric body where they are retrieved when needed. When I see photographs of our planet Earth made by the astronauts from outer space and look at that beautiful blue covering, I wonder if I am viewing the akasic body of our planet.

The body of our planet is composed of objective matter and energy and invisible substance and force we call kino-aka and mana. Our physical bodies of matter and energy also house the invisible kino-aka bodies and the life energy we call mana. The invisible bodies throw off light which is called "the aura." I feel that whenever I gaze at a sunrise or sunset, I am viewing the aura of my planet highlighted by the sun near the horizon.

Here is an experiment for you to use if you would like to see a human aura. Gather a few friends together some evening and create the most favorable setting you can for viewing the aura. The room should be comfortable, dimly lit, with one wall of a tan or gray shade. Place a candle or small lamp about six inches in front of the wall and have one person stand in front of it, masking it with skirt or pants.

The rest of the group should get comfortable about five or six feet away and should focus their eyes on the spot between the eyes, and the bridge of the nose of the person in front of the small light. Without changing the physical focus, switch your mental attention to the area around the head. Keep your gaze steady and your attention firm to let the lighted area around the head come into view.

Continued practice allows various parts of the aura to be seen. Sometimes just a ribbon of blue is seen surrounding the outline of the head. A clear light shadow may be seen. It extends outward and is thrown upon the wall behind the subject. Its edges may have a pinkish or bluish tinge. With much practice, your capacity to see more of the aura will reveal clouds of vivid color in the "surround" of the kino-aka bodies.

8

The Selves in the Brain

Brain research is exciting to students of Huna, for it appears to validate the Huna concept of the three selves and to add to our objective knowledge about them. Marilyn Ferguson's book *The Brain Revolution* reports recent discoveries in a readable, easy-to-understand fashion that can help us use our Huna techniques more efficiently.

In Chapter 19 of *Handbook to Higher Consciousness*, Ken Keyes gives a simple explanation of how the brain works. In his explanation the function of the High, middle, and low selves become very clear. Keyes calls the brain a "biocomputer." He describes the middle self as being like the president of a large business who receives preprocessed, abstracted information from the low self. Since the middle self can pay attention to only one thing at a time, the underlying, automated processing system (the low self) must determine what information it will pass on to the middle self. The crucial question is how does the low self choose?

The choices are made according to attitudes and beliefs that have been programmed into the low self by experience, repetition or the voice of authority. These programs are often strengthened by the middle self's agreement and affirmation, even though the original attitude or idea came from another person. However, we learn in Huna that we are not helpless, we are not forced to remain with any set of beliefs, we can change the program in our low self.

The middle self, whose consciousness is centered in the left hemisphere of the cortex or outer covering of the brain, continually reviews the information coming from the low self, whose consciousness is centered in the solar plexus. Every thought returns to the low self as future programming. Thus we often go around in circles, deepening a problem instead of resolving it.

The low self, your servant in one sense, follows directions literally and does whatever you ask. It takes your every thought as its command. Every thought from the low self as well as every action from ideas in the middle self results in further programming of your low self. And while the middle self is busy thinking and doing, the low self has difficulty in transmitting any but the most urgent messages to the middle self. To hear the more subtle messages, the middle self must be calm and still. We must develop the ability to still the middle self's thinking and allow awareness of low self activity to enter our consciousness. And to open the way to the deeper levels of the low self, we must clear away the attitudes and beliefs that currently demand our attention.

A good method for starting this clearing process is to have a notebook of unfinished business. Sit quietly and ask the low self to send into your awareness the problems it feels you should clear up. Make notes of these problems as they come into your mind and then try to do what your low self asks. I have found that my low self operates as a great reminder. I get messages from it like, "Make the car payment," "Write to a relative," and "Call so and so," all things I had decided to do and then forgotten. I have found that if I get busy and take care of those items of unfinished business, I am ready to hear more, and my low self can give me more of its preprogrammed information. I also noticed an odd characteristic of my low self. It will remind me just so often, then it gives up if I have not paid attention and done what it says.

The low self sends its messages to the middle self via the reticular activating system (RAS), a cone-shaped complex of nerves radiating from the brain stem and flaring up in a fountainlike display of nerve fibers that penetrate every part of the brain. The RAS is called the "doorkeeper to consciousness." All the information we get from the low self is channeled through it.

Through the RAS, the low self sends reports, puts you to sleep or wakes you up, and blocks out information that would disturb whatever activity in which you are engaged. The RAS determines how you perceive the world. You do not see the world as it is; you see it resonating with the hopes, fears, desires, demands, and expectations that have been programmed into your low self. Changing these will give you a changed world view and allow you to experience reality in wonderful new ways.

By eliminating labels given me by others, I was able to experience a wonderful new relationship to an ordinary house fly. Because of other people's attitudes, I had allowed a program of dislike and contempt for house flies to exist in my low self. Pondering this one day, I decided to eliminate for the moment all pre-existing ideas about house flies and get to know one. Soon a little fly came by and walked around for a moment on the back of my hand. What a delightful sensation its little feet were! And later, when I heard it buzzing around my head, I opened my awareness to listen without preconceived ideas. The sound resembled music, and I could listen to it deeply and intensely, giving me a new reality. After that, I observed the physical reactions of people who were totally immersed in chasing and killing flies. I was horrified to see their neck muscles tense, the blood rush into their faces, and other adverse physical reactions.

In the book *The Brain Revolution*, we learn about the two hemispheres of the brain. Here we find two distinct modes of consciousness that seem to relate to middle self functions. The left hemisphere, which controls the right side of the body, is logical, analytical, and work-oriented. Language skills reside in this part of the brain where most uhanes center their awareness. The right hemisphere, source of our feelings, controls the left side of the body and is usually sub-dominant in most persons, although it is called the primal hemisphere. (The left hemisphere is labelled the secondary hemisphere.) In the right hemisphere we have our spatial perception, understanding of whole systems, our intuition or receptivity to inspiration and our creative feelings.

The low self sends mana to each hemisphere (the mana-mana of the middle self). One stream of energy is furnished to our feeling nature, one to our thinking side. To find out if your mana-mana is having equal distribution make up a chart depicting the two hemispheres and ask your low self to indicate if these are equal or uneven. Increasing the power of our feelings to at least equal that of our thinking is the goal of every student of Huna. For it is through feeling that we become receptive to that which is of greater understanding than what we already possess. Our feelings can reveal to us the qualities in our relationships with other things.

Often I have been told by students that one of their dearest wishes was to know how "I really feel about that." Tuning into, and asking your low self to send mana to the feeling hemisphere, plus a willingness to know, will bring in to your experiences many of your true feelings. It is through the right hemisphere, the hemisphere that is receptive to love, that one can experience the compassion of the High Self. We have to open up our own feeling nature, and from it send out love to the best of our ability at that moment. The left hemisphere forms a prayer, but the right fills it with our feeling.

The High Self has these two faculties perfectly integrated, and so knows us well in both of our separated functions. The High Self sees us "whole," not as divided into separate feelings and thoughts. It perceives the relationships between you and your low self and between you and other people.

Increasing the activity of the right hemisphere is a major aim in Huna, for it is in this part of the brain that higher concepts are understood and creative thought takes place. The High Self can reveal to us relationships that we might never see otherwise; it can create larger patterns that include information stored in our memory banks.

If you wish the High Self to assist you in accomplishing your desires, "Ask and you shall receive." The High Self sees your life as a whole and the interrelationships of all events within it. Tuned to life and to all consciousness, the High Self has access to all the information you need to become self-actualized and self-realized. Its higher wisdom knows what you need and will assist you if you desire it. The High Self can manifest itself only through the right hemisphere of the brain, and that can be activated only by energy sent by the low self.

To bring both hemispheres to their optimium efficiency is the aim of many scientists and the goal of Huna students. Gopi Krishna, in *Higher Consciousness*, tells of one approach. Krishna's theory of the biological basis of kundalini energy explains it as the vital life force or, as in Huna, *mana*. Traditionally, kundalini is described as a coiled serpent resting between the genital organs and the base of the spine. In its passive state, it furnishes the power for normal consciousness, as well as the energy that moves human beings toward unity, and the sexual force that assures continuity of the human race and the evolution of consciousness. *Kundalini* is the pool of cosmic vitality that draws into itself through the chakras the life force that maintains and heals our body. When aroused, kundalini streams upward through the solar plexus and on up through the fibers of RAS, exploding into the whole brain. It brings light and evolves the brain cells to a higher state, increasing their capacity for conscious experience. This energy is then called liquid gold and resembles the description of the elixir of life in ancient alchemical texts.

The fountain rite of the Kahuna is the image of an aroused kundalini rising like a fountain to flood the brain, bringing into activity the High Self, the higher consciousness. As it rises, it cleanses the low self of impurities and erases restrictive and limited programs that prevent our perception of eternal realities. This primordial energy, greater than any other and giving rise to all other forces in our universe, is in every human being, working silently even now. Therefore, we must respect its tremendous power to either create or destroy, a power greater than any other creative or destructive energy.

Working with Huna, we are preparing the way for the creative life force to rise within us. If we remove obstacles from its path by eliminating all sense of sin or guilt and all prohibitive thought patterns and habits, if we love our own selves with the great love that is the essence of this kundalini force, we will begin to spontaneously experience bursts of this energy. When they subside, we are left with a memory of heightened awareness.

The brain has been labelled our electro-chemical system. It manufactures chemicals in pairs. The rise of one inhibits the rise of the other, and the fall of one stimulates the other to rise, giving us the phenomenon of sleeping and waking, for instance.

The solar plexus area that houses the low self is the source of *elan vital* or *mana* which it draws up from the second chakra or *ki* point in the etheric body. Between these two systems the body functions smoothly if each is functioning properly. Although autonomic systems, they are inter-dependent on each other.

When our left hemisphere has been over-stimulated, the chatter unceasing, the thoughts running to and from it, and sleep seems impossible, there are a few techniques that can help quiet it down. The activated sympathetic nervous system can be quieted so that the para-sympathetic nervous system can work to tranquilize and calm the left hemisphere.

Here is one exercise. Close your eyes and tilt your head to the left so as to elevate the right hemisphere. Breathe deeply and repeat silently in a monotone, "Left hemisphere relax, be calm, be quiet." Then create an image of a peaceful scene where tranquility is the keynote and stay with it. Allow it to come alive for you but don't comment verbally on it, just feel it. Sometimes a nap with your left side down will help you to relax and go to sleep more easily. The right hemisphere loves images, symbols and pictures filled with feeling. Give it those to rouse it into activity and produce calm and quiet on the left side.

To understand how these two hemispheres can operate separately, let us view three imaginary pieces of art. The first is perfection of form, but lacks feeling. The second, a riot of color recognized as feeling expression but uninterpretable because it has no form. The third, a masterpiece, has perfection of form and design and conveys powerful feeling content to the viewer. The first is a product of a left hemisphere working alone. The second is from the right hemisphere. The third is from both.

Scientists have divided hemispheric types into "divergent cognitive style" and "convergent cognitive style." Consider which one you may be! Experiments show that divergents have 95 percent recall of dreams and say they dream a lot. Convergents have only 65 percent recall, and many say they never dream. Verbal thinking (convergent types) activate the vocal chords giving rise to irregular rhythms in breathing. When talk is replaced with feeling, regular breathing resumes. When we are in action—sports for example—we should turn off our verbal consciousness and move into non-verbal consciousness for effortless function.

Our left hemisphere has a linear time record and explains things serially, like going around a clock, listing things in order. It labors with words to translate concepts into logical sense.

The right hemisphere knows no time. It deals with spatial relationships. It can call up a visual memory of a whole room and everything in it. Its memory is visual, holistic. It has a vivid and intuitive imagination and is artistically creative. The right hemisphere recognizes a disguised relationship (hidden relationships between two seemingly unrelated pieces of knowledge).

How do we take advantage of these two aspects of uhane's mind? Here is a practical outline of steps we can take to use both constructively.

1. In the left hemisphere, gather information and narrow the problem until obstacles are visible, then stand aside.

2. Next, in the right hemisphere, incubation. (Let it work outside your awareness, do not think about it or press for a solution.)

3. Intuition and insight will bring forth the answer.

4. Back in the left hemisphere, verify through logic. Test for logical validity. Then organize into a finished solution.

You can interweave this process. While one problem is in the incubator, another can be in the preparation stage.

The non-verbal generates ideas, the verbal verifies. It is a synergistic relationship.

A Huna student should be working toward balance in all things. Stability of the whole person. Here is a list of things that give each hemisphere joy and satisfaction. Your life style should be designed to furnish both the activities they love and help them to grow.

Right Hemisphere

Loves sunlight, daylight.
Loves physical action, motion.
Likes to dance, laugh, and cry.
Loves images gained through the physical senses—smells, sounds, sights.
Needs are personal and emotional.
Loves nature and natural things.
Loves to use the whole body in simultaneous action.

Left Hemisphere

Loves to read, write and speak.
Likes to read or listen to ideas, thoughts.
Likes to use fine muscle structures—dexterous hand work, speech.
Has social and ego needs.
Likes actions that use the parts of the body in sequential order.

Do you fulfill your potential as uhane and furnish your unihipili with goals and purposes? Are you receptive to being loved by your Aumakua and make an effort to care as much about a few as Aumakua cares about the many? It may sound difficult, but in slow easy steps, effortlessly and easily, we can move gradually, having fun on the Huna trip!

9

Memory, Recall and Dreams

Let's consider memory and try to discover facts about it that will be helpful in becoming a whole person.

First of all, the memory bank is in the *kino-aka* body of the low self. That is where the low self stores all perceptions and experiences. It controls all memory and can give us whatever we ask for. But although we can request any memory we want or need, we don't always get it. Have you ever been unable to remember someone's name, only to have it pop into your mind later?

Some memories are shared by the middle self and some are not. Some people can get only the shared memories. But the other kind are available, even if only through a session with a hypnotist. For instance, I was hypnotized once and I related, in a light trance state, events that had happened during surgery, when I was completely anesthetized.

Memories are never lost. Sometimes they are buried deep, but they are *never* lost. The low self has access to all memories and can give us any one we request. Why doesn't it always do so? Let's consider some of the reasons. By understanding the causes of poor memory or, to be more precise, poor recall, perhaps we can improve our performance.

The best possible condition for good recall is relaxation, a state in which the brain emits alpha waves of electricity. During physical relaxation, the brain waves slow down, and the mind of the middle self becomes more receptive to thoughts rising from the low self. Have you ever felt tense during an examination and had difficulty recalling answers you knew perfectly well? When you want easy recall, relax!

A conflict of desires can give rise to a memory block. Suppose I want to go somewhere at two o'clock but my low self doesn't want to go. I ask my low self to remind me of my plan at the proper time but what happens? My low self conveniently "forgets" to remind me.

Another factor is our low self's beliefs about memory and recall. What images does it have about your ability to remember? Some low selves have been "brainwashed" into believing that they have poor memory. At the University of Connecticut I see many examples of this. I've heard students moan, "I'll never remember a thing when I get to that classroom!" "I just know I'll go blank when he gives that test!" "I do fine in class, but when exam time comes, I just can't remember a single thing!" Do you make similar remarks about your own self's ability to remember? If you do, I recommend you change them to statements that show confidence in your low self's ability to send you any item in the memory bank at your request. Your low self can do it.

What about memories that come unbidden into your awareness? Why does your low self bombard you with so many memories? It is because memories of unfinished business retain unused energy; some of these memories have a little energy, some have a lot. A memory that has no energy can come into conscious awareness only through a deliberate request by the middle self.

Memories that have no feeling (mana or energy) are just recordings in aka stuff of experiences that can be recalled at any time. You might say that these are dead or colorless memories, devoid of life until they are energized again.

Memories that contain feelings live on as aspects of the personality. These memories pulse and live and connect to other living memories. The low self uses these unlived-out memories as the basis for behavior and goal achievement.

The energy contained in memories is feeling energy. The low self constantly responds to external events with feeling, which is usually expended as energy in action. However, action can't always expend all the feeling generated by the event. Then we have a memory of the event with a residue of feeling in it. The feeling aroused by the event is registered in the memory bank along with the event. The low self's memory bank is cluttered with all kinds of memories that are loaded with feeling energy, and it sends them up into the conscious mind whenever outer stimulus activates that old memory. If the feeling is accepted into awareness, and expressed in some form of action, it is drained from the memory which then returns to unihipili completed. If it is not admitted into awareness it often works as a stimulus for reaction based on content. These unfilled expressions of our feelings, stored in memory events, express themselves in our behavior and our reactions to current events. The stronger the denied feeling, the less uhane is able to deny it expression.

When the middle self suppresses a feeling rising from the low self, the feeling stays alive until it is returned to the conscious mind again. These stored, energy-filled memories express themselves in our behavior. The stronger the feeling, the less the middle self can deny its expression.

The job of the middle self is to absorb and express or channel outward all that feeling energy and return each memory to the low self for filing. The job of the low self is to get rid of all that clutter and get on with its work. The drive to discharge feeling is inherent in the low self. It is important to help the low self get free of memories that disturb its function and prevent top performance. When both selves fully participate in an experience, with the rise of an old emotion followed by action that uses up that energy, the memory of that experience is filed without energy.

Many of our experiences are painful to the low self, and often we are not aware of that pain. There seem to be different levels of pain, but nearly all painful experiences stimulate the low self to express pain by crying. We can often gauge the level of pain by whether or not we can stop the flow of tears.

Tears wash the soul clean, they say. Uhane can be cleansed by a good cry! Tears are a cleansing agent for memories, a solution that can dissolve some of the residue of feeling. If tears wash away the feeling, the meaning of a memory can become clear to the middle self.

Give your low self some time each day to present you with memories it feels are important. Sit quietly, alone and relaxed, and invite a memory, giving your low self the discretion to choose one you are able to handle at the moment. Observe the memory uncritically, examine it, and then start thinking, using your reason to try to understand why your low self sent it. If a feeling rises, admit it into your awareness. If tears come, let them flow.

Many people come to me with problems they have encountered when trying to meditate. One specific problem— being unable to clear the mind—is the result of too many current memories crowding up into conscious awareness, demanding the attention of the middle self. If these memories can be put into the past where they belong, they won't interfere with meditation anymore.

You can't blame the low self for bringing up these memories. After all, we don't usually give it much time to present its problems to us. Of course it will take advantage of our relaxed state of meditation, when the conscious mind is receptive. It is a good opportunity for the low self to return all those undigested thoughts to the middle self.

Worries come from the low self, flowing into conscious awareness with a plea to resolve, or take action on, some unfinished business. Have you ever been haunted by thoughts related to a decision that you must make? Have you ever felt relief in the pit of your stomach after you have made a decision? The low self, which cannot make decisions, will keep on pestering you, the middle self, until you make up your mind.

Have you ever had the experience of being reminded by your self of something that had to be done? You can use this function of the low self when you understand it. Here's an illustration of what I mean.

When driving from Connecticut to Gloucester, Massachusetts, I always used to miss the turnoff from the Massachusetts Turnpike to Route 128. Every time I made the trip I would worry about it and constantly watch for signs of the exit. It was exhausting and unnecessary. I tried an experiment. Seated at the wheel of my car before starting off, I spoke aloud to my low self. Giving clear, literal instructions, I said, "Today we will drive up the Massachusetts Pike. As we near the exit for Route 128, give me a reminder, draw my attention to it. Thank you very much." I then took off, had a lovely trip without a worry, and just at the right moment, the reminder to look for Route 128 flashed into my conscious awareness. And there it was on my right, with plenty of time to move over and take the exit.

Be fair to your low self, though. For instance, if I ask my self to remind me to mail a car payment on the proper day, I have to take action when the reminder comes, or my self will get discouraged. If the reminder comes at any inopportune time, I thank my self and request another reminder at a more convenient time.

Always thank your self for the favors it does for you, and praise it for doing its work well. You will find that the low self reacts to honest praise by becoming more confident of its ability to perform in the future. As you practice this, I'm sure you will come to share my feelings of awe and respect for the abilities of the low self.

Many experts in memory training emphasize the low self's ability to register an image and return it on command to the middle self's awareness. For good recall a picture is worth a thousand words. A picture is literal, unambiguous, and therefore, easier for the low self to comprehend. If you want it to do or remember something, create a picture in your mind and show it to your self. The imaging process can be used to remember lists, text, data, and even philosophical concepts. Use your imagination to create ways of making up pictures to represent ideas.

Unihipili's intelligence works to organize random material into coherent patterns. It does this while we sleep and we wake with what seemed confusing to us the day before neatly organized into a lucid, logical framework. During sleep the low self integrates all the activities of the day into the larger framework of the memory bank, sorting and classifying. Incomplete expressions of feeling go into clusters to which they are related. It organizes and re-organizes, trying many different patterns at times to bring these into line with what will be needed the next day. Because it activates the body, it will often rehearse future performances during the sleeping state to perfect its skills in jobs to be done. Every ninety minutes or so, the right hemisphere expresses its feelings in dream-drama, using symbolic forms that best fit the feeling that was experienced. Problems can be solved during the night. Give your low self a specific problem you would like organized into a solution before you wake up and it will often come up with a solution to resolve it.

In Huna, it is recommended that a course of dream recall be begun. To get in touch with the feeling side of our nature, we only have to "will" that it come into our awareness through recall. To show our earnest intent, we should get a notebook, label it "Dream Record" and place it near our bed with a writing implement. A small light will be helpful, too. An affirmation, silent or aloud, to the effect that it is our will that we recall our dreams will set into motion that process.

It is a good idea to also keep in your dream log a record of the day's events preceding the dream, for there lie many clues to the dreams themselves. To see each person and object in your dream as some aspect of your feeling nature, you can step into that object in your imagination and try to identify with how it feels as part of that particular dream. Its relationship to all the other parts of the dream should be explored. Each of our emotions has a specific relationship to all the others. Two people fighting each other in a dream, for instance, might be warring feelings within yourself.

Objects in your dreams may typify realities in your outer life. A car could stand for the "vehicle" by which you get where you want to go. Very often we use our personality to get what we want! Or it could represent the vehicle we call our physical body. Explore all alternatives. If the brakes don't work, perhaps you are losing self-control over your life. An empty gas tank could be telling you that you need to rest and re-fuel!

You can also program your low self for specific jobs during the night. To get a problem resolved fill a drinking glass full of water just before retiring. Holding the problem in your awareness, drink half of the water. Set the glass down and tell your self that you wish a resolution to your problem to enter into your awareness when you drink the rest of the water on arising in the morning.

If you would like to perfect some skill, such as public speaking or your tennis serve, ask your self to practice during the night so that the skill will be advanced to a better level of performance.

In the January, 1981 issue of *Psychology Today* there is an excellent article on "Lucid Dreaming" by Stephen P. LaBerge. A lucid dream is one in which you are aware that you are dreaming. Maybe some of you have had that experience. If not, working with a dream log over a period of time will prepare you for a lucid dream. Or, you can "will" to have one. Each night affirm that you deeply desire to be aware during a dream and know it is a dream. Do this for at least three nights. The advantage in having a lucid dream is that you can take voluntary action during the dream to guide its course to a conclusion satisfying to you. For instance, if you encounter some person you feel is threatening and ugly, you can approach that person with acceptance and love, and see clearly the meaning in that individual. You can direct the drama toward the action you desire, and begin to exert control over the events.

A simpler affirmation to use, that unihipili understands, is, "Tonight I will have a lucid dream." Again, repeat the phrase at least three times, intensifying the word *will* each time.

Another affirmation that may work better for you is the statement "I will *remember* to be lucid during one dream tonight." This is based on unihipili's ability to remind us to perform a function in the future, like my story of being reminded to see the exit signs on the turnpike. This is forming an association between what you want to remember to do and the future circumstances in which you want to do it. It helps you to visualize the intention clearly so that you are sure unihipili understands.

What does it mean to dream while knowing we are dreaming? Freud said of Hervey de Saint-Denys, a famous lucid dreamer of the 19th century, "It seems as though in the lucid dreamer's case the wish to sleep has given way to another wish, namely to observe his dreams and enjoy them."

Let's enjoy all of life, even our dreams. If they can contribute to our growth and happiness we should take advantage of them. Taking responsibility for a dream may prepare us for taking more responsibility during our waking hours.

Stephen La Berge concludes that the real significance of lucid dreams is that they guide us to higher levels of consciousness, for they suggest what it would be like to discover that in our daylight hours we are not fully awake. Perhaps the state of ordinary dreaming as compared to lucid dreaming is a parallel to an ordinary waking state to the fully awakened state. Many of us awaken from a dream with relief, but the lucid dreamer wakes within the dream with eagerness.

10

Extra Sensory Perceptions

Each kino-aka body has as many, if not more, sense perceptions as the physical body. The kino-aka body of the unihipili, called the etheric body, has etheric sight, hearing, smell and taste as well as the major sense of touch. The kino-aka body of uhane, called the astral body, also has all those senses. Nearly all of us are unaware of these extended sense perceptions, but they exist as potential in each one of us. By what criteria can we know them if they spontaneously bring us information? They are each sharper, clearer and more vivid than any physical sense input that we have ever experienced. In other words, the smell is more powerful, the taste is stronger, the image more delineated and the colors more vivid. The sounds are more harmonious than any heard with the human, physical ears. Anything less vivid than our own physical sense perceptions are from our own memory and are recall perceptions, or re-enactments within our brain of previously experienced sense perception.

The etheric sense perceptions are tuned into the natural world of the low selves. A realm of nature spirits (each physical body has one major spirit in it) and the kino-aka body of each animate thing. It is the world of forms in either. Because the etheric body of the planet is composed of designs, these designs can be detected by your own unihipili. Each pool of water forms a specific design in its etheric body, relating to its motion, its placement, its purity and its mineral content. Dowsers use their etheric sense perception to find the patterns in nature, whether it be a pattern of oil, water or earth. A dowser can locate a missing person by having their low self follow a cord of aka to the etheric body of the missing person.

The astral body has sense perceptions that reveal to us the conditions in the astral realm. Human spirits, in physical bodies or out of them can be seen "astrally." It is a world of color for its predominate theme is feeling alive. In communication with a disembodied human, one of the first messages one gets is that they feel "more alive" than when in the physical body!

There are higher sense perceptions, too, but most of us have not even experienced etheric perception yet, so to jump the gun would be unwise. Our first step is to increase our own unihipili's sense perceptions by training it to relay to us what it sees, hears, feels and touches. Dowsing is an excellent skill to develop to increase etheric perception. One of the reasons the majority of us have denied admittance into our awareness of etheric perceptions is that we would have to forego our conviction that there are no such things as elemental spirits, no elves, or sprites. To cut out from our awareness a whole realm of beings in nature is to lose something very valuable, but we can begin to restore that world into our reality by easy steps.

There has been a resurgence of interest in dragons, gnomes, elves and such in popular games and books. A recent book *Kingdom of the Dwarfs* by David Wenzel and Robb Walsh became a literary guild selection and has been a notable success on the open market. The tremendous interest in Hobbitts and the Middle Earth Kingdom was the first I noticed of the revival of interest in the natural kingdom, even though most people I know absolutely believe it is pure fantasy.

To go back now to where we were with a low self called unihipili, the elemental spirit that runs our physical bodies, we must begin wherever we find ourselves. If by now you have believed me through experimentation or taken my words on faith, you do believe you have a low self and every other human being has one, from whatever realm they originate.

The abilities of the low self are called the lower psychic talents. We should never ask our low selves to perceive in any way what is outside their "ken." Let's think of the etheric senses as those which can detect all that is too small for our physical eyes. Things we would need a magnifying glass to see, or else shrink into a tiny being like Alice in Wonderland did. All that is too small for our physical eyes to see and physical senses to bring into our awareness, can come in through the perceptive centers in unihipili's etheric body.

We begin training our low self by using images that correlate to the correct action to be performed. We imagine a thread of aka moving out and to the object we want information about and attaching itself there. This aka thread can form a little suction cup that resembles the foot of a fly. See this thread moving out and to the object, touching it and holding on with a tiny suction cup. Try this with objects within your living room, with plants, with anything you choose as you *practice.* For the first practices are simply that—practice. Like the first feeble attempts you made to ride a bicycle, when you were well aware you were not riding it!

When your low self makes contact with anything, it can relay to you, through a pendulum or other dowsing device (controlled by the nervous system) the information you seek. I used pictures in Newsweek magazine to direct my low self to extend a finger of aka and touch on the presidential candidates many years ago. I got a "reading" on each one. Unihipili can measure anything in nature. It can measure etheric bodies and it can measure physical bodies for they are under the supervision and control of the etheric body.

In Huna we work with a principle that states, *We all rise together or none of us rises.* Helping a weaker one to be stronger strengthens you. Unless you raise up the level of perception of your own low self, yours cannot rise any higher. As your low self develops its perceptions, yours will develop, unknown to you, but will keep pace with the etheric body development. First things first. Start working with unihipili in developing its sensistivity to danger to the physical body. Develop it to the degree that you will be alerted by it at the slightest "scent" of danger. Train your low self in using its etheric senses to alert you to what you cannot perceive through the physical senses. Remember, these will always be more vivid, more real than any perceptions coming through the physical organs of sense perception. You will not see, hear or smell as unihipili does, but the message will be loud and clear.

Max Long devised some good exercises for unihipili to develop these senses. He had objects hidden in boxes so that the physical senses could not relay information about them, and then he instructed his low self to reach into those boxes and attach a finger of aka to the object within. Willing that the low self bring back along that aka cord information about the object, the information finally came with long practice. Not always the name of the object, but whether it was small or large, cold or warm, hard or soft, and "like" some object with which uhane would be familiar. Objects hidden included buttons, keys, rings, clips, buttons, and assorted small objects. You can set up a row of identical small boxes and have a friend put in some objects you have never seen for your first experiments. Every time you practice, shuffle the boxes into a different arrangement. Another very simple experiment is to fill identical, opaque jars with different liquids, vinegar, water, bluing, etc. Use the same method of gaining information. For another experiment, again use opaque containers (I used film roll containers) and have at least 5 or 6 empty. In one place water, half full will do. Have them placed in a circle, shuffled around by a friend without you touching them. Now hold one of your palms about an inch above each container. Go around the circle a few times, then rest your hands in your lap. Ask your self to find an empty container and move it out of the circle. Keep moving them out of the circle until you pick up the one with water. How well did you do? Unihipili must practice, so praise your self for even making an effort. It will soon learn the difference between an empty container and one filled with water and you will be able to actually experience what your hand experiences as it hovers over each container.

Your hands are your physical dowsing instruments, but at first it is advisable to use an "extension" to your hands like a pendulum or a bobber (a ball stuck on the end of a fairly supple but rigid wire that is held in the hand).

The etheric body is like a relay station, too. It broadcasts and receives. To reach another uhane, you can use this station for transmitting distress signals, or your concern. We all have aka cords between us and every individual we have ever contacted, and those of our close relationships are like rope, containing many strands. Along these stronger cords flow instantaneous messages.

There are many stories or anecdotes about parents "knowing" their child is in danger and some report that the child actually was calling for one parent at that moment. We sense when a loved one is ill, in danger or in trouble of some kind. The built-in response to others' distress operates strongly at this level. It is fairly common for people to become uneasy or anxious without having any idea of the cause. Following this sensation, an image of a friend or relative may arise in the mind and be connected with the feeling by the middle self. ("There's something wrong with so and so! I just feel it in my bones.") Very often, a phone call proves the telepathic message to be correct. History is loaded with examples of ESP, the majority of which deal with threats to physical survival.

Another manifestation of this level of ESP is impulsive action by the middle self, for no apparent reason, which results in avoiding personal danger or in arriving just in time to assist someone who is in danger. We often call this "luck." This survival instinct in the low self functions at different levels of efficiency, depending on its programming as well as the middle self's attitude toward messages from the low self.

There is a traditional belief in a universal web of life, sometimes called the Golden Web, composed of strands of aka connecting each of us with every object and person we have ever seen or touched. This aka thread acts as a conductor of energy, colored by feelings and carrying the pattern of an idea. Some strands become strengthened by contact and the flow of feeling between objects and people. Wherever we turn our attention, energy flows. This principle is the basis of many mysteries like telepathy, healing, and magic.

Telepathic sending and receiving go on simultaneously in the low self. But if you want telepathy to function efficiently in your conscious mind, these two functions must happen separately.

One of the best ways to develop your ability to bring telepathic data to the attention of the middle self is by using the pendulum. With practice, you will improve your ability to receive information directly and instantaneously.

You have already used the pendulum to learn the vibrational rate of feelings and attitudes in your own low self. Using the same lists and charts, begin tapping the low selves of other people to find the intensity of their beliefs. Keep a notebook, adding new questions for this new activity. Practice at first on persons about whom you have no emotional bias. Remember that information coming up from your low self is always colored by its feelings, beliefs, and attitudes. You can use photographs, magazine articles, and signatures as data for drawing up personality profiles.

Treat this portion of your psychic development as training your low self in a new skill and don't expect perfect performance at once. Be prepared to teach the child within you to reach out along the aka threads, gather information, and bring it back to you. Be very clear in your instructions and be careful not to confuse the low self's literal mind. Don't cause anxiety by testing, examining, or expecting truthful results at first.

Pick up your pendulum and ask your self if it is willing to begin practice on gathering telepathic information. If the reply is No, do not force the issue. Leave it for another time. When you receive an affirmative answer, ask if it is willing to practice *now.* If you get a Yes answer to this question, ask the low self to go to the source of the data you are interested in, and indicate when it is there by a Yes swing. Wait patiently for this. When your self indicates that it is at the source, ask an unambiguous question that the low self can answer literally, either by use of the circular chart, or by Yes or No. Every few minutes ask your self if it is willing to continue. Always stop if its answers No. Usually, practice sessions should last no more than ten or fifteen minutes.

The middle self must participate in this by being receptive, attentive, and open-minded. If it has any preferred answers, this will influence the low self, which will tend to reflect them back to the middle self. It is not always easy to keep your awareness open, but it is necessary if you want unbiased information.

Very likely the excitement of realizing that your self can reach out and gather information on a universal level of consciousness will inspire you to try for precognitive data, that is, information about the future. If you are going to read the future accurately, you must learn and practice the skill. The temptation to try it too early is so irresistible that I caution you to expect very poor results at first, perhaps so disappointing that you will decide to give up. Very few people can foretell the future accurately, just as very few people can play the violin well. It takes practice.

Many areas of your life can be made more efficient through the use of the pendulum and the psychic faculty. After I had been using the pendulum for some time, it happened that I wanted to get a job as a bookkeeper. A newspaper advertised fifteen jobs that seemed appropriate for me. I cut out each ad, and spread them all out on the table.

When my low self indicated it was ready, I held the pendulum over each ad. I asked my self to reach out to each one in turn and determine whether or not the job was still open. In this way I eliminated four or five because they were already filled. At this point, I wrote down certain specific requirements: minimum salary, location and so on. Using these criteria, the pendulum eliminated several more. Then I asked my self to eliminate those jobs it would not like, and it did so. Now down to three choices, I asked my self to indicate the best one for us. With one strong swing it chose an ad placed by an automobile dealer. It did not specify salary or location.

Now share with me the eerie process that my low (and possibly High) self used to achieve the right result. Going to the phone, I asked directory assistance for the location of that telephone exchange. She said it was a town near me; so I called the number. I was shocked to hear that the position was filled.

However, the woman who answered inquired about my qualifications. On hearing that I had had automotive experience, she asked me to come over for an interview. The woman just hired did not have any experience and could be used in another position. I agreed to an appointment in two hours and asked for directions to get there. It wasn't until I hung up that I realized that the town was quite far away, inaccessible by bus, and at least an hour's drive. The telephone operator had given me the wrong information!

I was about to call back when my daughter suggested I consult my self through the pendulum before canceling the appointment. The pendulum indicated unmistakable urgency in this job opportunity, so I started out in a borrowed car.

Through the traffic I moaned about the difficulties I foresaw in commuting to that area. I conveyed that thought to the personnel manager, but she persisted in the interview. The low salary put the finishing touch to my disillusionment. As I rose to leave after refusing the job, she asked me to reconsider on the basis of a much higher salary, but it was not enough to compensate for the long ride. Then she offered me a travel allowance if I would just try the job for a couple of weeks.

So I went to work there. The job was perfect for me and the commuting wasn't as bad as I'd expected. But one problem remained: I did not own a car, and was using my son's. Driving with a faulty starter caused me to ruin his motor and obliged me to borrow money to buy him another car. But I could not get credit for a car for myself too, and the time had come to return his car. Dilemma of dilemmas! I informed the manager that I had to get another job that I could commute to by bus. He responded by arranging the purchase of a new car for me. Two cars purchased in my name within two weeks, when my job was barely begun! A miracle!

You will think of many ways that your self can use the pendulum to help you get useful information for planning and activities. It can help you choose books, schools, vacation spots, and many other things. The pendulum is a very useful tool that the low self soon learns to use skillfully. Once you have learned the technique and have established a good rapport with your inner self, you can begin to develop its latent psychic talent with exercises designed to bring in telepathic information.

Use your imagination and picture the process whereby the low self goes out along an aka thread to the source of the information, absorbs it, and returns to deliver it through the pendulum. By creatively using symbolic color, motion, and form, you can hold your low self's attention and teach it at the same time. Allow plenty of practice that your low self can enjoy, before using any of the data that comes through. Make up games patterned on the kinds of operations you will want to use.

The low self can also be trained to send out a new aka cord to any place or person you direct it to. One game you can play that will teach your low self to do this accurately is based on the yellow pages of the telephone book. Make a list of a few stores that might carry a particular product and ask your low self to go to each store, as you direct, to determine whether they carry the item, and whether they have it in stock. Keep your instructions literal, but make it all fun. If you want, you may verify the information, but be sure to do it in a spirit of game playing, and don't discourage your low self.

A similar game can be played with the newspaper. Clip several classified ads of one type and spread them out on the table. Hold your pendulum over each one in turn and ask an appropriate question for that ad. *For sale:* Is the item sold already? *Wanted:* Has the advertiser been supplied?

One of the most common uses of the pendulum is in finding lost objects. Remember that the low self holds the memory bank and has a wider perception than the middle self. We know that information about any lost article is stored in the memory. To find it, write a list of appropriate questions and ask your low self to probe the memory bank and give you answers through the pendulum. To help another person find a lost object, either picture the low self going directly to the other's low self to get the data, or picture it extending an aka thread to the object itself to learn its whereabouts.

The finger of aka extended by the self can touch; it can sense temperature, texture, and other qualities, as well as measure relationships to surrounding objects and places. The low self can analyze and measure another person's character, personality, or intelligence. Max Long's book *Psychometric Analysis* gives examples and instructions to assist the reader in becoming accomplished in that skill. During an election year, I have had a lot of fun using this technique to compare political candidates.

Don't practice too long, because it is in the nature of the low self to get bored by these games. Tests of psychic ability have shown that the self responds best when its actions fulfill a *real* human need. There must be a purpose to all efforts that the self puts forth. So, even in designing a game, make it clear to your self that the purpose is practicing for ease and confidence, as well as for enjoyment.

There is a side effect to using the pendulum which you will experience at some point. When you have established a good listening attitude and your low self has learned to give you information through the pendulum, you will begin to detect the answer within your mind before the pendulum starts to move. This effect is the result of your more open attitude toward accepting your low self's communications. A bridge has been constructed between the conscious and subconscious minds that allows messages to travel swiftly and easily between the two.

Using the pendulum also increases your understanding of the ways you communicate best with your self, and prepares you to reprogram attitudes that you feel need changing.

And now the other side of psychic skill: the ability to project a message, idea, or image along an aka thread to arrive at its planned destination in another person's solar plexus. The following technique is designed to aid you in efficiently sending thought forms to another person.

First we must define a thought form. Like a self, it must have intelligence, feeling, and will. We create it with an intelligent pattern or design, and then add the kind of feeling we want to accompany this design. Adding a charge of mana gives it the will or force to speed it on its way.

When designing a thought form that will separate and move away from your own aura, always remember the boomerang principle. Nothing in this universe moves in a straight line, and all curving motion returns eventually to its source. Make sure that any thought form you send would be welcome in your own aura, for it will return in some form, although perhaps changed beyond recognition. Whatever you send out will return to you.

Read the following instructions carefully. Then practice this particular thought form projection before designing your own.

Choose a person to whom you would like to send a thought of love or affection. Relax in a comfortable position and close your eyes. Using a countdown from ten to zero, deepen your relaxed state and expand your awareness to the area in front of your forehead. Raise your eyes slightly under the lids and imagine a blank screen in front of your face. Using the age-old symbol of love, a heart, you are going to give shape, color, texture, smell, and sound to love.

Imagine a heart with breadth, height, and depth. Perhaps it looks like a fat pillow, a dainty sachet, or a valentine. Give it the color of the kind of love you're sending: pink for affection, deep rose for intimate love, golden for the value of love, or pale blue for the calming effect of considerate love. Pick a color appropriate to your own feeling about the love you're sending. Now give it texture: pebbly, ridged, smooth, satiny, whatever you like. Let your creative imagination play humorously and lightly here. Decorate the heart if you like. Build its form, color and texture. Now add its essence, which will radiate out in a scent that soothes and warms the heart. Use your knowledge of smell to recreate an odor to accompany this heart. Imagine it beginning to pulsate, and create a sound to accompany the pulsation of this heart. Hold this image, pulsating with sound and radiating the nectar of love, for a moment, as you think of the person for whom it is intended.

A choice is now open to you. You have created a seed-thought that can either be sent now or be kept to grow in you and sent later. If you decide to send the seed to lodge and grow in another's solar plexus, picture the person in the distance and see your seed-thought move away from you, gaining momentum as it races through space to its destination. Allow a moment to complete the act, and let the total picture fade.

If you feel that the person to whom you are sending love may find it difficult to nurture this seed because of preconceived ideas of self-worth, use the following method to place it in the dark warm womb of your inner mind for gestation. Holding the image in its completed seed-form, ask your inner self to receive it and give it birth. See it descend out of sight, then move your attention to your solar plexus as you imagine it entering and coming to rest. Your own self will take whatever time is necessary to produce a full-grown thought that can be sent and added to the energy field of the recipient. You must let go of the image and forget it. Don't dig it up, for that would kill it. Allow your self to do the job. When the process is complete, you may become aware of its birth, and so, proceed to send it as in the first technique.

Whenever you use your creative imagination to construct a telepathic message, remember that the child within likes to play, enjoys humor and lightness, and is a willing co-worker when it enjoys the activity. Let the natural enthusiasm of the low self help to give to others what it enjoys receiving.

In deciding what projects to work on, keep in mind that the inner self responds to real human needs with a sympathetic surge of energy, but not to phony needs. For instance, dowsers succeed in finding water when plants, animals or people have a real physical need for water. However, when dowsers are tested by skeptical scientists under artificial conditions, they fail miserably.

You can recall, I'm sure, that sinking feeling in the stomach when you face an examination. That's the low self expressing its dislike of being tested. We often have to put up with exams and tests imposed by society, but we do not have to emulate society and doubt our own selves' ability, or subject them to an unpleasant examination before attempting to practice telepathy. Do not require your self to succeed in its first awkward attempts. Let it practice in the spirit of play until telepathy is memorized and effortless.

And always remember my Huna motto: *If you're not having fun, you're doing it wrong.*

Along with training your unihipili to stretch out strands of its blue kino-aka body, you can begin to exercise uhane's ability to extend cords or thread of its kino-aka body out to others. These must be of pure golden shimmering substance in order to carry your caring concern. Here you send the threads from the center of your forehead to touch and stick to the center of the recipients forehead (if it is a person). You can send a golden thread to a flower, a pet or any other animate creature, also. It will be received as an experience of feeling loved. Gold is also the color of wisdom and cannot be used for anything but the highest form of concern for another living being.

To do this, visualize a thread of gleaming gold light raying out from the center of your forehead and touching upon the forehead of the other. First send your love and concern for the other's happiness and well-being. Back along the cord will come information about any conditions that interfere with that well-being. You are then able to respond to what is being experienced within that person rather than to the outward appearance and behavior.

I developed this technique by focussing my attention, with the intention of finding out what was behind a little three year old boy's temper tantrum. I became instantly aware it was related to his inner experience of frustration over being smaller than I. Responding to that information, I picked him up, placed him on the kitchen counter and shouted, "You are bigger than I am now!" He laughed delightedly, temper tantrum over. He even hugged me, recognizing that I cared about how he felt.

Developing the ability to penetrate to the invisible, unspoken inner experience of another animate being can add a new dimension to your life.

The gold thread will not carry love or hate or any of the lower dualistic emotions. It can only convey caring. Caring is the ability we have to really care, without bias, that the other be happy, comfortable and at ease.

Gold is the color of wise caring; it envelopes your feeling-mind in one strand. So, first you need to resolve that you really want to be aware of what others experience within themselves, outside of your perceptions. Most of us fear to know what another feels for fear we will find it a very painful experience, so do not practice this until you feel you are ready to contact and respond to what really "is" for the other. It may be easier, for now, to continue "guessing" what other people experience—observing their behavior or body language and listening to their voice and words. These are excellent indicators of inner conditions, but often full of cover-ups and controlled action.

This technique leads you right into the heart of the matter. It affords the opportunity to respond to what is within, rather than react to the outer shell. It furnishes great understanding of the outer behavior and appearance.

Be absolutely sure that you really want to, and are able to take what will come to you, for it will move you closer to a realization of the unity between us all and eliminate many of your favorite biases about *bad* people and *good* people, and whether there is both evil and good alive today.

To perform this exercise you must get out of the way of any expectations or attitudes formerly developed about that person's reality. Lose all desire to "do" something for another, heal or cure, and just accept what you receive and respond to it as appropriately as your intelligence can guide you. The desire to "help" that person will be a barrier, for they need no help! Each individual, animate thing has its own potential for healing, growing and expanding. All you can do is to tune in to that process.

To use your own kino-aka body by stretching out tentacles to touch another, visualize yourself as a beautiful gem whose strands of light move out from the line of every facet. Visualize a clear, golden, faceted gem within your head that emits or transmits light outward in straight lines. Direct one of these golden lines of light substance toward the focussed object until it reaches and touches. Even in your practice, if you have no results, this ray of golden kino-aka substance will "bless" the other.

To make it felt consciously by the flower, animal or person, you must will your personal caring to travel along that thread. Your purpose must be firm and unshaken, for their freedom from any limitation, pain and suffering they are experiencing should be unbiased and uniformed. Desire for them their freedom, whatever it may be. You can use the following affirmation or make up one of your own.

"I care for you unconditionally. I send to you my caring concern for your well-being, your growth and evolution in your own way, not mine. I affirm to respond as appropriately as I can to any returning flow from you, in my action, words and deeds."

Energy follows along the focus of our attention. Delineated clearly and focussed "on target," it will "hit the mark." If you can do this with no expectations of any return of either information, gratitude or "favor" you will succeed in doing something needed so badly by so many. You will be emulating your High Self, who loves you unconditionally.

Let's not forget unihipili in our desire to help others. Send a golden thread from your heart center (middle of your chest) down a few inches to the solar plexus, home of unihipili, with the same caring concern. Be willing to know, in the most intimate way, the being that resides in and controls your physical body. Visualize it starting up into your head somewhere and flowing down to your heart where it picks up the pulsation of your heart to relay to your unihipili. After you have sent your golden thread from your kino-aka body, ask your unihipili to twist a cord of gold and blue and send it up through the heart and on up through your head to the high-self center in gratitude for all its help to you.

Know that your Aumakua can wind around that blue and gold cord a strand of its kino-aka body, a beautiful vivid translucent pink, and holding the cord safely within its own heart, establish this three-fold cord firmly connecting all three selves. Visualize this three-fold cord, winding its strands around each other like a telephone cable. See it as having one end in your high-self heart, a middle point in your head and the bottom end firmly glued into your solar plexus. The rhythm of your own heart will pulse this cord creating a harmony of sounds like a vibrating violin string, unheard, invisible, but very real.

The use of the golden kino-aka cord is your means of utilizing and developing what is called higher psychism, for it emanates from a higher place in your physical body. Blue etheric aka cords connect the whole natural kingdom of beings. The golden web enmeshes all human beings. And the members of the angelic kingdom are connected in one great unit, The Great Poe Aumakua, by the pink kino-aka substance of which their bodies are composed.

11

Huna Healing Techniques

Anything which is out of balance, disharmonious or distorted in any way can be brought into harmonious function. This is called a healing process. In Huna there are many different techniques which have been created to cleanse or restore harmony to any condition. Cleansing techniques remove obstructions and limitations that prevent harmonious function.

Our first objective is to define the situation, person or condition in full harmonious function. That is our target and a clear picture is needed. We must know what the final result should be. When we are clear within our own mind as to the desired results, energy must be generated to effect changes required to accomplish those results. We may use symbols instead of literal images if they will accomplish our purpose. Often the process needed to effect change can be included to expedite the healing or transformation of the condition. In physical healings our target is full, healthy function of all parts.

Some of the varieties of healing are mesmeric healing, hypnotic healing, mind-to-mind healing, the laying on of hands, distant healing and self healing. In mesmeric healing the emphasis is on the vital life force being transferred from healer to the person being healed by the laying on of hands in a concentrated state, or by the transfer of mana, the life vitality force, through the medium of metal, wood, silk or water. All of these materials may be filled with life vitality by using a technique. You can charge a glassful of water with mana by cupping your two hands on either side, about one inch away from the glass. Concentrate your attention on the flow of mana from your hands into the water within the glass. Holding that image of mana flowing from your hands into the water a few moments, and then releasing the picture so that the action can take place, will fill the water with energy. This energy can be used by you or offered to another to re-energize depleted physical energy.

Hypnotic healing uses the power of suggestion. Repeated suggestions, accompanied by the will that it should be done, will be effective. Only a small amount of vital force is needed in hypnotic healing, for the implanted suggestions will be effective to accomplish the healing. The energy within the subject is aroused to accomplish the goal of harmonious function.

The laying on of hands uses a direct transfer of mana from one to another. This technique is used with the goal held in mind by both healer and subject. Before the laying on of hands commences, it is wise to delineate and form a clear picture of what needs to be eliminated, changed or reformed to bring about the desired harmonious condition. It is not necessary that the hands be in actual contact with the physical body. Holding both hands about five inches away from the area that has been selected to be healed, the healer holds the position for a short period to allow the flow of healing energy to pass from one to another. The principle that hands can transfer mana to other people or objects is well-illustrated by the work of Baron Jules Du Potet. He charged trees with his hands and then had his patients hug or touch the trees for the transfer of energy to themselves. Healings were numerous.

To use a piece of wood as a healing object, get a green branch and strip it of its bark. Holding this branch or wand in both hands, build up a large supply of mana within yourself by deep breathing and visualizing it as rising within powerfully. Focus this flow of energy as entering into the stick with your eyes still closed. Just a slight touch of this stick will energize plants, pets or friends. It is well to discharge all mana from these sticks once they have finished their work. To do this, point the stick downward and visualize all the mana still in it moving down into the ground, to be dissipated there.

Distant healing is effected by using the flexibility of your own kino-aka body. With deep breathing and visualization fill up your own kino-aka body with mana. Next extend a portion of that body outward in a rod, thread or finger. Now visualize that extension touching, attaching and discharging mana into the target to be healed. This process should be accompanied by a clear picture of the result desired. One can also depict the process of how it is to be accomplished by using symbolic references. For instance, a broken bone can be pictured as having glue applied to the break. A vacuum cleaner can be employed as a symbol of drawing out dirt from an infection. Sandpaper can be pictured as scraping away an undesirable growth. These symbolic instructions are literal to any unihipili and will be used wisely in accomplishing the healing desired.

Self-healing has many different techniques. Choose the one with which you feel most comfortable. Each of us have many things that need re-balancing. We need more harmonious relationships, better balanced budgets, more opportunities to use our skills and most of us have some physical condition that could be bettered.

Each sound you utter has a correlating movement of lips, tongue and teeth. These movements, synchronized with the breath, cause changes in our body. They can be sounded aloud or silently, but the muscle action should always be the same.

Here is a short list of words that relate to our breathing and can be used in conjunction with the breath to effect a change as defined in the list. To use them, sound aloud or silently all the words, holding the meaning of each one as you proceed within your mind. Develop a clear understanding of what your tongue, lips, teeth and breath do simultaneously as you practice. It is very effective to sound the outgoing words as deeply as you can and allow the ingoing sounds to be non-verbal—absolutely silent, with the motions of the sounds shaped within your mouth.

MA: fire force rising, used to commit oneself, take an oath.
MA MA: quickens our enthusiasm, lightens our burdens.
NA: to be quiet, at peace, tranquil.
NA NA: slows us down, bringing peace, tranquility and feelings of well-being.
HA: the outpouring breath "transitory light." To get the point of a joke, the meaning within something, to understand what was not understood. In English this corresponds to our "Aha!"
NU: outpouring breath expressing deep feelings, roars as the wind, releases sound as feelings release.

NU NU: groaning, moaning, exhaling painful feelings.

HU: cause of rising feeling.

HU HU: flow of passion, feeling.

HOO: meditate.

E: pronounced *ay* as in hay. *Hanu* is a full breath. *E* is inhaling, *Ha Nu* is exhaling. To separate the two forms of exhalations practice *E Ha* and *E Nu* until you can exhale both your feelings and your thoughts in one exhalation.

The *ay* sound is silent as it is drawn in. Notice how it opens up the throat for the passage of air. Practice the inhale shape of your mouth silently, focussing on that until you get a fully open throat.

Combine *E* and *Ha* next. Feel the change in contractions and expansions in your mouth and throat. Then practice *E Nu* and begin to feel the sounds that naturally come out of you with the outbreath of *Nu*. Go back to the definitions and perceive that the outpouring breath sounds like wind, as feelings release. As painful feelings are released it turns into moaning or groaning. Let that happen. That moaning and groaning is releasing the pain within that is a form of crying. *E Ha* repeated can bring on a case of laughter, or gaiety, a rise in spirits!

The *Hoo* Meditation is conducted in this manner. Focus on the outbreath only, rapidly breathing out and sounding Hoo Hoo Hoo as rapidly as you can, and build up your capacity for longer and longer trembling, or dancing and moving in rhythm to it. Let your body release all its pent-up energy as you do the *Hoo* Meditation. When you have done it as long as you feel it is possible, continue for just a few more *Hoo*s. Then drop down and relax completely, breathing naturally. Continued practice of the *Hoo* meditation will clear your mind and bring you to a state of peaceful relaxation where your consciousness will be altered.

To bring your nervous system into rhythmic harmonious function we use the next technique. *Ma Ma, Na Na.* First *Ma Ma* outbreath, long *ay* (E), inhale. Then *Na Na* on one outbreath, then inhale. As you do this rhythmic exercise, tune in to the two powers within you. Get into the sound of the peace and quiet and also to the sound of your own enthusiasm and zest.

If you feel you have a lot of locked up pain, select a time when you can be alone and use this technique. *Nu Nu E Nu Nu E Nu Nu E . . .* and so on. Let your moaning and groaning out, let it become loud and urgent, and if it turns into deep sobbing, allow that to happen. Let your system release it all.

Some of the most basic Huna work is concerned with finding out what our social programming is, and then doing something about correcting the parts of it that are harmful to our personal welfare.

One of the most harmful programs most of us have absorbed is that it is all right to worry and be concerned about others. Most of us have developed this excessive concern over the welfare of others. Society teaches us to be serious and to work hard. To get things correct, not committing errors. These values are imbued into us from early childhood.

We must release these programs, dissolve them, and replace them with real caring for others. Not concern over their unhappiness and their problems, but focussing on their joy and happiness.

Give yourself, as well as others, permission to be joyful, happy, ecstatic, and enthusiastic. Experience the positive emotions that nurture growth. We should all be deliciously, deliriously happy, but some of us feel a bit sinful when we are so. Being unhappy does not improve a bad situation. In fact it usually makes it worse. We are the cause of our own happiness or unhappiness. We can begin to take responsibility for it once we realize it is all right to be happy.

Try experiencing joy and happiness just for the exercise. See if you can do it. Laugh, think of something funny, some lovely thing, or someone or some place that has given you joy in the past. Work at re-experiencing the joy, and then let joy and happiness take over just for their own healing qualities. Determine that the past program is gone and a new day is starting for you.

How can we do this while we are aware that terrible things are happening all around us, to those we love and people we don't even know? First, by realizing that our worry and serious concern do not improve any situation or event by one tiny bit. In fact, they impede and inhibit any positive action we might make. Be happy, be joyful, and laugh. All the world loves a laugher, and the world will begin to laugh with you, for laughter is very infectious. It really is. It is just as, if not more, infectious than all the germs floating around in our atmosphere.

"Laugh your cares away" is an old proverb with deep meaning. It is actually true that laughter can dispel care and worry. And it can heal relationships, personalities and bodies. If you can laugh, you can know you are OK. When you find yourself in a state of mind where laughter is impossible, where you can see no humor anywhere, you are in deep trouble, for gravity in the physical world will really oppress you, and seriousness of attitude will drag you down.

Levity is laughter and humor. Your right hemisphere has a fantastic sense of humor, and it is available to every uhane, if you but desire it. Many people are really attached to the program they are in. They worry, taking everything dead seriously (and it is death-like to be serious) and find it very difficult to be comfortable unless they retain their old program.

We have all experienced situations where we have really benefitted by being in the company of someone who is not worried, is not serious, who is not fearful and fretful about the future. We all know someone, or have met someone like that. We know how relaxing it is to be with them, for they have nothing negative to give to us, no burden to put on our shoulders. We feel free with them, knowing nothing will be added to the load of worry we already carry. Remember these experiences as a lesson to reinforce what you have just read. Of course, others who are socially programmed to take everything seriously will not perhaps appreciate your new outlook. They will not perceive the humor in situations that you do, and they may resent you for it. But with your new-found confidence through Huna, you will be able to empathize with them without being influenced by them. It is your own responsibility to choose whether to be unhappy or happy at every moment of your life. Decide to make choices now instead of staying in your social mode of habitual worry and serious concern about everything that comes along the pike.

You won't be unaware of trouble and difficulty in your world or with your friends or intimates, but you can choose whether others' troubles can have the power to make you unhappy.

Use this affirmation to help you re-program your self: "It is my responsibility to choose whether to be happy or unhappy. At every moment I have that choice anew. I can begin now to choose what I really prefer. And I take responsibility for that choice."

Using this, you will come to realize how often you have blamed others for your unhappiness, your negative emotions. We are so used to saying things like "He made me so mad," "She makes me unhappy every time she does that," "If this or that would happen, then I'd be happy." "Events out of my control are what make me unhappy." I could go on and on, and you can think of many remarks of this nature you have heard others make and have made yourself.

Just for fun, start actually "hearing" others blame something outside themselves for their own happiness or unhappiness, and tell yourself to draw your attention to any similar remarks you might make out of habit.

You have always been the cause of your own experience. Now begin to realize that, and take over control of your life. Stop being the victim of other people. If anyone can *make* you unhappy, they control the strings that make you jump.

When I was growing up, I developed a lot of guilt concerning my actions and behavior. So often I heard from those adults who were my relatives, teachers and others, "You know when you do that I worry!" (guilt!) "You do that just to make me unhappy!" (guilt) "Are you doing that to make me angry?" (guilt), etc., etc. ad-infinitum, until I believed I was responsible for the happiness or unhappiness of others. This is a terrible burden to put on a growing child. Have you ever done that to anyone you know? Or loved? I still react guiltily when someone is depressed or unhappy—wondering wildly within my mind, did I do something wrong? Is it my fault?

It's called "putting your trip on someone else's shoulders," and many children grew up as I did, carrying everyone else's trip on their shoulders. Have you ever felt guilty when someone chose to become angry or sad because of what you did? Did it ever occur to you that they had a choice of reactions? There is a wonderful book titled *When I Say No I Feel Guilty*. As I read it, I felt the author was telling the story of my life. I still feel that refusing someone what they want makes them unhappy and their unhappiness is then my fault! Isn't that silly when you really look at it? But I am still having difficulty getting that program out of my computer.

There is a wonderful technique to get you over the barrier to change. First we determine what is, and what we want it to be. Suppose you have a relationship that is not going well, for quarrels are frequent. Use that for an example. First take paper and draw a bridge. A simple arc will do. On the left side, at the foot of the bridge, clearly describe in words the situation as it is now. Then move to the right side of the paper, and under the foot of the other side of the bridge, describe literally what change you would like to see become real. Now across the top of the arc write "Hypocrite."

Most of us have been taught it is sinful to act like a hypocrite. We feel guilty when we do. Now you must drop that attitude and say to yourself, *For a period of time I am going to be a hypocrite.* A hypocrite is one who knows full well what really is, but acts in accordance with something which is not true or real.

It is important that you deal with the problem as a hypocrite for you must not lose sight of, or suppress what really *is* at any time, all the while you are pretending that another situation, the solution at the end of the bridge, is the reality. Keeping both in your awareness, begin to act the hypocrite. Pretend in all your actions and words that the other situation is the true one.

One of the best applications of this hypocrite technique is in dealing with those you find it impossible to love, to care for, and yet are tied to through job or some other relationship to dealing with that person. Your objective: to truly care for them. The reality: you dislike them intensely and can't stand even the sight of them. Get up on the hypocrite bridge and begin to act as if you cared about them. Feel like a hypocrite, know you are being hypocritical. It is important not to forget reality while you act in a role that is insincere and inauthentic, for if you can stand being a hypocrite, you will find that you land, almost without realizing it, at the end of the bridge on the other side. The former reality has disappeared and the new reality is now authentic and true.

Your low self, with its elemental mind, is a superb builder. It has been trained through many eons to build many different forms. In the mineral kingdom, it learned how to create a perfect gem. Then in the vegetable kingdom, in one particular phase of its evolution, it learned how to create and maintain a flower through its whole life cycle. Moving into the world of unrooted creatures, it may have enspirited a bird, an insect, an animal or a fish. To help our low self remember its wonderful skills, we use the following technique to honor the progress that brought it into our body to exercise its skills there.

Find a comfortable place and take a position in which you can physically relax without going to sleep. Be sure the temperature and your clothing are comfortable. Close your eyes and focus your attention on your feet, telling them to relax. Move your attention up to your ankles, relaxing them, and continue up to your calves. It may help to imagine invisible hands stroking and releasing tension in tight muscles. Next the knees and then the thighs. Move to the buttocks and then up to your waist. Relax the waist, back and front, and then work on the abdomen.

As you proceed, repeat the affirmation, "As relaxation becomes deeper, so does my awareness deepen and become keener." Use this as often as you like. Go on to relax your stomach, chest, upper back, and shoulders. Focus your attention on each part of your body in turn, and gently *will* each part to relax. Relax your neck, throat, scalp, and face, paying close attention to your forehead, eyelids, cheeks, mouth, and tongue. Allow the jaw to go limp as you move into total physical relaxation with an alert state of conscious awareness.

To deepen your awareness, imagine you are in an elevator, looking at the elevator door. Lift your eyes under the lids to a spot above the imaginary door, and see the word PEACE printed there. Pretend you are at the tenth floor and count yourself down to one, reenacting the sensation of moving to lower levels in order to move into deeper levels of consciousness.

At level one, picture the door opening and in front of you a gemstone. Allow the gem to appear and then observe it. Note its shape, color, and texture. Observe anything else in the scene before you. Now merge with the gem and identify with it, perceiving the world through it and sharing its view of reality. After a few moments, move away, de-identifying, and once more view it as a separate object. Has it changed? Observe and remember any insights you may get. Have a telepathic dialogue with it about any topic you choose. Affirm, now and then, that you will recall this experience, in perfect clarity, any time in the future that you decide to remember it.

Let the gem fade from view and be replaced by a flower. Following the same procedure, merge with the flower and perceive another reality, experiencing the processes within the flower, and its awareness. De-identify and have a conversation with the flower as you did with the gem.

Let the flower fade from view and be replaced by a tree. Merge with it. Imagine the base of the tree, hidden from view by the earth. Sense the taproot, branch roots, and rootlets moving and touching the roots of other trees. Sense the underlying unity of all plants and trees. De-identify and talk with the tree.

Let the tree fade away and be replaced by an animal. Follow the same sequence. Here you can experience the freedom of an unrooted being.

When the animal fades from view, imagine you are now back in the elevator. The word *Peace* is over its closed door. As you practice the technique, this word *Peace* will become a symbol for this level of consciousness. Now start counting yourself up to the tenth floor with suggestions that you will return rested and reinvigorated. Add the suggestion that clear recall will enable you to make notes of your experiences for future reference. Continue the count until you merge into everyday reality at the count of ten.

Keep a log of your experiments with this technique. You can use the objects suggested below plus others of your own choosing.

a beach stone	a fly	a bush
seaweed	a wasp	a forest
fish	a bird	a snowflake
the ocean	a bee	an icicle
the wind	a chair	water
a scooter	a table	fog
a tricycle	a room	rain
a car	a house	a wall
a bus	a weed	a fence

Throughout this technique keep in mind that your low self has built and maintained many things before it entered into a physical body of a human. It has had many lives in human bodies, always accompanying you on your travels through the evolutionary process. You can ask your low self to show you movies of some of their past lives using this same technique. You will see the bodies it built for you in the past, in their growth to maturity and their history. In these recalls, be sure to remember you were there, too, and dip into how you felt in that particular body in that time and that place. The development of both you and your low self to the present time is in the *akashic* memories held in the etheric body of your own low self. To share with it and appreciate all the forms it has given life to and maintained throughout a specific cycle, is to bring your low self into greater harmony with your present purposes and desires.

In Assagioli's *Psychosynthesis,* you can find many fantasy games to use to explore the roles you play. Here Assagioli expands on his theory of subpersonalities, which is compatible with the Huna theory that the low self creates subpersonalities from the unexpressed experiences of the middle self. Conflicts that are programmed within the low self become opposing subpersonalities, warring for expression, and causing problems for the middle self. By experiencing these selves in fantasy, we can learn to love, accept, and integrate them. *Transactional Analysis in Psychotherapy,* by Eric Berne, discusses another fertile area in searching for possible or probable subselves. I have also found many techniques in the book *Awareness,* by John O. Stevens.

There is a logical idea behind the theory that the low self creates subpersonalities. The programming that goes into the low self comes from many people, particularly parents and teachers. The low self builds images of a parent, a model citizen, a winner, a loser, and so on. Whenever feeling energy is aroused about a particular image, the low self tries to incorporate it into the personality. Whatever cannot be incorporated into the conscious personality remains below, living and thriving on the continuous nourishment of life's experiences. Some images may fade away through neglect, but others come alive as they are fed, and demand autonomy as occasions arise that fit that image. For example, each of us has a policeman inside us. Whenever our behavior offends the policeman, he goes into action, usually in our dreams, but sometimes in our behavior and body language. Try some of the following roles in your own fantasy games, and then add some more from your own imagination, or from the recommended books.

willing victim	top dog
striver	achiever
loser	winner
helpless victim	martyr

In order to get in touch with your super-personalities, the higher aspects of your personality that you have rejected as impossible, improbable, or unnecessary, you can use archetypes such as the Wise Old Man and the Wise Old Woman. We can add the adjective "wise" to the title of any role we play, and picture a scene in which the wise parent, the wise boss, or the wise child plays a part. Another adjective to use in role-playing is "loving," as in loving wife or husband, loving son or daughter, and the like. Here is an example of a procedure you can use.

When the elevator door opens, you are facing a long dark tunnel, with a light shining at the far end. You move swiftly through that tunnel, and come out into a landscape of incredible beauty.

Observe this scene so you can remember it later. Then allow an image of one of your super-personalities to appear and communicate with you. Talk to your new guide, and then merge with him or her, and view the landscape through the senses of the guide.

Now in the distance a row of hills appears, stretching to the horizon, each one higher than the one in front of it. Integrated with your guide, fly to the top of the first and lowest hill, where another of your super-personalities awaits you.

Observe this super-personality, talk with it, then merge with it and view the landscape from its point of view.

Go on to the next hill and the next super-personality, and through a dialogue and the merging technique, add this super-personality to your experience.

Continue this process as long as you like, stopping whenever you feel you want to. When you decide you've had enough, fly easily and swiftly back over the hills, allowing each super-personality to depart from you to its own space as you travel back to regular waking consciousness.

This technique helps you to recognize and integrate higher aspects of your person that you have previously rejected. You can also make an affirmation of your desire to become united with all higher aspects of your personality in the daily functions of your life.

If you begin to recreate your reality to include and unify all aspects of your being, anything you can imagine, within the realm of possibility, can be true for you.

By this time, you will have cleansed yourself of much, through learning how to breathe properly and deeply, how to discharge old grief and sadness, and you will have learned to lighten your day through laughter and joy.

You have worked with techniques to change your relationships and the social roles you play to more satisfactory conditions. Being responsible will have helped roles you play and your relationships to more satisfactory conditions. Being responsible will have helped you feel more in control of your own life.

Knowing your own low self and its powers of construction, of building into form your every thought, feeling and action, you now need to know how to destroy the limitations that still prevent your progress, hold you back from expressing your true potential. Getting rid of these is called cleansing or dissolving and disintegrating those twisted, warped, humanly created forms that when gone can release you into the freedom to be yourself in all your fullness.

It is difficult to cleanse anyone from something they cling to, or are attached to like a security blanket. Examine your own "security blankets." Do you feel if you worry about a future event it will not be as painful to experience when it occurs? You are attached to worrying, and perhaps will not be able to cleanse it right away, but keep working on all your attachments, for they do not assure you of a hold on reality. Clinging to what locks you in step with old patterns is a prison in which many of us live, and some of us even enjoy!

First you must do all you can to let go, to relax and allow to disappear all the dead stuff that is no longer useful to you. Make a list of what you feel attached to, and consequently worry about losing. They go together! Fear of loss results from clinging. It is paradoxical that what we cling to the tightest is often the thing we lose the quickest. How would you like to be wrapped around with tight threads of aka until it became a smothering cocoon? Of course you would struggle to get free of it! So will your friends and relatives if you try to wrap them in cotton wool—preventing them from experiencing their life fully. Clinging brings you loss! If you can begin to understand that concept you are well on your way to releasing your home, your spouse, and your friends. Surprisingly, you will not lose them! I was very attached to one home I had, over-insuring it and worrying about it constantly. Fears of it burning to the ground, being invaded by strangers, and many other thoughts crowded my mind constantly. I worked to release my attachment to it, and was so surprised to find the house did not disappear, I still lived in it and enjoyed it tremendously! And so with my friends. When I released them to behave however they wished, not obligating them to call me or join me in any activity, they came around frequently and happily.

Take your list and look at it realistically. Will any item on it disappear if you lose your attachement? Stop thinking about it? Stop worrying about it? Cross out those you conclude honestly will stay just the way they are without your attention on them. Your negative attention filled with fear of loss. Care more about their freedom than your possession of them!

Keep working on your list daily. Really look at the things you are attached to, including the people. Do you observe any chafing under the attention you give them? Can you sense they do not feel fully free when with you? Keep working.

Before you ask your High Self to help you, you must do all within your own power first. When you feel you are now up against some block to your development, some fear or guilt you cannot seem to drop, then, and then only, begin the prayer to the High Self for its cleansing power of forgiveness, mercy and compassion to disintegrate and dissolve all barriers to your freedom.

Do this alone, and make sure your privacy will be at least for half an hour. Stand up straight and tall, letting that imaginary sky hook latch on to you for effortless standing. Let it hold you up. Stretch up your arms until your hands are about a foot apart above your head. Imagine they are a cup, empty and waiting to receive or be filled.

Direct your attention to your High Self and keep it focussed there through this whole ritual. Repeat this affirmation or a similar one you devise that suits you better.

"I am willing that all the limitations to my freedom to express my true self be cleansed from my subtle vehicles and my physical body. I am willing that my High Self do whatever it can within the wisdom pattern of my evolution. I ask that nothing be dissolved that is needed for my further growth and understanding, but only those limitations that are barriers to that growth and understanding."

Now visualize an untra-violet healing ray creating a pillar of light that descends over you, descending until it is below your feet, enveloping you with its purifying power. It can cleanse your whole being of impurities. Stand there and allow this light to do its work. Breathe deeply with your desire to inhale the fragrance of your own High Self. Focus on the idea of that real fragrance which is beyond perception ordinarily. Desire that you become aware of it. With repeated rituals, this fragrance is bound to become perceptable to you, and will enhance the healing process.

After a few moments, end the ritual with the affirmation: "To my High Self, who acts as my wise parent: I leave myself in your charge. You know what is best for me at this time, and I accept in gratitude the fact that I can rely fully on your wisdom. So be it."

Always, in every ritual with your High Self, offer up your preparatory work as a contribution to your High Self, assured that you have done all you can before asking for help.

To cleanse others of their limiting conditions, ask your High Self to intercede on your behalf, if you truly care for that person. Ask your High Self to send the beautiful violet light of mercy, forgiveness and compassion to melt away all restrictions to their growth and freedom. Ask your High Self to work with the High Self of the other in full cooperation for the good of all.

One very ancient Hawaiian technique for cleansing and healing is called *Hooponopono.* The objective of *Hooponopono* is to release and cut all aka cords or ties or connections with imbalancing, inharmonious, negative situations. It is used to achieve balance and peace of mind, within and without and among others and nature. The healing manifestations are both spiritual and mental, then ultimately physical and material. If used in an exorcism, it helps release earthbound spirits from individual places or situations. If used in conjunction with past life recall it resolves and removes from the memory bank the traumas that result in the inharmony, without causing stress.

Hooponopono may be used for adults or children with average disorders, malfunctions, etc. It should always be used in a family get-together for a dying patient and is helpful for accident, suicide or drowning victims. It can be used to heal a disagreement between individuals, groups or friends. It relieves intense emotional, mental, vocal or physical expressions such as hatred, anger (mild to violent), guilt or depression. If a victim of a curse desires to be released, *hooponopono* should be used.

You begin with pen or pencil and paper. A clear picture of the existing condition and all individuals connected with it are put on to the paper. List everyone you can think of and their relationships to that which is to be cleansed. When you have made as total a survey of the condition or person as you can move into the next step.

You can memorize or read aloud the following affirmation, filling in the blanks with the appropriate words: "The Great Poe Aumakua working as one, listen to my request.

I_____and my family, relatives and ancestors wish to do a *Hooponopono* for this_____and all my family, relatives and ancestors involved. Cleanse, purify, sever and cut all negative unwanted memories, blocks and energies that have been created and/or accumulated from the beginning to the present...transmute these unwanted energies to pure light...and it is done."

When you have a very complicated situation around someone, stretching back in time a long way, the following *Hooponopono* can be used to clean up a lifetime: "The Great Poe Aumakua working as one, listen to my request.

I_____and my family, relatives and ancestors wish to do a *Hooponopono* for_____and his/her mother from the time of conception till the present. Cleanse, purify, sever and cut, and transmute all the unwanted memories, blocks and energies to pure light...and it is done."

For the exorcism or cleansing of land or person, the following formula is recited with intense sincerity:

"The Great Poe Aumakua, working as one, listen to my request.

I_____my family, relatives and ancestors wish to do *Hooponopono* of these premises/persons, his/her family, relatives and ancestors. If there are any earthbound spirits within, on and around these premises/persons...we humbly ask forgiveness on their behalf and ask they be released to the path of light. No longer will they be earthbound...and it is done."

Hooponopono is particularly important to release and calm a dying person. This cleansing process allows them release through repentance and forgiveness as they participate with you in the ceremony. It can be used for ridding a person of bad habits and for appraising oneself of past and present error.

Ritual for Healing Someone

A call for help from the all-seeing eye "Red Eye of the Sun" is to be spoken soundlessly.

First center your focus on God, or the divine essence.

Then, hold your breath while repeating:

(hold breath) *Koon ohi, ula, oka la.*

(breathe, then hold) *Li hi lihi, ula, oka la.*

(breathe then hold) *Uanini, Uakua, ua ola.*

Now speak the name of the person to be healed and the name of the illness.

If on the right side, designate by a *kua*.

If on the left side, designate by *hema*.

Exhale, silently sounding *ha* (brings force to carry mana to the part to be healed).

Repeat this five times, moving your focus from feet to chin and then to part to be healed.

Give thanks for the healing by silently intoning three times

Aumakua and *"thank you."*

12

Toward a Huna Society

Wherever I place my attention, energy flows in preset patterns. The impact of my energy out in the world is determined within my selves. The pattern of the effect is inherent in the cause. If my total awareness is involved in an experience, my total energy flow is directed to that experience. I can affect my world in small or large degree by the manner in which I center my attention. Fuzzy, vague ideas have little effect.

To use Huna effectively, I know I must clarify the design in my mental fields that will be broadcast to others. I know I must fill that design with strong feeling to give it force. I must stop the leaks of energy that dissipate my forces. Understanding Huna enables me to use the faculties of each self in its proper role at the proper time.

You and I, like everyone else, need a constant flow of energy to continue living, and if we are unable to gain it directly from the cosmos, we seek it from other people. We use many methods to get this energy, most of them unconscious, and since our survival depends on getting it, we continue to use any method that has proven effective. The essence of mental energy is neutral; the labels "bad" and "good" apply only to the patterns in which mental energy is emitted. Emotional energy runs the gamut from hate to love, but since we need energy, we often accept hate-colored energy because it seems easier to get than love-colored energy.

Think of some child you know who stimulates tremendous hostility in others. A real bad actor, he deliberately behaves in a way that provokes adults' wrath. But look more closely. He succeeds in getting attention, and is obviously using methods that in his past experience have proved to get him the life energy he needs to survive. I've watched children try to get their parents' attention in many different ways, and I have observed many parents who refuse to give their attention except when the child is annoying. In my own interpersonal relationships I have experimented with deliberately withdrawing my attention from other people, and deliberately placing my full attention on them. By observing their reactions, I have begun to learn about their energy needs and satisfactions.

I have found that when I really listen to another person, placing my full attention on his or her concerns, a very effective flow of energy passes between us. Surprisingly, I feel no loss of energy. It is as if I have opened a faucet, and energy is flowing out in a steady stream from an unknown source.

The Kahuna of old practiced their magic by ensuring that the flow of energy was strong enough to be effective. When they impregnated their throwing sticks with energy and a clear purpose, and threw them with force and direction, the sticks hit the target with exactly the intended results. In modern times also, some individuals have the ability, called psychokinesis, to influence the behavior of matter with their minds. Stopping a clock, bending a spoon, and controlling the needle on a compass are some of the tasks being undertaken experimentally now. Many individuals have been very successful in these efforts.

Placing your full attention on your own High Self will transmit energy to it. If you place your full attention on your low self, energy will be activated there. Focusing attention on a particular part of the physical body sends a stream of energy to that part, and can heal it if it is not well. With your pendulum, you can measure the amount of energy in each of the three aka bodies at any time. When you find a deficiency, concentrate a stream of energy to that body and then measure again.

As we begin to take responsibility for all energy flowing outward from our selves, and for choosing its design and feeling-color, we begin to realize the importance of our choices. Lack of knowledge keeps most people in the position of taking in undesirable energy, and reflecting the moods and feelings of those around them. Are you projecting radiations and energies that you would like to get from others? Are you accepting energy into your system that drags you down, discourages you, depresses you? Let me outline a practice that you can use to help your selves and others at the same time.

Using your creative imagination, visualize all energy flow in terms of color. Think of all words, ideas, thoughts, and feelings as having a particular color that symbolizes the kind of energy that is flowing. The next time someone turns his attention on you, let your low self tell you what color that attention is. If you don't like the color, transmute it. Let me illustrate the technique by an example from my own experience.

One evening, I was reading alone in my living room when a friend walked in. He looked irritated and began to criticize the condition of my room. I imagined that the color of his flow of energy toward me, reflecting a black mood, was a dirty dark gray with flecks of angry red. I opened my mouth slightly and visualized the energy entering my body and flowing down into my solar plexus, where it whirled around and changed color to lovely rosy red, symbolizing love and affection. It then rose up through my throat, flowed out toward him, and infused his field of energy. Without saying a word or using any kind of body language, I just kept picturing this energy-changing process. Within a few moments, his mood had changed radically, and his behavior reflected a positive attitude toward me and my room.

The transmutation of energy is a skill we all can develop and use for changing the world. Taking in the destructive and transmuting it to constructive, taking in the negative and turning it into positive energy is something everyone can do. As our skill improves, our low selves will learn to do this automatically, below the level of awareness, allowing us to move on to other skills.

We can change our selves, and we can change the world. We can start where we are, with Huna, and begin to change our design of living. As our lives change, other people will change their responses to us. And so we can help society begin to change in the direction of becoming a Huna society modeled on universal unchanging principles, which are leading us all in an evolutionary path toward the fulfillment of humanity.

The Huna concept applies to everyone, for we all have the same three selves. The programming of people's selves may be different, but the methods by which they are programmed are the same. This knowledge brought power to the Kahuna of old, and that power is available to you now.

The Huna concept applies to both male and female. Although physiologically we have either a female or a male body, psychologically we are both masculine and feminine. On the outermost fringes of manifestation, masculine and feminine energy are more strongly differentiated, but as forces move toward higher levels, there is a greater merging of masculine and feminine, until at the highest divine level they become one and indivisible. Consciousness evolves up to higher and higher states. We have the choice of flowing with it, or resisting it by holding onto familiar patterns.

Society tends to cling to established values and attitudes. We feel secure in patterns that worked well for our ancestors, even though they are out of date. Adults persist in behaviors that paid off in childhood, even though they are no longer useful. In order to be a Kahuna, each of us must now take responsibility for our own attitudes, for with responsibility we gain power. These two always go hand in hand.

Whenever I blame my difficulties on the fact that I am a woman, I am letting my feminine role control my life. All of us are exposed to social programming about gender identity, and most of us allow it to dictate our images of self and others. As long as I allow my self to be indoctrinated with the idea that men and women are psychologically different, I am controlled by that belief. Using Huna, I can begin to re-examine the social limitations imposed on both sexes and develop a new self-image as a person and as a woman. When I take responsibility for my own gender identity, it no longer has power over me.

As I look at the women's liberation movement, I see a rising awareness of the need to change society's beliefs about masculine and feminine. Roles are beginning to change. Society, through parents, teachers, and peers, has been telling me who I am and who you are. We have all looked for our identity in external events, and we have found it. But now this identity is proving false and useless because it is not soul-satisfying. Every time my low self sends me a message concerning what I *should* be, I now know it is revealing the programming I have accepted in order to feel accepted by others.

But something inside me always rebelled whenever I was told I *must* be this, that, or the other. "You must accept this because that's the way things are!" has always aroused feelings of anger and rebellion in me. "You can't," is a phrase that has been my downfall more than once. I've asked friends to please eliminate the phrase, "You can't miss it," from directions they give me, for it invariabley aroused an impulse to prove them wrong. I finally got sick and tired of getting lost, so with Huna, I looked into this pattern of behavior and learned to understand it. That was the beginning of the cure. Now I refuse to *accept* any statement that begins "You can't..."

In order to change society, we must change our selves. Society is its members and their belief systems. Society is a self-perpetuating pattern designed to preserve itself, but within us lies the urge to grow and change, to flow with evolution. This inner quality shows outwardly in individuals and groups who question social standards and refuse to accept tenets that limit individual self-actualization.

It is not enough just to become aware that society is strangling and destroying individuals, we must understand how society does it, and recognize the part each of us plays in the process. Each of us perpetuates limiting beliefs by passing them on to others. As we become aware of these beliefs we can eliminate them and substitute others designated to bring about growth, progress, and ultimate fulfillment.

It has been difficult for me to accept a full responsibility for all of my behavior. And the paradoxical principle that says I am also responsible for the behavior of others has puzzled me for a long time. Huna helped me to realize that I create my world, and help others to create theirs, from many levels of my personality, only one of which is the conscious level of operation. My High Self is in constant telepathic communication with other High Selves, and my low self is broadcasting constantly to all other low selves. These vibrating patterns join with others to create the world I share with all other human beings. To take responsibility for these unconscious actions I must investigate what they are. When I find out what I am doing, I can choose what I will do. I have free will, but I can exercise it only when I am aware of the choices I have.

Becoming a Kahuna means that I am releasing my selves from the power that others have had over them. I am freeing my personality from the limitations others would impose on me. I am detaching myself from the restrictive programming in my low self, in order to dissolve it and allow the higher potentials within me to be freely expressed. I am rejecting other people's image of me by refusing to replicate it in the projections I send out to my world. I am now beginning to create a personality in my own image. I am not my selves. I created my selves from the stuff of living that I have accepted and internalized. What I create, I can change.

> I am.
> I always will be.
> I am creator among many creators, all reflecting the potential of the All.
> The three selves are and always will be.
> They are created in a divine pattern that is universal.
> Understanding this universal pattern enables me to use it to manifest my being.

The secret that is Huna is the concept we need to achieve happiness, a fuller life, and spiritual growth.

As we use Huna in our own lives, we understand how it can help others, so we share it to the extent that others are willing to consider a new point of view.

And as we change our lives into satisfying, exciting adventures, we perceive the possibility of changing our society into one that is progressive and full of opportunities for all to achieve self-fulfillment.

We begin to view other people's behavior in the light of Huna, and to understand the underlying causes that shape and preserve or move our society.

I have an exciting vision of a society that, like the Kahuna, knows only one sin, the sin of hurting one's own self or another's self.

I see a future time when everyone will understand how selves are created, and will use this knowledge to create a world where all individuals have the opportunity to achieve self-understanding, self-actualization, and self-transformation.

I see a time when the integration of ancient wisdom and modern science will bring in a new age, an age that will give us greater opportunities for the growth of every part of our universe.

I feel each one of us has a unique and wonderful role to play in this process.

As middle selves, each one of us is "will-in-action," needing the love of the High Self and the wisdom of the low self to bring into reality our will-to-be.

And each being has these three forces of mana, mana-mana and mana-loa to work with in the three selves, to bring into reality the context within which they experience the greater reality which is divine will, wisdom and love. There is a greater reality than the one we design with our individual wills, and Huna can help us design it in accord with that greater reality rather than outside of it.

To design in accord with the rule of *harm to none, help to all,* is to work with the Huna concept and fit in with the universal tendency toward good. No resistance is offered to the middle self whose designs help others as well as their own selves. Life flows and fear is lost. We then can eagerly accept the challenge life offers us in this particular incarnation. The challenge to build structures in accord with reality and move and have our being in those patterns which are constructive and helpful in carrying us all forward on the one great trip, the trip from ignorance to wisdom. On this trip, we leave a bit of ignorance every time we gain a bit of wisdom, like peeling an onion away to its core. At the core is the wisdom and our job is to unveil it and let its light shine. We can also keep encircling it with dark shadows of designs that mute and weaken the natural light within, so that we see as through a glass, darkly, our own personal creations.

From egocentric, where the world flows into our center, and all that is admitted is sifted through a dark mesh, allowing only our preconceptions, expectations and assumptions to enter, we can move to a new position. The new pose is one in which we are centered in the light within, looking outward without any assumptions of what reality is, open to new experiences of the here and now. From our own center we must look forward, for we cannot perceive in any other way. When we circle the periphery, gathering up selected materials to draw into our selves, we are limiting our three selves to the concepts developed in our past, and operating within a rigid belief structure which seldom changes. Think of the pendulum, moving from a point in ever widening circles, and realize that is freedom for the middle self. When the pendulum rotates in ever narrowing circles, that is the retreat into ego-centricity which binds us into a cocoon of our own making. We spin the silk of our lives into a golden web to attract that which we need for fulfillment. And if we have woven ourselves into a cocoon and cannot see any light on the path ahead, we must find a way to break out of that cocoon.

Huna is one way. Huna can help us to break through a previous life style into a new and exhilarating one. The world will be seen fresh and new. Here and now will be present. Ask your High Self for the love that frees and your low self for the wisdom to take this gigantic step. As you begin to emerge from your dark cocoon of the long sleep, and are really aware of your environment, keep on seeing it with fresh eyes each day, recognizing your own power to create the context within which you experience power or helplessness, responsibility or dependance. Begin to design a new life based on avoiding the one Huna sin and using the principles of Huna to assist you in your will-in-action.

As you create a better personal world for your three selves, with more opportunity and freedom, more responsibility will come to you with its concomitant personal power. Wield this power wisely and bring satisfaction to your own three selves simultaneously as you bring satisfactions to those around you. Your enthusiasm for life will be as contagious as your joy in it. This radiance will allow your High Self to transmit its love, and your low self to share its wisdom through you. And your will will be perceived as benign and comforting. Enclosing others in your charmed circle, you will nurture and protect all growing buds of light, allowing them the same freedom you enjoy, but admonishing at the same time that freedom can be curtailed every time a self is hurt.

Appendix I
Huna Chants

In the following appendices are further Huna techniques for you to use. The first is a sample of Huna chanting. The Kahuna of old used chanting to delve deeper into the meaning of each chant, for by repetition and the sounding of the various words they gained an insight that brought to them more fulsome meaning of the chants.

In Appendix III, I recommend the use of teaching stories to flesh out understanding of age-old truths, no matter where they are found. Many religions have found that the use of parable, story and anecdote makes truths more easily revealed. We can search for these teaching stories in many places.

The Huna dialogue is similar to a technique found earlier in this book, but Appendix III has variations of that technique that were not stressed in the previous description.

Instructions on keeping a Huna diary (Appendix IV) and keeping a Huna memoir journal (Appendix V) will aid the person who likes more variety in their pursuit of self-understanding.

The five charts that are shown for pendulum use in Appendix VI will give some idea of the extent to which the pendulum can be used. You will probably be inspired to find and create more charts.

Huna Chanting

The Peace of I, in Hawaiian, *Ka Maluhia O Ka "I"*

      O ka Maluhia no me oe,
      Kuu Maluhia apau loa,
      Ka Maluhia o ka"I."
      Owau no ka Maluhia,
      Ka Maluhia no na wa apau,
      No keia wa a mau a maulos aku.
      Haswi aku wau i Kuu Maluhia ia oe,
      Waiho aku wau i Kuu Maluhia me oe,
      Aole ka Maluhia o ke Ao,
      Aka, Kau Maluhia wale no.

Ka Maluhia O Ka "I", in English, The Peace of I

      Peace be with you,
      All my peace.
      The peace that is "I"
      The peace that is "I AM"
      The peace for always,
      Now and forever and evermore.
      My peace I give to you,
      My peace I leave with you,
      Not the world's peace,
      But, only my peace.
            THE PEACE OF "I"

Appendix II
Hawaiian Dictionary

Aku: clear unclouded. A full moon.

Akua: supernatural being, object of fear or worship.
Embracing an idea incomprehensible, powerful yet complete, full-orbed.

Akua noho: departed spirit of a person. Adj; the qualities of some gods, syn; unihipili. Architect, builder, a place of residence, to dwell.

Akua-aumakua: ancestors who died long ago and who have become Gods.

Aumakua: A person who provides for a chief, a trusty steadfast servant, not easily provoked to leave.

Au: personal pronoun singular. An ocean current, grain in wood, action of mind, time (lifetime) territory (space).

Ma: fire force rising.

Makua: parent begettor, mature person, to call a person master, to honor.

Akua lapu: God, ghost or spectre apparition who wants to frighten.

Akualele: Flying God.

Akuanono: gods. Deceased spirits who dwell with and act over men as guardians.

Akua ulu: god of inspiration.

Huna: hide, conceal, keep from sight of, to be reduced fine, as powder.

Huna Huna: small parts of knowledge.

Hu: the seed or cause of rising, growing up, maturity.

Na: the incoming breath.

Hanu: natural breath of the "spirit"; people.

> *Nu:* the sound of breath emitting, expressing deep, intense feelings of the soul.

> *Nu:* roar as the wind, to think, to reflect on.

> *Hanu synonym: Ea:* fiery spirit, vital breath, breath of life, life itself.

Nahu: pain (if you aren't using Huna, you are in pain!)

Huhuhuna: to conceal, to hide often or much.

Hulahula: sacred prayer.

Hulani: to rise to heaven, to praise, exalt.

Huli: to repent, change your course.

Huhuhula: to dance and sing often.

Hua: an idea, a flowing out, a going out from seeds or egg.

Hu-aka: adjective; clear as crystal, bright, white and shining.

Huhu: flow of passion, feeling.

Hoo: meditate.

Hua: a full moon, bud, sprout; bear fruit, to grow or increase in size. Expand. Consequences of an action.

Kahuna: to exercise a profession, to work at one's appropriate business, to sprinkle salt on a sacrifice, a trade, an art, a profession.

> *Kahu:* to be, or act as servant. Spoken of a king, to take care of his people.

Kahuna pule: a priest.

Kahuna lapaau: a physician.

Hoo kahuna: to sanctify.

Kahunaao: to teach, a preacher, one whose business it is to impart knowledge to men.

Kahuna ana ana: sorcery, divination.

> *Ka:* a beginning.

> > Enough, stop!

> What, that which, the person or the thing which.

> To strike, as to strike a fire with flint and steel.

To finish or end a thing.

To rest, to flee.

To radiate, to go out from the center (as light from the sun or cinders from a hot iron).

To braid or knit from a center point.

To go out every way, as from a center.

A vine, the branches spread and run.

Kahu: to bake in the ground, to kindle or make a fire, to burn, honored upper servant, or guardian, keeper, provider, shepherd.

Ma: fullness, solidity, accompanies, take an oath. Prep: at, by, in through, unto, by means of.

Maa: to gain knowledge by practice of skills.

Mau: repeat often, endurance, eternal.

Mana o: will or wish, to think, to meditate, spirit of wisdom. A purpose.

Mana: supernatural power, power, strength, spirit, strength of character, glory, majesty, intelligence, a line projecting from another line to branch out, to be divided, worship, reverence, adoration. Verb: to be divided.

Mana o io: real, substantial, true, full of confidence.

Manao lana: buoyancy of mind.

Mana lo: sweet, as fresh water is; firm, hard.

Mana wa: feelings, a spirit, an apparition.

Mama: light (in opposition to heavy) quick, active, nimble, it quickens us.

Nana: quieting, comforting, consoling, slows us down, brings peace, tranquility, feelings of well-being.

Malama: sunlight, moonlight, or starlight. Solar month, prophet, star gazer, astrologer. To keep, preserve, watch over, to serve as a servant, to care for another. To reverence, to obey, to observe (as a festival) to be awake to danger. To put things in order.

Lama: light.

Mala ma lama: supernatural light, light of the mind, knowledge of salvation, knowledge, enlightenment.

La: the sun.

U: to protrude, rise on toes, prepare to stand, desire earnestly, to drip, drizzle, ooze or leak water slowly. To be tinctured or impregnated with anything. Grief, sorrow, or expression of affection. Unwillingness.

Unihi: grasshopper, small, thin, spindle legged, weak, without strength.

Unihipili: leg and arm bones, not able to speak, name of class of gods called Akuanoho.

Uhane: (see Hane and Hane hane) The soul or spirit of a person, holy spirit. Deceased person, ghost, lives on after body dies. Adj: spiritual (partaking of the spirit or soul).

Uha: belch wind, swell, distend, squander, waste, misuse property, not easily held, greedy, craving, eating often.

Uhini: locust. Something like a grasshopper, thin, slender, small. Leg and arm bones bound together and worshipped in that condition.

Pili: to cleave to or adhere to, to belong to, accompany, follow, belongs to one person or thing.

Pili pili: constantly adhering.

How to Pronounce Hawaiian Words

Consonants: as in English.

Vowels: as in Latin, Spanish, Italian, and other Romance Languages—*a* as in *father, e* as in *they, i* as in *machine, o* as in *no, u* as in *moon.*

Stress: always on the next-to-last syllable. Examples: ooHAney, ooneeheePEElee.

Appendix III
Utilizing Teaching Stories

There are many stories that hold a teaching or lesson within them. Some of these stories are events right out of our own life or the daily newspaper. Others can be found in fable, paradox or parable.

Consider every story a teaching story until it proves otherwise. Review stories you have told of events in your own life and probe them for the wisdom that might be revealed as a teaching. Probe the stories told you by another and consider them as holding bits of wisdom about human nature that can help you to a greater understanding of universal principles.

In looking for the teaching essence within each story, inquire as to its universality, for it is there we truly learn. What is not universal only applies to the particular. Although this is interesting and informative, what we are seeking is a solid foundation for learning about all, or everyone. We seek things which, when truly there, apply to all.

The sufi stories, called teaching stories, always have a lesson for us as do the Aesop's fables. The parables told in the Bible each have a universal lesson to teach if we can but perceive it. For a teaching story to be a teaching story must have wisdom for each person reading it.

Each story is a teaching story if we could but perceive this. Even a small tale told by a child about his or her experience of life can teach us some universal theme about experiencing life if we but tune into the essence we share.

Begin by focussing in on some proverb, tale or story that is known to hold a lesson for all. Get the feel of what is to be gained from a teaching story then seek out the same quality in all stories. Teaching stories are notable for their briefness. It is too difficult to extract the juice of wisdom from overladen stories, so look for the brief, concise story that will reveal its lesson effortlessly.

The Huna Dialogue

The Huna dialogue is a technique for bringing a middle self into closer intimacy with its low self and High Self. We become separated in time and space or consciousness, because we are a middle self, revolving around the periphery of experience, collecting data which will feed and nurture the belief structure constructed by the middle self of all the bits and pieces offered by events and others. On this periphery we become unaware of the processes going on within the High Self and the low self. Here, on the periphery, we develop what can be called an ego or personality which is the vehicle we use for interaction with our world. And our world becomes our reaction to it based on former conclusions and constructions of what the world is really like rather than what the world or reality actually holds for each of us in the here and now.

The low self is attuned to current realities, and we can reach the low self through dialogue, among other techniques available. The High Self recongizes the potentials in the environment for our growth and development, and can, through dialogue, reveal to us its broader vision of reality. Our experience of others can be heightened and gain greater breadth through imaginary conversations with their low and High Selves so that interpersonal relationships can be developed that nurture and sustain both individuals.

This method can bring great satisfaction to all three selves, and it is one in which equal participation brings rewards. It can be used daily in conjunction with regular meditation, or just by itself in periods of seclusion and quiet.

Select a time when you will have at least half an hour of uninterrupted leisure in which to pursue your own dialogue. Find a place that is comfortable and easy, with no distractions to the middle self or low self.

Select a time when you are neither hungry, nor tired. A period in which there are no physical demands on you which need gratification. Then, with the right time and space determined, settle down and relax as much as you can. Get comfortable.

Stretch your body and move around until you are as relaxed and comfortable as possible. Use a seated position for the most favorable results.

You are now seated and comfortable. Ready to begin your dialogue with your other selves. You, as middle self will become an interested observer to the stream of ideas, thoughts and feelings presented to you by your other selves. Before you begin, determine the placement in space in front of you that your selves will occupy. I find the following arrangement best for me, but you can vary your configuration to please yourself.

Closing my eyes, I visualize three empty chairs in front of me. One to my left, one directly in front of me and one off to the right. I see these three chairs clearly. At this point I check to see if my comfort is sufficient to allow me to continue undisturbed, and rearrange my position if necessary.

With eyes closed, ask that your low self seat itself in the chair to your left. Ask it to become a symbolic form representing the part it will play in the ensuing dialogue. Observe closely the age and dress of your low self. The position it takes in the chair and all the body language it sends to you as it settles in for the dialogue. You will want to record this experience for further study and as references for later conversations, so observe all the details you feel may be helpful in those events.

Once your low self has attained a form in your imagination, proceed to ask a question of your low self. It can be any question, even the simple one of "How are you today?" Listen with all your perceptive faculties. Listen with your sense of smell, sight and touch, your total perceptive faculty open to images of any kind. Become as open and willing to observe in a neutral fashion as you would like to be received by someone you love. Become totally accepting of all action and ideas emanating from your low self. Continue to hold a dialogue once it begins with the low self, being sharply aware of every nuance so that your memory will furnish you with details to be written down later. During this dialogue you may ask your low self to project into the chair on your right any images of you, as middle self, that it would like to draw to your attention. Here the low self has an opportunity to portray you as it sees you and give you added insight into the way you play the role of middle self at various times and under various circumstances.

Following this, you can ask your low self to project an image of someone else's low self or middle self into the chair at your right. Once that image is fully formed, hold an imaginary conversation with that self, allowing the other to respond fully to your interested and caring inquiry into its experiences of you or another aspect of the relationship between you. In this manner, you can gain added insight into the workings of interpersonal relationships and improve the quality of those you desire to continue.

Body language is an important aspect in all these imaginary dialogues. What the form depicts through movement and posture can often relate more than the ideas that emanate from the form. See the clothing chosen by your low self to garb the form depicting you as middle self, or the form of another self. Notice the age in particular that the low self shows to depict some facet of this image.

Often you will realize the information garnered will correspond to what has been hovering in the background of your awareness. Now it will assume a foreground stance to reveal its importance in the relationship between you.

There is much background material which is very close to our awareness but just escapes detection by a busy middle self. Our own body language is so automatic it usually escapes our notice, but here, bringing it into objective view it can be observed and analyzed. Do not reject anything, but see it all with a dispassionate gaze. Reactions of an emotional nature will cloud the very objective of the internal dialogue taking place.

Use all your abilities of an uninvolved spectator to perceive the realities within the dialogue. When writing your account of the dialogues, allow other bits of awareness to flow into your account, broadening and widening your experience.

Always keep in mind that your awareness will bring recall later according to its ability to remain keen and observant. Take your time and don't rush these conversations, for the slower and easier kinds of dialogues result in fuller and richer rewards.

The length of your conversations will be guided by your natural desires to continue or stop. Let these sessions be as natural and spontaneous as possible.

When you feel your dialogue with the low self has given you enough material for this period, thank your low self and allow it to disappear from view.

Focus now on the empty chair in front of you. Here is where you ask your High Self to form an image of itself that will portray the role it will take in this particular dialogue. It will appear differently every time you hold a dialogue, as perhaps your low self will, just as each of us presents different faces to the world under differing conditions. Here the imagination is allowed to create a symbolic role for the High Self to hold the qualities which will be emphasized in this particular conversation. The High Self eyes will contain the love which is a dominant feature of the High Self, and is the binding force between your High Self and your heart center. You may feel the piercing glance of your High Self penetrating your chest at some point. This will be the aka cord that connects you, being animated by the dialogue.

Ask your High Self a question to begin the dialogue. Then allow it to take a natural course of spontaneous flow of images and ideas that are relevant to your current situation. The High Self is a fount of wisdom for insight into the meaning of what you are experiencing in your life. From here, the total acceptance of you and your experiences will become apparent. The High Self never forgives you for anything. From its view of reality you are fully acceptable just as you are. It will give you a feeling of warmth and acceptance you can get from no other source. Along with that acceptance it can give you insight and guidance for your further flowering, your added awareness and awakening to the potential your environment and world holds for you.

In this exercise you can come closer to actually experiencing the nature of both High and low selves, and through that awareness increase your working capability as a team.

When the experience is over, stretch your body and return to normal waking consciousness, readying yourself to record all that transpired.

To gain the most benefit from these sessions, a journal recording all you become aware of and your response to these awarnesses can be a great help. Reviewing this journal before continuing into another experience can reactivate unfinished or unclear dialogues, so they can be repeated or reviewed within the next experience. Another way of benefitting from journal keeping is to review and then add, in writing, your further insights derived from the review. This will allow for newer material to arise in your next dialogue.

Take your problems and indecisions into these dialogues for feedback from your other selves. Ask your low self to show you the middle self as it appears to the low self, and perhaps to others. The low self plays many roles, and these roles can be depicted with amazing accuracy through the mimicking abilities of your own low self.

Use the name you have chosen for your low self in addressing it or making any requests. You may want to decide on a name for your High Self or ask the High Self to give you a name with which to address it. A title such as "my wise one" is another appropriate way to conduct a dialogue with the High Self.

The low self is expert in building forms within the mind, and can be depended on to mimic the outer world in devising symbolic portraits of itself and its middle self. The High Self will be powerful in the sending of unformed images and ideas which you can translate, with the help of your low self, into images and forms if you desire to do so. Stunning clarity is the hallmark of messages from the High Self, and you "know" with a firmness and certainness of the accuracy of the idea. As you proceed with this dialogue day by day, it becomes easier and more productive. As in any technique, practice makes perfect. So if at first it seems labored and artificial, full of doubts as to source of material, just continue until the process attains a type of fluidity and grace typical of all mastered skills. Learn to listen well with all your perceptive faculties combined into one great listening organ as you absorb the information which will pour from the other levels of your consciousness where your High and low selves dwell. You can plumb the depths!

Appendix IV
Keeping a Huna Diary

Both macrocosm and microcosm have aka bodies which hold subtle substance called ethers. In Hawaiian this substance is called kino-aka. Around our planet there is a kino-aka body called the "Noosphere" which corresponds to the mental body or mind of the planet. Each one of us has a miniature Noo.

The Noosphere is divided into layers or spaces, and each kino-aka body interpenetrates all other kino-aka bodies. These bodies each hold "thought forms" which can be seen by the aware individual who searches for them diligently.

The low self guards and keeps all thought forms like grapes clustered on a stem. The stem represents the theme or principal thought and the grapes symbolize each small thought that is connected to the main idea. Through attaching our observation to one grape, the other grapes in quick succession reveal themselves until we reach the main stem connecting all the grapes, or thoughts.

Keeping a Huna diary is an effort by a middle self to connect up with the various clusters of thoughts held by the low self, and trace them to their root. To connect with the contents of your own noosphere, get a notebook for the specific purpose, label it to your liking and begin a process of collecting information from your own self.

It is like tapping an underground stream of images and recollections of your interior life with which you have been out of touch. In keeping a Huna diary, you allow that stream to carry you deeper and deeper into the stream of thoughts that will lead you to their various cores of being. Through a Huna diary you can tap the well of "being" within, and alleviate your sense of poverty of being, your aloneness, your sense of meaninglessness. With the Huna journal we can get in touch with our other selves, all aspects of them, and begin to know that our lives have meaning. We are not as isolated as we thought, and we can begin to enjoy the companionship of our low and High Selves.

The Huna diary is a journal written by the low self, not the middle self. The middle self takes dictation from the low self and records it for future use. The stance of being a recorder for thoughts flowing from the low self must be clearly understood before you begin. Speak to your low self silently, addressing it by name, and clearly state "This is YOUR diary." Make it clear that only the thoughts of the low self will be recorded in this diary.

Begin each session by printing clearly and literally a question or topic at the top of a fresh page. Some of the questions that are productive are as follows:

Where are we now in our life?
Significant scenes from our past.
What roads we did not take that we could have?
What decisions did we make that proved important?
Which persons are important to us, and why?
How eventful experiences affected our lives.
Suppressed emotions.
Suppressed assertions.
Unfinished commitments.
Unresolved problems.
Unfulfilled hopes and wishes.
Goal expectations.

Major worries and concerns.
Memories of importance.
A specific relationship (name the individual here).
Hopes for the future.
Last regrets.
Imaginative headings for biographical chapters of our life.

After you have the title of the work to be done printed at the top of the page, the subject matter to be explored, pause and meditate for a few moments. Be quiet and still, reaffirming your role as recorder for the thoughts which will flow from the low self.

Now, open your eyes and proceed to write down whatever comes into your awareness. A word, a thought, an idea or an image. Record as objectively as possible. Just keep recording and writing the thoughts that flow in, resisting the impulses to analyze or think about them. Let them flow. Write them down.

If they stop, tap your pen and pencil until they begin again. Then write. If one thought is intruded on by another thought, move to the new thought, dropping the old one with a dash to complete it. Keep it going by being persistent. Write down all thoughts you consider distractions or intrusions. They are part of the stream. You will find your low self trying to distract you from this effort. It may resist opening up to you. If you touch a tender spot, it may recoil and offer you a diversion. You need not be swayed into giving up on this technique, for the longer you continue it at one sitting, the more productive it will be. It is better to devote one hour a week to it instead of fifteen minutes a day, for the low self can resist you easily for fifteen minutes, but you wear it down persisting longer than that.

Set a time period for this technique, then stick with that space of time until it has concluded. Later you may review the material, making notes on separate paper about future explorations you would like to make based on that material. You may find a single word popping in that often seems to be out of context with the material. This word is a good topic to head a fresh page with as it may be one "grape" that can lead to the stem of a cluster of many ideas. Any word or group of words is the vehicle which carries essence or meaning. To get to the essence or meaning is to reach the stem. Colors often hold much essence or meaning within them and make excellent page headings. What does black bring to your mind? Red? Deep blue? Certain shapes could be substituted also. A triangle, a square or a circle, for instance. Ancient symbolic shapes also can prove fruitful.

Appendix V
Keeping a Huna Memoir Journal

Another technique for plumbing the depths of our experience of reality is to keep a journal of our memories. The method for doing so is as follows.

Sitting down with your notebooks, start with some memory that pops into your mind. Write out how you, as middle self, recall that event. Instead of facts, move to how you experienced that event, your thoughts and feelings that arose in you during the event. Record all you can remember and then put down your pen or pencil, sit back and close your eyes.

Call your low self by name, and request further elucidation of the event as it is recalled by the low self. Then open your eyes, pick up your pen or pencil and poise it over your notebook. Write down what comes into your awareness from the low self, whether it be a word, a thought or an image. If a stream of thought is interrupted, leave off and move with the intruding thought. If there are blank phases, just tap your pencil in a series of dots until something arises, then move into recording that. Allow plenty of time for the low self to respond in order to overcome the resistance and blocks keeping you from full contact with this particular memory.

When you feel no more information will be forthcoming, lay down your pen or pencil again, sit back and close your eyes. Now you will call on your Higher Self with a specific request. "What can I learn from this recall experience that will enrich my knowledge of my selves and my life experience?" Waiting for a moment in the stillness of contemplation about the wisdom you need to grow with, allow the idea of growth through added wisdom to penetrate your awareness and become a need or hunger within you. Then open your eyes and poise pen or pencil over the notebook until ideas begin to flow into your awareness. Expound on these ideas as they come tumbling forth and add to them your understanding of what they mean. Leave room following this experience to record your views when you reread at a future time the material written. Review these as often as you feel they are still relevant in your life.

Appendix VI
Charts

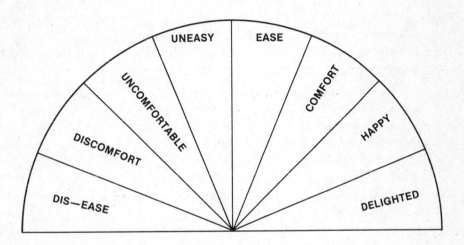

Sometimes the most important question to be answered by the low self is its rate of comfort with an idea, a plan or a program.

To find out if you're on the right track, use the pendulum to find out from your low self its estimate of the correct time and space in which to make a decision.

You can use the circular swing for good or bad to find out how unihipili feels, but a more precise rating can be obtained with the above chart. An uneasy low self can lead to disease or accident if forced to go through with some decisions made by the middle self.

From studying the Sufi religion, I found that the here and now is the time and space best suited for a full spiritual life.

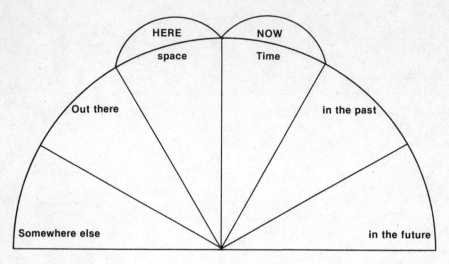

So, when planning to purchase something important, go somewhere on a trip, take a vacation, or any other planning, ask your self if the time is right and it's your space to be in. I used this method to determine whether the purchase of a new home would be effortless and easy, for the here and now includes the effortless. It was the right time and space for me, and all went smoothly, my confidence boosted by using this chart. Being in a hurry to gratify our desires instead of our needs, we so often pick the wrong time for space that is not for us.

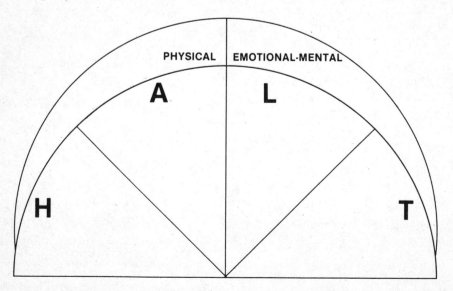

H for hungry, A for angry, L for lonely and T for tired, spells Halt, and covers most reasons for depression. Hunger for food or companionship, anger at another, lonely and in need of companionship, or just plain tired, physically, emotionally or mentally.

The first swing is for whether the origin is from the environment (physical) or from within. With that determined, you then swing your pendulum again for the symptom to be treated. If hungry for food, eat! If angry, express it in some way that causes no harm. If lonely or hungry for companionship, be assertive and go and seek it. If tired, no matter how, rest and recuperate. Use a regenerating exercise to gain more mana, or sleep if that is indicated.

Research has shown that animals live longer with a lowered body temperature. You can experiment with lowering your own through the use of this chart.

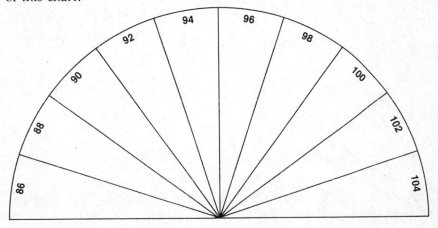

First acquaint the low self with the chart. The numbers stand for degrees. You can use a thermometer to show your low self what your body temperature is now, then deliberately swing the pendulum to that figure on the chart. Now ask unihipili to indicate it understands by swinging to the correct temperature.

Then ask your low self to swing it back and forth as it lowers your body temperature, giving a reading that is continuously lower. Every time after that you can take your temperature by the pendulum, and lower it a degree or two if you feel it is good for you. Pay close attention to your physical well being with this experiment, and realize the power inherent in it. Don't abuse it!

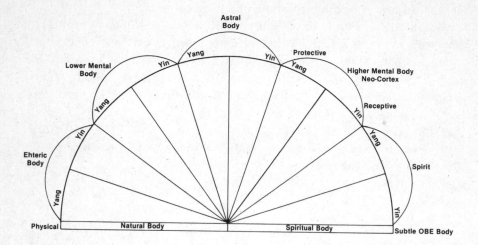

This chart is determining, with the pendulum, the dominance and/or malfunction of any of the subtle bodies. The etheric body has a yang aspect, called the "immaculate concept." It is the divine design or pattern the body will revert to when released from all other patterns or designs. That side is yang. Its yin side is the receptive side, which brings into form all the concepts it attains from the next higher body, the lower mental body, from its yang side, and imposes the limitations and conditions that have been built into it since birth.

The conceptual mind is sub-dominant in the physical human being design. It is ruled by the astral body ordinarily. It has a malfunction built into the original pattern at birth. That malfunction, on the etheric level, will impose itself on to the physical body or the brain, creating a malfunction in the higher bodies to correspond to it as long as they are connected to the physical.

During incarnation, the animal body should be dominated by the higher mind and the spirit, but seldom is. Our divine inheritance is dominance over the animal kingdom, and the power to change the natural patterns of that kingdom.

Bibliography

*Anderson, Marianne S. and Louis M. Savargy, *Passages: A Guide for Pilgrims of the Mind.* New York: Harper & Row, 1972.

Assagioli, Roberto, *Psychosynthesis: A Manual of Principles & Techniques.* New York: Viking Books, 1963.

Atcheson, Richard, *The Bearded Lady, Going the Commune Trip and Beyond.* New York: John Day, 1971.

Bailey, Alice, *Consciousness of the Atom.* New York: Lucis, 1973.

Berne, Eric, *Transactional Analysis in Psychotherapy.* New York: Ballantine Books, 1975.

Blakemore, Colin, *Mechanics of the Mind.* Cambridge University Press, London, 1977.

Blakeslee, Thomas R., *The Right Brain.* Achor Press/Doubleday, 1980, NYC.

Boone, J. Allen, *Kinship with All Life.* New York: Harper & Row, 1954.

Branden, Nathaniel, *Breaking Free.* New York: Bantam, 1972.

Brunler, Oscar, *Radiations.* Cape Girardeau, MO: Huna Research Associates, 1974.

Bucke, R.M., *Cosmic Consciousness.* New York: Dutton, 1974.

Castaneda, Carlos, *Journey to Ixtlan.* New York: Simon & Schuster, 1972.

Castaneda, Carlos, *A Separate Reality.* New York: Simon & Schuster, 1971.

Castaneda, Carlos, *Teachings of Don Juan.* New York: Ballantine, 1969.

Cayce, Hugh Lynn, *Venture Inward.* New York: Harper & Row, 1964.

Cerminara, Gina, *Many Lives, Many Loves.* Los Angeles: Sloan, 1963.

Cousins, Norman, *Anatomy of an Illness.* W.W. Norton & Co., NYC, 1979.

Faraday, Ann, *Dream Power.* New York: Medallion, 1973.

Farrow, E. Pickworth, *Psychoanalyze Yourself.* New York: Lancer, 1972.

Ferguson, Marilyn, *The Brain Revolution.* New York: Taplinger, 1973.

Finch, William J., *The Pendulum and Possession.* Phoenix: Esoteric Publications, 1973.

Fodor, Nandor, *Between Two Worlds.* Los Angeles: Parker, 1964.

Ford, Arthur, *Known but Unknown.* London: Psychic Press, 1969.

Frankl, Viktor E., *Man's Search for Meaning.* Buffalo: Washington Square Press, 1963.

Freeland, Nat, *The Occult Explosion.* New York: Berkeley Publishing, 1972.

Gardner, Adelaide, *Meditation: A Practical Study.* Wheaton, IL: Quest Theosophical Publishing House, 1968.

Hill, Napoeleon, *Think and Grow Rich.* New York: Hawthorn, 1966.

Huxley, Aldous, *Doors of Perception.* New York: Harper & Row, 1963.

Ingalese, Richard & Isabella, "From Incarnation to Incarnation," 1904 Occult Book Concern NYC.

Janov, Arthur, *The Primal Scream.* New York: Dell, 1971.

Jones, Gladys, *The Flowering Tree.* Los Angeles: Sloan, 1965.

Jung, C.G., *Memories, Dreams, Reflections.* New York: Vintage, 1965.

Karlins, Marvin and Lewis M. Andrews, *Biofeedback: Turning on the Powers of Your Mind.* Philadelphia: J.B. Lippincott, 1972.

Keyes, Ken, Jr. *Handbook to Higher Consciousness.* Berkeley: Living Love Center, 1973.

King, Serge, "Mana Physics." Baraka Books, Ltd., NYC, 1978.

Kirsten, Grace & Robertiello Richard, *Big You Little You.* Dial Press, NYC, 1977.

Krishna, Gopi, *Higher Consciousness: The Evolutionary Thrust of Kundalini.* New York: Julian Press, 1974.

The Kybalion: Hermetic Philosophy. Three Initiates, Des Plaines, Illinois: Yoga Publication Society, 1908.

Laing, R.D., *The Divided Self.* New York: Pantheon, 1969.

Leadbeater, C.W., *The Chakras*. Wheaton, IL: Quest Theosophical Publishing House, 1972.

Leadbeater, C.W., *Man Visible and Invisible*. Wheaton, IL: Quest Theosophical Publishing House, 1969.

LeShan, Lawrence, *The Medium, The Mystic, and the Physicist*. New York: Viking, 1975.

Lilly, John, *The Center of the Cyclone*. New York: Julian Press, 1972.

Linde, Shirley Motter and Savary, Louis M., *The Sleep Book*. Harper & Row, 1974.

Long, Max Freedom, *Growing into Light*. Santa Monica: DeVorss, 1955.

Long, Max Freedom, *The Huna Code in Religions*. Santa Monica: DeVorss, 1965.

Long, Max Freedom, *Psychometric Analysis*. Santa Monica: DeVorss, 1959.

Long, Max Freedom, *The Secret Science at Work*. Santa Monica: DeVorss, 1953.

Long, Max Freedom, *The Secret Science behind Miracles*. Santa Monica: DeVorss, 1948.

Long, Max Freedom, *Self-Suggestion and the New Huna Theory of Mesmerism and Hypnosis*. Santa Monica: DeVorss, 1958.

McBride, L.R., *The Kahuna, Versatile Mystics of Old Hawaii*. Hilo, Hawaii: Petroglyph Press.

Maltz, Maxwell, *The Magic Power of Self-Image Psychology*. Englewood Cliffs, NJ: Prentice-Hall, 1964.

Maltz, Maxwell, *Psycho-Cybernetics*. Englewood Cliffs, NJ: Prentice-Hall, 1960.

Maltz, Maxwell, *Psycho-Cybernetics and Self-Fulfillment*. New York: Grosset and Dunlap, 1970.

Manning, Al G., *Helping Yourself with Psycho-Cosmic Power*. Los Angeles: Parker, 1968.

Maslow, Abraham, *Religions, Values and Peak Experiences*. New York: Viking, 1970.

Masters, Robert and Houston, Jean, *Mind Games: The Guide to Inner Space*. New York: Viking, 1972.

Monroe, Robert A., *Journeys Out of the Body*. New York: Doubleday, 1971.

Ornstein, Robert E., *The Psychology of Consciousness*. San Francisco: W.H. Freeman, 1972.

Ostrander, Sheila and Schroeder, Lynn, *Psychic Discoveries behind the Iron Curtain*. Englewood Cliffs, NJ: Prentice-Hall, 1970.

Pearce, Joseph Chilton, *The Crack in the Cosmic Egg*. New York: Pocket Books, 1973.

Perles, Frederick S., *Gestalt Therapy Verbatim*. New York: Bantam, 1971.

Powell, A.E., *The Etheric Double*. Wheaton, IL: Quest Theosophical Publishing House, 1969.

Prinz, Thomas, *Precipitations, The Science of Succeeding in Your Purposes*. Bridge of Freedom, Inc., King's Park, N.Y., 1973.

Smith, Manuel J., *Kicking The Fear Habit*. Dial Press, NYC, 1977.

Smith, Adam, *Powers of the Mind*. Random House, NYC, 1975.

Rogers, Carl, *On Becoming a Person*. New York: Houghton Mifflin, 1970.

Roszak, Theodore, *The Making of a Counter-Culture*. New York: Doubleday, 1969.

Steiger, Brad, *Secrets of Kahuna Magic*. Para Research, Rockport, MA, 1981.

Stevens, John O., *Awareness*. Moab, Vermont: Real People Press, 1971.

Tart, Charles T. (Ed.), *Altered States of Consciousness*. Cresenta, California: Anchor Books, 1972.

Tompkins, Peter and Bird, Christopher, *The Secret Life of Plants*. New York: Harper & Row, 1973.

Watson, Lyall, *The Romeo Error: A Matter of Life and Death*. New York: Anchor Press, 1975.

Weed, Joseph J., *Psychic Energy: How to Change Desires into Realities*. Englewood Cliffs, NJ: Prentice-Hall, 1970.

Weed, Joseph J., *Wisdom of the Mystic Masters*. Englewood Cliffs, NJ: Prentice-Hall, 1971.

Weil, Andrew, *The Natural Mind: A New Way of Looking at Drugs and the Higher Consciousness*. New York: Houghton Mifflin, 1972.

Westlake, Aubrey T., *The Pattern of Health: A Search for a Greater Understanding of the Life Force in Health and Disease*. Berkeley: Shambhala Publications, 1961.

White, John (Ed)., *Highest State of Consciousness.* New York: Doubleday, 1972.
White, Stewart Edward, *The Unobstructed Universe.* New York: Dutton, 1959.

Many of these titles can be ordered from Para Research. Write for our catalog.

Index

and extra sensory perception (ESP)
70
and frustration of human needs
46-47
as gateway to High Self   40,
50-51, 83
and hypnotism   69
and kino-aka body   153, 163
and mana   139
naming of   43-44, 93
programming of   150-151
as record keeper   45
training of   155
will of   118

*Magic Power of Self-Image
Psychology, The*   111
Mana
definition of   130
conversion to mana-loa   87, 91
function of   15, 141
properties of   19, 132
supply and use of   130-132
use of for relaxation   59-60
and water symbolism   86-87
Mana-loa   131
function of   15
healing process of   20
properties of   19
Mana-mana   130-139
function of   15
distribution to neo-cortex   66
properties of   19
Maslow, Abraham   83
Maltz, Maxwell   111
Memory
block of   145
energy of   146-147
and kino-aka body   145
and relaxation   146
See also Low self, Middle self
Meta needs   83
Middle Earth Kingdom   154
Middle self
communication from   23
center of consciousness of   17,
21-22, 81, 138
conflict with low self   113
definition of   63
and dialogue with High Self   87-89
duality of   35, 44-45, 66

environment   76
and extra sensory perception (ESP)
70
intellect   23
kino-aka body of   153, 163
language skills   139
relationship to low self   64, 67-70
and need for human love   59
self image of   35
and silence   90
sleep and dreams   69
and surgery   69
Moss, Dr. Thelma   132

Nature spirits   153
Notebook of Unfinished Business   138

"Original sin"   29
Orgone box   133
Out-of-body experience (OBE)   19

Pain   147-148
Pendulum   189
and beliefs and choices   96-106
charts for use   209-213
definition of   93-94
and finding lost objects   160
and how to make   94
and how to use   94-96
and psychic communication
157-159
side effects of use   161
and training low self   156-160
verification of low-self understanding
69-70
Pierrakos, Dr. John   130
Prana   130
Prayer   88-92
and mana offering   131
Presley, Elvis   50
Psychic development   157-159
Psychometric Analysis   13, 161
Psychosynthesis   176

Radiesthesia   93
RAS. *See* Reticular Activating System
Recovering the Ancient Magic   13
Reich, Wilhelm   57, 133
Relaxation techniques   59-61, 109-110,
141-142, 162, 174-180
Sequential relaxation   31-34

DEVELOP YOUR PSYCHIC SKILLS

Enid Hoffman

Psychic skills are as natural to human beings as walking and talking and are much more easily learned. Here are the simple directions *and* the inside secrets from noted teacher and author Enid Hoffman.

Develop Your Psychic Skills gives you a broad overview of the whole field of psychic experiences. The exercises and practices given in this book are enjoyable and easy to do. Use them to strengthen and focus your own natural abilities and turn them into precise, coordinated skills. You'll be amazed at the changes that begin to happen in your life as you activate the right hemisphere of your brain, the intuitive, creative, psychic half, which has been ignored for so long.

This book shows you how your natural psychic powers can transform your life when you awaken the other half of your brain. It teaches you techniques for knowing what others are doing, feeling and thinking. You can see what the future holds and explore past lives. You can learn to locate lost objects and people. You can become a psychic healer. It is all open to you.

Develop occasional hunches into definite foreknowledge. Sharpen wandering fantasies and daydreams into clear and accurate pictures of events in other times and places. Choose what you want to do with your life by developing your psychic skills. When you finish this book you'll realize, as thousands of others have using Enid Hoffman's techniques, that the day you began to develop your psychic skills was the day you began to become fully conscious, fully creative and fully alive.

ISBN 0-914918-29-X
183 pages, 6½" x 9¼", paper

$7.95

KAHUNA MAGIC

Brad Steiger

Based on the life work of Max Freedom Long, *Kahuna Magic* lays open the secrets of the Kahuna, the ancient Hawaiian priests. Long used the secrets of the Hawaiian language to unlock the secrets of this powerful and mystical discipline.

Long was a much-respected psychic researcher. His student Brad Steiger chronicles Long's adventures on the way to understanding the magic of the Kahuna. By following Long's trek, the reader will learn how the Kahunas used their magic for both the benefit of their friends and the destruction of their enemies.

Central to the Huna beliefs was the thesis that each person has three selves. The Low Self is the emotive spirit, dealing in basic wants and needs. The Middle Self is the self operating at the everyday level. The High Self is the spiritual being that is in contact with every other High Self.

The subject matter of *Kahuna Magic* is contemporary and compelling. The book incorporates many of the concepts and concerns of the modern Western psychological tradition of Jung and Freud while bringing in subjects as diverse as Eastern philosophies and yoga in a manner that will help the readers understand themselves and those around them.

ISBN 0-914918-34-6
127 pages, 6½″ x 9¼″, paper $5.95

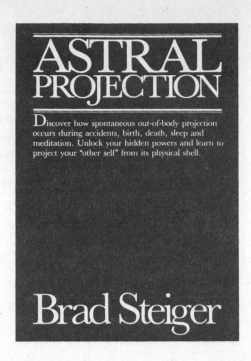

Discover how spontaneous out-of-body projection occurs during accidents, birth, death, sleep and meditation. Unlock your hidden powers and learn to project your "other self" from its physical shell.

Brad Steiger

ASTRAL PROJECTION

Brad Steiger

Parapsychological researchers have established that one of every one hundred persons has experienced out-of-body projection (OBE). These experiences are not limited to any single type of person, but rather they cross all typical boundaries.

In *Astral Projection*, Brad Steiger investigates the phenomenon of OBE and correlates those events into broad categories for analysis and explanation. In his clear and non-sensational style, Steiger relates how these spontaneous experiences occur and when they are likely to re-occur. In addition to the standard and well-documented categories of spontaneous astral projection at times of stress, sleep, death and near-death, Steiger devotes considerable time to the growing evidence for conscious out-of-body experiences, where the subject deliberately seeks to cast his or her spirit out of the physical shell.

Along with his study of astral projection, Steiger sets guidelines for astral travellers, tells them the dangers they may face and how this type of psychic experience might be used for medical diagnosis, therapy and self-knowledge.

Author Brad Steiger is your guide to controlling astral projection and using it for your own benefit.

ISBN 0-914918-36-2
234 pages, 6½" x 9¼", paper

$9.95

A reporter's encounters with ghosts who walk, speak, move objects and even kill. How spirits haunt the scenes of their violent death. Here's convincing proof of a spirit world that exists all around us. With an introduction by Hans Holzer.

Brad Steiger

TRUE GHOST STORIES

A Psychic Researcher's Hunt for Evidence of Hauntings

Brad Steiger

Brad Steiger's years of research into the infinite expanse of the spirit world is now available in this fascinating compilation of verified hauntings. These are not only the classic ghostly manifestations often discussed in paranormal literature, but also cases Steiger has researched, often using well-known mediums as contact points with the ethereal energies. *True Ghost Stories* does not stop at just relating the details of ghostly hauntings, it goes beyond other books on ghosts and hauntings to present the prevailing hypotheses about spirits in a scientific, yet highly readable manner.

The author investigates and explains three predominant theories that claim such manifestations are "telepathic infection," "idea patterns" or "psychic ether." Steiger concludes that no single one of these theories should be held dominant, but then again, none should exclude the other. *True Ghost Stories* proves the existence of ghosts and reveals significant facts and features of their nature. This new book leaves the reader with the chilling realization that we have yet to fully understand ghosts; more can be learned only through future contacts with the spirits.

ISBN 0-914918-35-4
168 pages, 6½" x 9¼", paper

$7.95

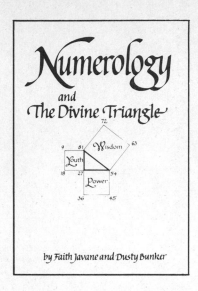

NUMEROLOGY & THE DIVINE TRIANGLE

Faith Javane & Dusty Bunker

Now in its fourth printing, this major work embodies the life's work of Faith Javane, one of America's most respected numerologists, and her student and co-author Dusty Bunker, a teacher and columnist on metaphysical topics.

Part I introduces esoteric numerology. Topics include: the digits 1 through 9; how to derive your personal numbers from your name and date of birth; how to chart your life path; the symbolism of each letter in the alphabet; the life of Edgar Cayce, and more.

Part II delineates the numbers 1 through 78 and, illustrated with the Rider-Waite Tarot deck, synthesizes numerology, astrology and the Tarot. *Numerology & The Divine Triangle* is number one in its field.

ISBN 0-914918-10-9
266 pages, 6½" x 9¼", paper $10.95

NUMEROLOGY AND YOUR FUTURE

Dusty Bunker

In her second book, Dusty Bunker stresses the predictive side of numerology. Personal cycles, including yearly, monthly and even daily numbers are explored as the author presents new techniques for revealing future developments. Knowledge of these cycles will help you make decisions and take actions in your life.

In addition to the extended discussion of personal cycles, the numerological significance of decades is analyzed with emphasis on the particular importance of the 1980s. Looking toward the future, the author presents a series of examples from the past, particularly the historical order of American presidents in relation to keys from the Tarot, to illustrate the power of numbers. Special attention is paid to the twenty-year death cycle of the presidents, as well as several predictions for the presidential elections.

ISBN 0-914918-18-4
236 pages, 6½" x 9¼", paper $9.95

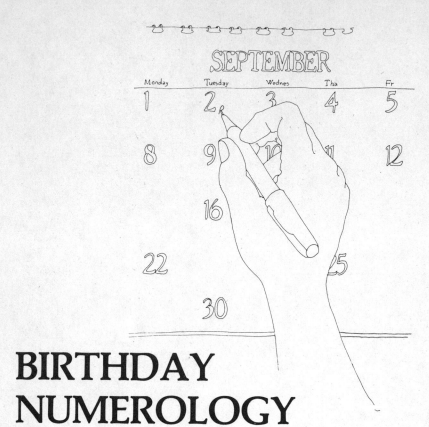

BIRTHDAY NUMEROLOGY

by Dusty Bunker and Victoria Knowles

One of the unique things about you is the day on which you were born. In *Birthday Numerology*, well-known numerologist Dusty Bunker and psychic counselor Victoria Knowles combine their knowledge of numerology, symbolism and psychic development to present a clear and coherent presentation of how the day you were born affects your personality.

Unlike other methods of divination, the beauty of this book lies in its simple and direct presentation of the meaning behind personal numbers. Rather than having to perform complicated calculations, all you need to do is know your birthday. The book is uncannily accurate, written in a warm and engaging style and, above all, is easy to use.

The introductory chapters discuss the foundation and validity of numerology and will help you discover why the date of your birth is crucial in determining your personality. From there, *Birthday Numerology* examines the traits and characteristics inherent in people born on each day of the month.

Dusty Bunker and Vikki Knowles have written a book that is much more than just a delineation of various personalities, it is truly a guidebook to your journey through the 31 days.

ISBN 0-914918-39-7
228 pages, 6½" x 9¼", paper

$9.95

DREAM CYCLES

Dusty Bunker

Dream Cycles offers a new and exciting approach to dream interpretation through the use of numbers, colors and symbolism combined with scientific research into dreams and their effects. Author Dusty Bunker brings the same engaging style she used in *Numerology and the Divine Triangle* and *Numerology and Your Future* to present a comprehensive treatment of the meaning of your dreams.

We all dream—some dreams we remember and others we do not. An old saying maintains that "an uninterpreted dream is like an unopened letter." Dusty Bunker provides you with all the letter openers you need. She gives you practical instructions for improving dream recall and helps you build your own dream dictionary for interpreting the personal symbolism of your own dreams.

Using the archetypes of numerology and metaphysics, *Dream Cycles* tells you that the personal rhythm of your dreams is determined by the numerological significance of the day on which you were born. Dreams and waking experiences both stem from the same inner sources and follow the same cycles. Understanding one will help you understand the other. Understanding your dreams will lead to an understanding of your waking reality.

ISBN 0-914918-30-3
229 pages, 6½" x 9¼", paper

$9.95

Your birthdate is more than a number

Your Numerology Portrait is all about you—the real you. It vividly reveals your inner potential, your key personality traits, and it helps you see your unique talents and abilities.

The Numerology Portrait results from a series of calculations based on your name at birth and the numbers in your birthdate. By using the concept of the Divine Triangle and proven mathematical derivations, Para Research has developed a clear and concise delination of the four personal numbers and the meanings they hold for you.

From the time you take your first breath, you are influenced by vibrations from the earth's field of energy. Your birthdate provides the pattern called the Life Lesson Number. Your name given at birth is translated into numbers using an ancient number-letter code. This code provides the three vibrations called the Soul Number, the Outer Personality Number and the Path of Destiny Number.

The Numerology Portrait provides an in-depth analysis of your own personal numbers that you were born with and will carry through life. The Portrait devotes at least one full page of interpretive text for each number. All of the calculations in the Portrait are performed by our IBM System/34 computer.

Your personal numbers are unique to you. They tell you the lessons you must learn during your life and the spiritual growth and development you can attain. They also reveal the state of consciousness which you have reached and record the growth of your soul. When you begin reading your Numerology Portrait, you'll discover among other things why you are likely to make a lot of

money, why you will enjoy a good marriage, or why you tend to be idealistic.

From your Life Lesson Number, you will find out what you have to learn in this lifetime. This number is extremely significant in your choice of a career. It also represents the cosmic gift you are given in order to accomplish your destiny. Your Soul Number is what you, in your inner secret self, desire to be. This part of your personality is not easily recognized by others unless they know you very well. The Soul Number also indicates what you may have done in previous lifetimes. The Outer Personality Number represents the personality you present to the world. It's the you as others perceive you and is important in understanding how other people react to you. The Path of Destiny Number represents your aim

in life. It shows the path you must walk, what you should accomplish and what you must be.

Your Numerology Portrait encompasses these and other aspects of your personality. It is authoritative and unerringly accurate. Every word, every explanation embodies the work of Faith Javane, one of America's most respected teachers of numerology and her student and co-author Dusty Bunker, a teacher and author of three books on numerology.

Your Numerology Portrait is inexpensive. Of course, we realize that there is no substitute for the one-to-one interchange between a numerologist and his or her client. However, a good numerologist would charge as much as $40 to $50. Compare that to the incredibly low price of $5.00 for the Numerology Portrait. This low price is possible because the text and the mathematical formulas are both stored in our IBM System/34 computer. You pay only for the cost of putting your personal information into the computer, compiling one copy, hand checking it and then sending it. You will receive your copy in approximately two weeks.

Along with your portrait is a money-back guarantee that is unconditional. This means that you can return your Numerology Portrait at any time for any reason and get a full refund. Para Research takes all the risk, not you!

Order today. Your Numerology Portrait just may be the most important picture you ever look at. It will show you aspects of your personality that you may never have thought to exist.

© 1982 Para Research, Inc.

The Numerology Portrait

You were born on a certain date, at a certain hour and minute into the earth's field of energy. The conditions and vibrations of this energy field determine to a great extent those actions and reactions that will characterize your entire life. In addition to your birthdate and time of birth, your name is as individual as you are. It represents your personality and your potential to the rest of the world.

The Numerology Portrait presents an overview of your personality using the ancient science of Numerology. Through a series of calculations of the four personal numbers that affect you, this portrait can lead to a greater understanding of yourself and how you relate to the world.

The numerological analysis in your portrait is based on the concept of the Divine Triangle. In the sixth century B.C., the mathematician Pythagoras invented the equation, $c^2 = a^2 + b^2$, for the right triangle. Rather than simply use this elegant formula to solve geometric or physical problems, Pythagoras also considered the right triangle a map of the universe that incorporated all facets of human existence. In the same way, you can consider the Numerology Portrait a map or blueprint of your life.

The Numerology Portrait calculates the four personal numbers that you are endowed with at birth. *Life Lesson Number* represents what you must learn in this lifetime and is derived from your full birthdate. Your *Soul Number* is your real personality, the underlying force that influences all your actions in life. This number is derived by assigning a numeric value to the vowels in your full name at birth and by adding those numbers together. The *Outer Personality Number* indicates how you appear to others and shows what people expect from you and is found by adding the values of the consonants in your full name at birth. The *Path of Destiny Number* indicates what you must do in this life and shows the contributions you are destined to make. This number is derived by adding your unreduced *Soul Number* and unreduced *Outer Personality Number* together.

All calculations and interpretations in the Numerology Portrait are done by the computer at Para Research. You receive an extensive computer printout that provides in-depth explanations of the meaning behind each of the four personal numbers. The explanations and analyses are based on the definitive book *Numerology and The Divine Triangle* by Faith Javane and Dusty Bunker, published by Para Research.

The Numerology Portrait will give you a diverse understanding of yourself and of how you function in the world. Use it as a map of the future that will make your upcoming experiences even more rewarding. To have your Numerology Portrait compiled, use the order form on the adjoining page.

COMPLETE RELAXATION

Steve Kravette

Complete Relaxation is unique in its field because, unlike most relaxation books, it takes a completely relaxed approach to its subject. You will find a series of poetic explorations interspersed with text and beautifully drawn illustrations designed to put you in closer touch with yourself and the people around you. *Complete Relaxation* is written for all of you: your body, your mind, your emotions, your spirituality, your sexuality—the whole person you are and are meant to be.

As you read this book, you will begin to feel yourself entering a way of life more completely relaxed than you ever thought possible. Reviewer Ben Reuven stated in the *Los Angeles Times,* "*Complete Relaxation* came along at just the right time—I read it, tried it; it works."

Some of the many areas that the author touches upon are: becoming aware, instant relaxation, stretching, hatha yoga, Arica, bioenergetics, Tai chi, dancing, and the Relaxation Reflex.

Mantras, meditating, emotional relaxation, holding back and letting go, learning to accept yourself, business relaxation, driving relaxation.

Family relaxation, nutritional relaxation, spiritual relaxation, sensual relaxation, massage and sexual relaxation. *Complete Relaxation* is a book the world has been tensely, nervously, anxiously waiting for. Here it is. Read it and relax.

ISBN 0-914918-14-1
310 pages, 6½" x 9¼", paper

$9.95

COMPLETE
MEDITATION

Steve Kravette

Complete Meditation presents a broad range of metaphysical concepts and
meditation techniques in the same direct, easy-to-assimilate style of the
author's best-selling *Complete Relaxation*. Personal experience is the teacher
and this unique book is your guide. The free, poetic format leads you
through a series of exercises that build on each other, starting with breathing
patterns, visualization exercises and a growing confidence that meditation is
easy and pleasurable. Graceful illustrations flow along with the text.

    Complete Meditation is for readers at all levels of experience. It makes
advanced metaphysics and esoteric practices accessible without years of study
of the literature, attachment to gurus or initiation into secret societies.
Everyone can meditate, everyone is psychic, and with only a little attention
everyone can bring oneself and one's circumstances into harmony.

    Experienced meditators will appreciate the more advanced techniques,
including more sophisticated breathing patterns, astral travel, past-life
regression, and much more. All readers will appreciate being shown how
ordinarily "boring" experiences are really illuminating gateways into the
complete meditation experience. Whether you do all the exercises or not, just
reading this book is a pleasure.

    Complete meditation can happen anywhere, any time, in thousands of
different ways. A candle flame, a daydream, music, sex, a glint of light on
your ring. In virtually any circumstances. *Complete Meditation* shows you
how.

ISBN 0-914918-28-1
309 pages, 6½″ x 9¼″, paper

$9.95

Source Books in Astrology
from Para Research

ASTROLOGY, NUTRITION & HEALTH
by Robert Carl Jansky

Explains how to use the natal horoscope to foresee and prevent health problems. This concern is as old as Hippocrates and Ptolemy, but there are few books on the subject written for the layman. The author, a professional astrologer trained in biochemistry, demonstrates, in readable nontechnical language, how a knowledge of astrology can help the reader understand the components of metabolism and health. Paper, $9.95

CONTEMPORARY ASTROLOGY
by Jerry J. Williams

A modern look at astrology which takes the reader on a tour of the heavens. Illustrated with diagrams, charts and drawings, this book will help the reader construct *and* interpret an astrological chart. This new paperback edition of *Contemporary Astrology* not only presents the basics of astrology but also encompasses psychology, metaphysics, mythology and politics. This book is a meeting ground for tomorrow's social sciences. Paper, $8.95.

ASTROLOGY BOOKS IN PRINT
by Para Research Staff

A comprehensive annotated listing of all astrological books available to the public as of early 1981 and including projected publications from major publishers. Collected by our research staff and collated through computer control, this inexpensive bibliography will not only be in high demand by astrologers, but also by all bibliophiles, librarians, bookstore clerks and researchers. Paper, $3.95

ASTROLOGY INSIDE OUT
by Bruce Nevin

This is an excellent introduction to astrology and much more. Its theoretical framework, integrating esoteric tradition with modern harmonic research in astrology and recent developments in physics and psychology, will interest every astrological reader. Through its many ingenious visualization and meditation exercises, even seasoned astrologers will learn new ways to recognize and interpret astrological patterning from the "inside out." Paper, $13.95

THE AMERICAN EPHEMERIS FOR THE TWENTIETH CENTURY
by Neil F. Michelsen

For the first time, an inexpensive paperback ephemeris which covers the entire 20th century with the accuracy and detail you expect from *The American Ephemeris*. Sun and Moon longitudes to 1 second; planet longitudes to .1 minute; calculated for GMT time; Solar and Lunar eclipses; aspectarian of Jupiter through Pluto and much more. Noon or Midnight, each volume: Paper, $15.95

PLANETS IN ASPECT: Understanding Your Inner Dynamics
by Robert Pelletier

Explores aspects, the planetary relationships that describe our individual energy patterns, and how we can integrate them into our lives. Undoubtedly the most thorough in-depth study of planetary aspects ever published. Every major aspect—conjunction, sextile, square, trine, opposition and inconjunct—is covered: 314 aspects in all. Paper, $12.95

PLANETS IN COMPOSITE: Analyzing Human Relationships
by Robert Hand

The definitive work on the astrology of human relationships. Explains the technique of the composite chart, combining two individuals' charts to create a third chart of the relationship itself, and how to interpret it. Case studies plus twelve chapters of delineations of composite Sun, Moon and planets in all houses and major aspects. Paper, $13.95

PLANETS IN HOUSES: Experiencing Your Environment
by Robert Pelletier

Brings the ancient art of natal horoscope interpretation into a new era of accuracy, concreteness and richness of detail. Pelletier delineates the meaning of each planet as derived by counting from each of the twelve houses and in relation to the other houses with which it forms trines, sextiles, squares and oppositions, inconjuncts and semisextiles. Seventeen different house relationships delineated for each planet in each house, 2184 delineations in all. Paper, $13.95

PLANETS IN LOVE: Exploring Your Emotional and Sexual Needs
by John Townley

The first astrology book to take an unabashed look at human sexuality and the different kinds of relationships that people form to meet their various emotional and sexual needs. An intimate astrological analysis of sex and love, with 550 interpretations of each planet in every possible sign, house and aspect. Discusses sexual behavior according to mental, emotional and spiritual needs. Paper, $13.95

PLANETS IN TRANSIT: Life Cycles for Living
by Robert Hand

A psychological approach to astrological prediction. Delineations of the Sun, Moon and each planet transiting each natal house and forming each aspect to the natal Sun, Moon, planets, Ascendant and Midheaven. The definitive book on transits. Includes chapters on the theory and applications of transits. Paper, $19.95

PLANETS IN YOUTH: Patterns of Early Development
by Robert Hand

A major astrological thinker looks at children and childhood. Parents can use it to help their children cope with the complexities of growing up, and readers of all ages can use it to understand themselves and their own patterns of early development. Introductory chapters discuss parent-child relationships and planetary energies in children's charts. All important horoscope factors delineated stressing possibilities rather than certainties. Paper, $13.95

To Order Books: Send purchase price plus fifty cents for each book to cover shipping and handling to Para Research, Dept. HU, Rockport, MA 01966. Massachusetts residents add 5% sales tax. Prices subject to change without notice.

LIFE AFTER DEATH

S. Ralph Harlow
with an introduction by Enid Hoffman

The possibility of an afterlife is a universal concern. In *Life After Death*, Ralph Harlow makes a convincing argument for the existence of another plane of being. And that argument has special relevance today with the renewed interest in death and dying.

Harlow reviews his own experiences of contact with the afterworld, combs the Bible for references to a life after death and surveys the work of leading literary figures for their views on the subject. From telepathic contact with the dead to near-death experiences, Harlow explains the various possibilities and factors involved. All this work is collected in one readable volume that makes the death experience understandable and explains rationally the likelihood of an afterlife.

Originally published in the early 1960s, this book was truly ahead of its time. *Life After Death* has a renewed relevance following the work of Elisabeth Kubler-Ross on the experience of death, the acceptance of the near-death experience as a reality and recent psychic research into astral projection and its various forms.

In her introduction, Enid Hoffman says the book gave her a "deeper understanding of life after death and all the possibilities it holds." Read it and see why Ralph Harlow concludes that he "still believes in immortality."

ISBN 0-914918-40-0
173 pages, 6½" x 9¼", paper

$8.95